SELF-DIRECTION

SELF-DIRECTION
A Revolution in Human Services

Valerie J. Bradley
Marc H. Fenton
Kevin J. Mahoney

Published by State University of New York Press, Albany

© 2021 State University of New York

All rights reserved

Printed in the United States of America

No part of this book may be used or reproduced in any manner whatsoever without written permission. No part of this book may be stored in a retrieval system or transmitted in any form or by any means including electronic, electrostatic, magnetic tape, mechanical, photocopying, recording, or otherwise without the prior permission in writing of the publisher.

For information, contact State University of New York Press, Albany, NY
www.sunypress.edu

Library of Congress Cataloging-in-Publication Data

Names: Bradley, Valerie J., author. | Fenton, Marc H., author. | Mahoney, Kevin J., author.
Title: Self-direction : a revolution in human services / Valerie J. Bradley, Marc H. Fenton, Kevin J. Mahoney.
Description: Albany : State University of New York Press, [2021] | Includes bibliographical references and index.
Identifiers: LCCN 2021007122 | ISBN 9781438483436 (hardcover : alk. paper) | ISBN 9781438483429 (pbk. : alk. paper) | ISBN 9781438483443 (ebook)
Subjects: LCSH: Human services. | Autonomy (Psychology)
Classification: LCC HV40 .B814 2021 | DDC 361.973—dc23
LC record available at https://lccn.loc.gov/2021007122

10 9 8 7 6 5 4 3 2 1

To the people with disabilities and older adults across the country who have chosen self-direction in order to create services and supports that help them to lead their best lives

Contents

List of Illustrations		ix
Acknowledgments		xi
Preface		xiii
Chapter 1	Self-direction: What It Is and How It Works	1
Chapter 2	The History and Policy Antecedents of Self-direction	9
Chapter 3	The Federal Role: Less Visible, Just as Important	23
Chapter 4	The Status of Self-direction across the Country	37
Chapter 5	Setting Individualized Budgets to Support Self-direction	65
Chapter 6	The Impact of Self-direction: Results for Participants	83
Chapter 7	The Impact of Self-direction: Financial Results	99
Chapter 8	Factors That Can Influence the Growth of Self-direction	119
Chapter 9	The Expansion of Self-direction to Other Participants	139
Chapter 10	International Examples of Self-direction in Human Services	157

Chapter 11	Reflections and Recommendations	185
Postscript		205
Notes		207
References		211
Index		229

Illustrations

Figures

1.1	Elements of Self-Direction.	3
4.1	Number of self-direction programs in the United States.	39
4.2	Number of participants in self-direction programs in the United States.	40
4.3	Number and proportion of National Core Indicators survey respondents (adults in the United States with intellectual and developmental disabilities) who are self-directing.	43
5.1	Five-level support needs framework.	74
7.1	Percentage of participants receiving paid assistance after 9 months.	103
8.1	Faces of participant direction.	121
10.1	Seven-step model.	171

Tables

7.1	Non-Personal Care (Institutional) Medicaid Costs—Year One Differences per Person	104

7.2	Non-Personal Care (Institutional) Medicaid Costs—Year Two Differences per Person	104
7.3	Arkansas Medicaid Expenditures Per User Per State Fiscal Year: Agency and Independent Choices	107
7.4	California Monthly Expenditures by Group	112
10.1	Comparable Utilization From 1994 to 2013	161

Acknowledgments

The three authors would like to recognize people who made important contributions to this book and to thank them for their collaboration. First, Pam Doty in the Office of the Assistant Secretary for Planning and Evaluation deserves our sincere gratitude for all the questions she answered and the fact checking she was willing to do as we were writing the book. Pam also guided us to international experts who were able to help ensure the accuracy and completeness of chapter 10 on international efforts in self-direction in the Netherlands and Germany.

We give special thanks to Jessica Maloney, director of communications at the Human Services Research Institute, who provided extraordinary editorial support and consultation throughout. Her expertise was invaluable.

Other colleagues made contributions to specific chapters:

Mark Sciegaj, PhD, MPH, professor of health policy and administration at the Pennsylvania State University, contributed the section on national inventories charting the growth of self-direction in chapter 4;

Jamie Petner-Arrey, PhD, policy associate, and John Agosta, PhD, executive vice president—both from the Human Services Research Institute—were the main authors for chapter 5 on how budgets are set;

Bevin Croft, PhD, research associate at the Human Services Research Institute, was the lead author of the section on self-direction in behavioral health in chapter 9;

Kali S. Thomas, PhD, associate professor of health services, policy, and practice at the Brown University School of Public

Health and research health science specialist at Providence VA Medical Center, coauthored the section on self-direction for veterans in chapter 9;

Martin Routledge, head of operations at In-Control and director of the Coalition for Collaborative Care, was the main author of the section on self-direction in England in chapter 10;

Matthias Von Schwanenflugel, a senior official in the German government, reviewed and edited the section on Germany in chapter 10.

We are also grateful for editorial support from Virginia Mulkern, PhD, senior advisor at the Human Services Research Institute, and Hassan Ragy, former research assistant at the Human Services Research Institute.

Preface

This book comes from the deep experience the authors have had in human services and self-direction. We felt a need to reach out to the public policy community to explain how self-direction provides an extraordinary alternative for long-term services and supports that shifts the power and control to participants but is not yet well understood. Each of us has had more than 40 years in the human services field, at least 20 of which were spent developing and consulting to states on the self-direction option across the country. Each of us was nearing the end of our professional careers. Each of us is passionate about passing on the lessons and legacy of this empowering approach and the ways that the option to self-direct can reach more people. As individuals, we have observed the emergence of self-direction from different vantage points. We hope that in this book we succeeded in combining those observations and experiences in a cohesive whole that advances the understanding of self-direction and helps create a path forward for its growth and development across the country

The initial idea for the book came when Marc and Val spoke at an international conference on self-direction at British Columbia University in 2015. Seventeen countries attended, many presented, and Marc and Val realized how little was understood about the approach to self-direction in the United States. They decided that a book on the American experience with self-direction would fill an important void. They reached out to Kevin and invited him to join them to write a comprehensive overview of self-direction.

Val began her work in human services in the late 1960s as a staff member in the California Legislature during major reforms of the state's mental-health and developmental-disabilities systems. She left and became a consultant and eventually founded the Human Services Research Institute (HSRI), a nonprofit public-policy organization. HSRI has been in the forefront of major reforms in behavioral health and developmental disabilities, including conducting research on the outcomes of deinstitutionalization, supporting the expansion of family support initiatives, designing quality assurance and improvement tools, and creating the National Core Indicators program that collects data on people with developmental disabilities and their families in 46 states. Her interest in self-direction began when she was an evaluator of self-direction pilot programs for people with developmental disabilities funded by the Robert Wood Johnson Foundation in the 1990s. She saw that self-direction was key to the empowerment of people with disabilities. Since then, she has continued to help states to refine policies that support self-direction as part of person-centered initiatives. She is now President Emerita of HSRI.

Marc has been in public services and public policy for his entire career. His work began at the Massachusetts Department of Mental Health and Mental Retardation where he focused on closing state institutions and building the foundation for community alternatives. He joined the Public Consulting Group, Inc. (PCG) in Boston in 1995 and consulted with state governments across the country on deinstitutionalization, building cost-effective community programs, and developing long-term strategies for community-based systems. He moved to self-direction in 1999, providing consultation to states that were awarded self-direction pilots for people with developmental disabilities funded by the Robert Wood Johnson Foundation. Seeing how self-direction satisfied people's needs and desires in a public system at a competitive cost, he established a new firm at PCG—Public Partnerships, LLC—to provide financial management and support brokerage to states creating self-direction waivers and programs. At the time of his retirement, the enterprise was in 26 states supporting 130,000 participants, 150,000 workers, and a joint venture supporting self-direction in Australia.

Kevin came to self-direction research in 1995 when he was recruited from California by the Robert Wood Johnson Foundation and the US Department of Health and Human Services Office of the Assistant Secretary for Policy and Evaluation (ASPE) to head the Cash and Counseling Demonstration and Evaluation that was about to get underway. ASPE and the Robert Wood Johnson Foundation wanted an impartial, respected researcher to lead this randomized control experiment, a person with significant experience working with state governments and federal agencies. Kevin came to Cash and Counseling as an agnostic regarding self-direction, but the results of this eight-year research endeavor turned him into an advocate. He then went on to be the national program director for the 12-state replication of Cash and Counseling and testified frequently before congressional committees seeking to make it possible for all states to take up this option. In 2009, Kevin became the founding director of the National Resource Center for Participant-Directed Services, which was established at Boston College to help programs around the country and across the world implement this option. Kevin attributes a significant part of his learning and understanding to his own son, who now manages his own budget. Kevin is presently professor emeritus at the Boston College School of Social Work, where he served for 18 years.

Returning to our vision, we believe self-direction is an approach that can significantly alter how services and supports are provided to people who are aging, people with mental illness, veterans, and people with physical and developmental disabilities. It shifts the power and control from the system and the professionals to the participant and family. This change in the power relationship has the potential to "disrupt" and alter the trajectory of many aspects of human services. Public managers, researchers, human services professionals, and advocates willing to build the necessary infrastructure, to heed the growing evidence, and to listen to the voices of participants will be needed to expand self-direction.

As our book neared completion, the COVID-19 virus struck the United States. At the time of writing, nursing homes and assisted-living facilities accounted for well over a third of all coronavirus deaths. In many states, more than half of coronavirus deaths occurred in nursing homes. As the number of cases mounted, the Center for Medicare and Medicaid Services (CMS) regulations limited visitations to nursing facilities and addressed the need for COVID-only facilities. Adult day care and other congregate programs for people with disabilities closed. People looked for an alternative. CMS issued guidance allowing states to adapt and expand their home- and community-based services to provide supports to meet this crisis. This guidance specifically mentioned expanding the availability of a self-direction option under the Appendix K for 1915(c) waivers and 1135 waivers for state plans. This made sense for three major reasons:

1. People with preexisting conditions want to limit the number of people in and out of their homes to reduce their exposure to COVID-19. Agency workers often see several clients, and high turnover rates in these roles mean staff change frequently.

2. Close family and friends, many of whom live with or near individuals with disabilities and already provide unpaid care,

may be newly unemployed. By paying family caregivers, recipients can compensate those close to them instead of worrying that the care is an added burden. Research has shown that receiving assistance from people that the individual with disabilities already knows is beneficial (Newcomer et al., 2012). Conversely, family members experience less stress because they do not have to worry about the adequacy of care (Foster et al., 2007).

3. Self-direction provides significant flexibility. The individual with disabilities can switch between agency-delivered and self-directed services at any time. When the program participant has control of the budget, (s)he can purchase needed goods and services including personal protective equipment (PPE), a cellphone, or internet connection to facilitate telehealth.

Within one month of the release of the CMS coronavirus toolkit, 14 states had modified their waiver programs to permit the temporary hiring of legally responsible relatives—for example, a spouse or parent of a child with a disability—thus expanding the labor market significantly, and 21 states had increased self-directed budgets, benefit limits, and/or rates expanding participants' ability to purchase the supports needed during the pandemic.

We do not know what the long-term implications of these changes will be. We do know that for those participants facing fewer support alternatives and who have numbers of family and friends out of work, self-direction is playing a major role in helping people with disabilities and older adults to receive needed services and supports in the community. Anthony Fauci, MD, and other experts have warned that the United States may never entirely return to "normal." At first, this may seem ominous, but it need not be so. If we reflect back in time, it was the polio epidemic that led to the self-direction movement as the people affected by that disease fought for greater control over their lives (Shapiro, 1994). Just as crises in the past have spurred new ways of thinking, COVID-19 may be opening our eyes anew to the value of self-direction. Who knows what the new "normal" will be?

Chapter 1

Self-direction

What It Is and How It Works

The emergence of self-directed supports as a mode of service delivery in human services constitutes a major if somewhat overlooked national shift. Simply put, self-direction is changing the way services are planned, managed, and delivered. Specifically, it is changing the way that individuals who need long-term care in the public sector—usually Medicaid recipients with disabilities or who are elderly—interact with public-service systems by encouraging them to exercise choice among providers and, in turn, to exercise more control in the marketplace. Unlike system participants served by traditional providers, individuals who self-direct can use their individual budget to secure services from a wider market to meet their needs. This approach goes against the typical ways in which public authority managers, program administrators, and case managers have functioned. Typically, public authorities have circumscribed choices and offered limited service menus. In self-direction, professional roles are changed, and the balance of power is altered in favor of the participant. The outcomes of self-direction that have been documented so far are very positive. This change, which until recently has flown under the radar, will potentially revolutionize assumptions about public sector services and is likely to have a permanent impact across the country.

Self-direction is the newest and fastest-growing platform for the delivery of community based services and supports to individuals needing long-term care in the public sector. It creates a direct connection between the public entity and the individual rather than channeling resources to providers who in turn offer services. In other words, self-direction eliminates the middleman and places the purchasing of resources at the disposal of the individual. With self-direction, public funders enter into agreements directly with participants through an individual budget. The participant then develops a plan with their supporters and within the guidelines and approval of the funding agency. Purchasing decisions and resource management are now the responsibility of the person receiving services. Public agencies allocate resources, approve service plans, and oversee the management and quality of self-directed services. Participants decide who to hire as well as what to purchase and from whom. In some self-directed programs, individuals can select services and supports provided not only from health care or social service agencies but also from local businesses and community agencies of their choosing.

Self-direction creates two options for people directing their own services: *employment authority* and *budget authority*. With employment authority, participants are allowed to recruit, hire, manage, promote, and dismiss their personal support workers. They are recognized to have full employer responsibilities and authority. When participants have budget authority, they can purchase a wide range of services and supports from traditional providers and nontraditional providers; these may include improvements and equipment for residential services that enable them to remain in their homes. In both models, all payroll and purchases must be made within an allocated budget based on an individual service plan.

Figure 1.1 also shows the management supports required by the participant: financial management, support broker, and authorized representative. The financial manager is usually an agency that holds the funds and makes the purchases, runs the payroll, and deducts and pays the taxes and benefits as required. The support broker, often a case manager, helps the participant develop the plan and understand the spending, hiring, and firing decisions. Some participants require personal assistance in making final decisions. The authorized representative is chosen by the participant to speak or act on his/her behalf without pay. This creates an entirely new structure and process for the management of Medicaid and other public funding sources for services and supports.

This approach started informally about 70 years ago in California, first for people with polio and then for people with disabilities living on college campuses. It became a state program service model in California, Massachusetts, and Wisconsin in the 1980s. In the 1990s, the Robert Wood Johnson Foundation gave the self-direction movement significant momentum. First, the foundation was one of the sponsors of the Cash and Counseling pilot

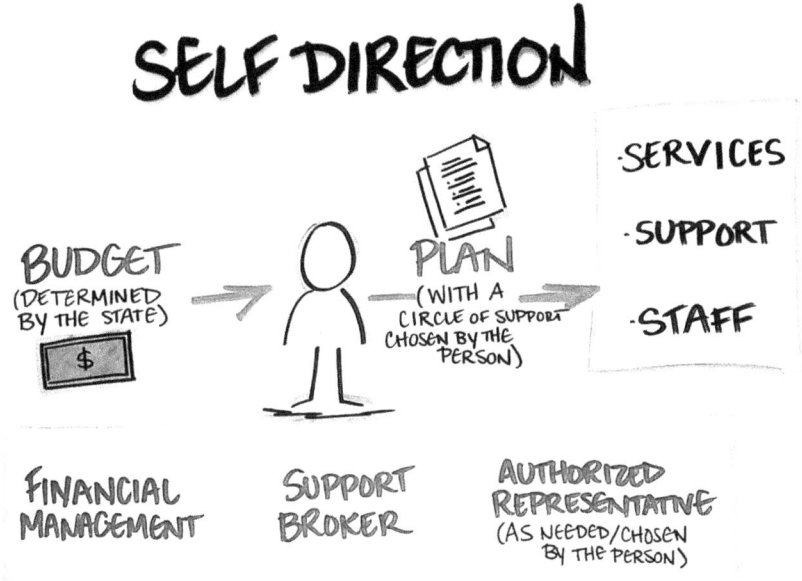

Figure 1.1. Elements of Self-Direction. Illustration by InkyBrittany commissioned by the authors.

program, which was a randomized control experiment that explored a new way of serving individuals with physical, developmental, and intellectual disabilities and problems of aging in Florida, Arkansas, and New Jersey. After several successful and well documented years, the program was expanded to 12 more states. The Robert Wood Johnson Foundation then funded 19 state self-direction pilot programs focused on individuals with intellectual and developmental disabilities.

Since 2003, self-direction has been a service option for all states under federal home and community based services (HCBS) Medicaid waivers[1] that serve the elderly, people with intellectual and developmental disabilities, people with physical disabilities, autistic individuals, individuals with serious mental illness, individuals living with HIV/AIDS, and individuals with acquired brain injury. Over the past decade and a half, the number of individuals using waiver funds to self-direct their services has grown consistently across the country. Today more than one million people, living in every state and the District of Columbia, have chosen to purchase and direct their own services.

The rapid expansion of self-direction is in part due to the rapid growth in the nation's older population and their desire to stay in their homes as they age. The Veterans Health Administration—working with the aging and disability networks—created the Veteran-Directed Home and Community Based Services program (VD-HCBS); and self-direction has recently expanded to persons with mental illness. (Both groups are detailed in chapter 9.) We expect that self-direction will expand to an even broader range of groups as the outcomes of self-direction—in terms of both individual outcomes and the cost efficiency of service systems—become more widely understood and as states develop the infrastructure to manage self-direction on a larger scale.

Most individuals who require long-term public supports are now given a choice: "You can have your community based services and supports provided by local agencies, or you can receive a budget that will allow you to schedule your services, hire people to come into your home to provide them, and, in many cases, purchase certain goods and services from individuals, agencies, and businesses in your community." Initially, many participants were wary of taking on this responsibility, and many state human service agencies did not have the infrastructure to support self-direction; however, the program is now growing and expanding. It is reaching a broad range of participants with diverse support needs and has spawned a new industry focused entirely on supporting individuals who are making their own choices and managing their services.

Satisfaction with self-direction, as indicated by the review of research in chapter 6, is high among participants and family members, and they uniformly said they would recommend self-direction to a friend who needed services. Respondents went on to say that they valued the choice and control that self-direction gives them. Further, total costs are managed within the projections established by the Medicaid waivers and the rate structures of Medicaid state plan services as reviewed in chapter 7. Rather than creating budgets without limits or budgets that are continually renegotiated, self-direction creates a discipline. The spending budget is agreed upon by the individual and managed throughout the process. Most states set aside a small amount of savings that can be used for unplanned emergencies or changes. This enables state agencies to accurately project costs and manage changes in the program.

Another reason self-direction has become so popular is that it meets the needs and values of different stakeholder groups: public agency managers, elected officials, clinicians, consumers, families, and advocates. It can meet conservative goals by using the marketplace to manage costs and expand choice. It can meet progressive service goals for individual consumers who seek more independence and inclusion in their communities. There is no other program model that so effectively straddles these different goals.

For self-direction to work well and continue to grow, several new policies and processes have been required; these are described later in this book. States have implemented new technology and business approaches to track expenditures, meet reporting requirements, and manage payrolls. Further, to support individuals who cannot communicate their needs during the planning process, states have created a role called an "authorized representative" to provide participants with assistance to direct their services and communicate their desires. The authorized representative is usually a family member or close friend who agrees to play this role without compensation.

To determine the allocation of resources to an individual, the service plan must be monetized to determine what it costs and how it can fit within the budget of the public agency that is managing the services. The monetized plan or individual budget is sometimes simple, covering just a few services, and sometimes complex, involving a large number of services and supports. Budgets range from several hundred dollars a month to more than $10,000 per month depending on the goals and needs of the participants. People who self-direct their services may need just intermittent support to remain in their home or they may need round-the-clock care every day; both work well in self-direction. The different approaches and processes for setting individual budgets are discussed in chapter 5.

The individuality and complexity of these budgets are unprecedented in public administration. Literally every budget could be different in terms of the kind and quantity of services and supports that are delivered. This creates an enormous database on services provided, their costs, and their providers. It also required several new public management service inventions: the financial management services agency (FMSA) and support brokers.

Financial management service agencies, usually hired by state Medicaid or service agencies, support participants in a number of ways: (a) they help participants manage their budgets; (b) they support the employee recruiting, hiring, and payroll processes; (c) they ensure compliance with state labor laws; (d) they file federal, state, and local taxes and pay fringe benefits; (e) they assist the participant to purchase goods and services; (f) they provide "live" reports to participants on their budgets and expenditures; (g) they identify expenses that are not authorized by the individual's budget; (h) they provide customer service and assistance to participants and workers; and (i) they provide a Medicaid billing process for the state agencies. The Internal

Revenue Service qualifies most FMSAs as "fiscal employer agents," which means they serve as the hiring agent on behalf of participants, accountable for all employer responsibilities while participants make decisions on the hiring, supervision, and termination of their workers. FMSAs have developed in every state. Some are small local agencies focused on a particular community; others are national organizations able to enroll and support tens of thousands of participants per program.

The other new entity created for self-direction is usually called a support brokerage. Support brokers work directly with participants and their families to (a) help them to develop a person-centered service plan and individualized budget; (b) provide assistance in hiring, managing, and terminating personal support workers; (c) provide assistance in making purchases of services and supports; (d) help participants coordinate and back up their services, particularly for people who require services and supports daily; and (e) perform other employer-related and budget management tasks requested by participants that enable them to meet their goals and changing needs. These services are provided in-person, on the phone, and sometimes online. Some states have created a separate Medicaid reimbursable service—referred to as support brokerage, individual counseling, or personal guide—to perform these functions and act as a liaison between the individual and the program. Support brokers can be local individuals usually qualified by the state agency, specially trained state workers, or private agencies hired to provide this service to all participants in the waiver.

Participation rates, satisfaction, and outcomes continue to improve every year. Costs are managed within state budgets. And yet self-directed services remain poorly understood by eligible individuals, helping professionals, and the general public. We hope this book will change that for individuals eligible for long-term care, for professionals providing services, for public officials creating legislation and public programs, for administrators managing services, and for taxpayers paying for services.

We will follow the social history of the self-direction movement as well as the judicial and legislative history at the federal and state levels. We will examine the current research on the impact on participants and direct care workers as well as studies on the costs and outcomes of self-direction. As a national case study, we will look at the implementation and growth of programs for similar participants in different states and try to understand why the utilization rates vary widely and how utilization can be increased. We will look at how service plans are developed and how their costs are determined, or "monetized." Since this is an international movement, we will look briefly at the Netherlands, Germany, England, and Australia—countries that have made a national commitment to self-direction.

At the end of many of the chapters, we will use interviews with participants and family members to illustrate the lessons that have been learned and the changes that have been experienced across the country. We believe these interviews will clearly explain how self-direction works, why participants in self-direction embrace the freedom to make choices about their supports, and how it can be improved. In the final chapter, we will summarize what we have learned from policy leaders and evaluators across the country on the future of self-direction and how it can be expanded and improved.

We hope to inform current and future policy makers about what self-direction has accomplished and how it could be used for current and new populations. We believe we are at the beginning of a new chapter in the delivery of human services for people with disabilities and those who are aging. This is a population that is very large and becoming larger, that is more outspoken about their needs, and that is aware of what works and what doesn't work for them. And we are at a time when the demand and cost of long-term care is becoming part of a national conversation for a rapidly growing population.

Chapter 2

The History and Policy Antecedents of Self-direction

The increasing embrace of self-direction in the human services field has been fueled by a range of ideological trends, public policy initiatives, and social movements over the past several decades. Unlike many programs for people who depend on public services, self-direction draws on solutions from both the political Left and the Right as justification. For those on the Left, self-direction offers individual empowerment and the ability to negotiate for needed services on an equal footing with providers. For those on the Right, self-direction offers a free-market solution to state funded and managed services by putting the purchasing power in the hands of the individual. In an era of intense partisanship, this convergence of philosophical assumptions lends possible support for continued expansion of self-directed options in the future.

With this as a backdrop, there are several historical events and trends that have fed the interest in self-direction.

Early Activism

The 1960s are remembered as a period of disruption—disruption that took the form of social protest against racial segregation and an unpopular war. This period also saw the mobilization of people with disabilities and their families. In the mental health field, consumer groups like the Mental Patients Liberation Front took on involuntary treatment and forced medication. They argued for housing, jobs, and income supports in addition to psychiatric services (Chamberlin, 1990). In the developmental-disabilities field, the fledgling Association for Retarded Children (now The Arc) organized families around the country to advocate for a more positive public perception of children with intellectual disabilities and their potential (The Arc, n.d.). They sought concrete reforms such as access to education, preschool, and jobs. In the physical disability community, important figures such as Ed Roberts—one of the founders of the historic Berkeley Center for Independent Living in 1972—rallied people with physical disabilities to take charge of their own lives, to demand the supports they need to live independently, and to reject the medical model and the notion that they needed to be fixed (Anderson, 2013). Finally, activism among the elderly burgeoned during this period as well, as groups like the Gray Panthers argued against forced retirement and in favor of better health care, housing, and income supports (Sanjek, 2009).

The political activism and advocacy spawned by these groups would combine with the reform zeitgeist of the era to support major changes in federal policy in the next two decades, including the following:

- Section 504 of the Rehabilitation Act (1973), which prohibited discrimination against people with disabilities in any program or setting that receives federal funding. This broad language ensured that people with disabilities had access to federally funded housing, schools, public accommodations (such as airports, playgrounds, and public libraries) and guaranteed individuals a private right of action.

- Supplemental Security Income (1974), Title XVI of the Social Security Act, which "federalized" previous state income support programs for the aged, blind, and disabled. These changes also made it possible for families with children with disabilities with financial need to collect income supports on behalf of a child under 21 years of age.

- Education for All Handicapped Children Act (1975), (reauthorized and retitled in 1990 as the Individuals with Disabilities Education Act), which ensured that children with disabilities were entitled to receive free and appropriate public education. The legislation stipulated that education should be provided in the least restrictive setting and that each student should have an individual education plan. Over the years since the inception of the law, there has been an increasing emphasis on serving children with disabilities in mainstream settings, and more recently about opportunities for these students once they move into the adult world.

- Developmentally Disabled Assistance and Bill of Rights Act (1975), which defined developmental disability and asserted the right of such individuals to independence, productivity, and integration. The law also established a robust infrastructure of research, advocacy, and planning and program development.

- Title VII (Centers for Independent Living) of the Rehabilitation Act (1978), which allocated funds for "independent living services," a National Council on the Handicapped (now Disability), and a research agency devoted to issues affecting people with disabilities within the then Department of Health, Education and Welfare.

- Section 1915(c) of the Social Security Act (1983), which allowed Medicaid funds to flow into the creation of community supports as alternatives to institutions for people with disabilities, people with chronic health issues, and elders. In the last three decades, Section 1915(c) has been the major funding source for the rapid growth of home and community based services (HCBS) for people with disabilities and older Americans.

- Americans with Disabilities Act (1990), which significantly strengthened earlier nondiscrimination mandates and guaranteed that people with disabilities have the same opportunities as everyone else to participate in the mainstream of American life—to enjoy employment opportunities, to purchase goods and services, and to participate in state and local government programs and services.

This impressive succession of major legislative victories gave people with disabilities, the older adults, and other disadvantaged groups the opportunity to be included in their communities and schools, to have a predictable income stream, and to take advantage of a growing system of supports in their home communities. These groundbreaking advances provided a solid and predictable foundation that made it possible for individuals to take the next steps toward empowerment and control. Increased independence and expanded expectations were important precursors to self-direction.

Philosophical Shift

A variety of philosophical forces combined in the 1970s and 1980s to reinforce the importance of inclusion and the recognition of the basic "personhood" of individuals with disabilities and other disadvantages. The movement to close institutions and to move people into more humane and individualized settings assumed that institutionalization stripped people of their basic humanity and their uniqueness as citizens. To counter the human cost of congregate facilities, the notion of "least restrictive setting" as a criterion for judging residential and school settings became a powerful mandate (Bradley, 1978).

Another major conceptual change was the advent of normalization—a Scandinavian construct translated and elaborated on by Wolf Wolfensberger and colleagues (1972)—which asserted that the stigma associated with disability could only be ameliorated by supporting people in "normal" communities, homes, jobs, and service settings that were as close as possible to those available to people without disabilities. This relatively simple thought soon permeated the developmental-disability world and was also applied in the broader human services field. It was revolutionary in that once you accepted the premise, it was impossible not to see custodial facilities like state hospitals, state schools, and nursing homes as infantilizing and isolating settings. With normalization came a commitment to assist individuals with disabilities and other disadvantages to be true members of their communities and to have the same experiences and opportunities as their nondisabled peers. If people have the opportunity to lead ordinary lives, then it follows that they should also be able to make important life choices. This assumption was an important underpinning of self-direction and a focus on choice.

Programmatic Precursors

Prior to the emergence of self-direction nationally, there were program models in the disability field that embodied some of the same elements that can be found in self-direction. One of these models grew out of the physical disability advocacy movement. In their desire to control more of their own lives, advocates argued that they should be able to hire, train—and, when necessary, fire—their personal care attendants. Several states in the early 1980s, including California and Massachusetts, developed service options that gave individuals with physical disabilities the opportunity to become employers and to direct their own personal care staff.

Another early model of self-direction grew out of the family support movement composed of parents of individuals with intellectual and developmental disabilities. In the 1980s, parent advocates worked to persuade several states to initiate flexible family support programs. These early programs recognized the importance of tailoring services to individual family circumstances and provided stipends that could be used to purchase a wide range of services. Depending on the state, funds could be used to install ramps and other home modifications for children in wheelchairs, to hire homemaker and personal care support in the home, and to purchase respite services and other supports that met the individual needs of the family. The premise of family supports was that families know what is best for their family member and should be able to purchase services and supports to meet their needs (Bradley et al., 1992).

Reform through the Courts

A cascading series of federal court cases that began in the 1970s contributed to an increased regard for the full citizenship of people with disabilities. The first major case was *Wyatt v. Stickney* in 1971. The *Wyatt* decision established the principle that deprivation of liberty, as experienced by people in institutions, could only be justified if residents received treatment. This right to treatment would be the basis for court-ordered reform of institutional settings in a number of states, including Massachusetts, Connecticut, Michigan, New York, and Maine. In 1972, a landmark case was *Lessard v. Schmidt* in which a federal district court in Milwaukee struck down Wisconsin's commitment law as unconstitutional. For the first time, a court required that commitment proceedings provide individuals with mental illness with the range of due process.

The Supreme Court weighed in on the rights of people with disabilities in 1975 in *O'Connor v. Donaldson*. In their ruling, the Court found that a state cannot constitutionally confine a nondangerous individual who can survive safely in freedom by themselves or with the help of responsible family members or friends. These cases all served to reinforce the rights of individuals with disabilities to more humane treatment and ultimately—in *Halderman v. Pennhurst State School and Hospital* (1977)—the right to live in the community given the inability of segregated institutions to provide constitutionally acceptable treatments. Finally, the most recent assertion of the right of people with disabilities to live outside of institutions came in the Supreme Court decision in *Olmstead v. L.C.* (1999). The finding in that case made it clear that individuals who wanted to move to communities should be given the freedom to make that choice.

Demonstrations

In the 1990s, the Robert Wood Johnson Foundation (RWJF) began to explore self-direction by funding research into how the concept was implemented in Europe—specifically in Germany and the Netherlands (Cameron & Firman, 1995). The foundation ultimately funded three US demonstration programs that fostered the development of participant-directed home- and community based services for older adults, people with chronic disabilities, and people with intellectual and developmental disabilities. The first demonstration was Independent Choices: Enhancing Consumer Direction for People with Disabilities (2004). The second was the Cash and Counseling program (1995), and the third was the Self-Determination for Persons with Developmental Disabilities program (1997). These demonstrations documented the key components of self-direction, including individual planning, the role of case managers, and the ways in which budgets were configured and managed.

Independent Choices. Independent Choices, a $3.4 million program, ran from 1995 to 1999. It supported nine demonstrations aimed at giving people with disabilities more choices about their services and supports and the authority to manage how they were provided (DeMilto, 2004). It also funded three research projects. Independent Choices demonstrations included a restructuring of the Ohio Medicaid waiver program to add choices to the services available to older participants and the creation of a "rapid-response" program to address unmet service needs of home care clients in Alameda County, California.

Cash and Counseling. Named for the Dutch experiment it was patterned after, Cash and Counseling was a partnership between RWJF and the US Department of Health and Human Services Office of the Assistant Secretary for Planning and Evaluation (ASPE). What follows is a summary of key issues and findings. The story of the origins, implementation, and results of Cash and Counseling are described in detail in a dedicated issue of *Health Services Research* (2007).

From the ASPE perspective, Cash and Counseling grew out of the ashes of the Clinton Health Plan which, due to advocacy mainly from the World Institute on Disability, contained a self-direction option in its long-term care provisions. ASPE staff wanted to shed more light on this option, and they believed the only way to do this was through a large controlled experiment. RWJF came to this issue having just financed a review of long-term care initiatives in European countries that revealed varying self-direction approaches in Germany as well as the Netherlands. RWJF officials also believed that a large, randomized, controlled experiment was needed. In 1995, RWFJ created a program office to oversee the demonstration and to provide technical assistance. In 1996, four states were selected for this demonstration: Arkansas, Florida, New Jersey, and New York. Given delays in implementation and other factors, New York subsequently dropped out (Sciegaj et al., 2008).

A series of focus groups and surveys of home care recipients took place in each of the states to help determine the kinds of supports that participants would want to self-direct and the kinds of information that people would need to help them decide between traditional agency-managed services and managing their own budgets. Based on these conversations, the states developed their own approaches to outreach and supportive services, including service brokers and financial management.

During the roughly three years between site selection and the start of the demonstration, federal Medicaid, Food Stamp, and SSI waivers were obtained; key Medicaid Research and Demonstration (1115) Waivers included the ability to offer cash benefits and the ability to hire and pay legally responsible relatives (used in Florida and New Jersey). SSI and Food Stamp waivers were needed as participants could save money and carry it forward to purchase more expensive assistive devices or home repairs. Sometimes the amount saved could exceed the $2,000 asset limit allowed in these programs.

By the end of 2003, more than 6,700 people had volunteered and taken part in the demonstration—with half randomly assigned to manage and control budgets equivalent to what agencies would have spent on their behalf and half assigned to the traditional model. The strength of the results of the controlled experiment surprised nearly everyone. Participants in the self-direction component were far more satisfied with their supports and had far fewer unmet needs. Health outcomes were the same, or better, for those who self-directed; overall satisfaction with life improved even though the budgets were modest, and all of this was achieved without major increases in cost.

This first phase of Cash and Counseling was followed by broad dissemination of the results to policy makers and advocacy communities. In addition, a manual was written for future program administrators, and key results were circulated by and through national associations and membership groups. The positive results provided the impetus for legislative initiatives that quickly followed (Deficit Reduction Act of 2005 and 2006 Reauthorization of the Older Americans Act) and convinced the two major funders (who were joined by the Administration on Aging) to continue to fund Cash and Counseling, this time by replicating the approach in Medicaid programs in 11 states across the country. The Retirement Research Foundation funded a similar demonstration program in Illinois to bring the number of replication states to 12. The replication phase lasted from 2004 to 2008, and the results, documented by evaluators at RTI International, will be discussed in a subsequent chapter.

The success of the replication phase led RWJF, together with Atlantic Philanthropies, to fund first a business planning process and then the creation in 2009 of the National Resource Center for Participant-Directed Services, whose mission is to assist programs across the nation to implement the self-direction option.

Self-Determination for Persons with Developmental Disabilities. In 1997, RWJF invested in a broad range of demonstration activities around the country aimed at exploring the ways in which the self-direction model could be implemented for people with intellectual and developmental disabilities (Shumway, 1999). As with Cash and Counseling, RWJF provided funds to 19 states to create a foundation for the development of self-directed services. The introduction of self-direction in the intellectual- and developmental-disabilities field was a significant departure from traditional agency-based services and supports. RWJF allocated more than $5 million in support of the demonstrations. Allocations for each project amounted to $400,000 for a 3-year period, $200,000 for a 2-year period, or $100,000 for a 1-year period. While each local project was based on the same broad outline of values and objectives, there were significant differences given the variations in geography, sociodemographic factors, resources, service configuration, and economy. Further, the 19 states represented in the project also differed insofar as their history and evolution of publicly funded services, the extent of reliance on public institutions, the extent of provider acceptance of notions of self-determination, the extent of regulation, and the presence of supportive advocacy and professional/provider organizations.

The Human Services Research Institute conducted an evaluation of the pilot programs (Bradley et al., 2001). Some of the key findings included the following:

- Flexibility was the key. The most successful demonstrations were in states that could reengineer their funding systems to facilitate the development of individual budgets. Where systematic approaches to budget development (e.g., based on costs and/or individual characteristics) were already in place, the task of making these individual resource allocations was facilitated.

- Where self-determination was embedded throughout the system—rather than existing as a "boutique" service—the programs saw better outcomes.

- Across the country, the ability to lead a self-determined life was significantly influenced by the availability of direct support professionals.

- The juxtaposition of the self-determination demonstrations with the emerging aspirations of people with developmental disabilities combined to spur the growth of organized self-advocacy.

- Implementation of self-determination contributed to an enrichment of service planning and enhanced staff understanding of "person-centered" practices.

The evaluation also included policy recommendations for future implementation of self-determination initiatives. One suggestion to public managers was to simplify the processes surrounding self-determination, including budgeting and employee management. Where the process is too complex, there is a risk that families and service brokers—rather than participants—will be making the decisions. Another recommendation was to give service brokers the leeway to do the important work of supporting participants to explore their options by delegating some of the more onerous administrative responsibilities to another entity.

In summing up the impact of the RWJF demonstration, the evaluators made the following observation:

> Prior to these demonstrations, antecedents to self-determination can be found in innovations explored within family support, supported employment and independent living systems. One can argue that "self-determination" is less a revolutionary concept and more an evolutionary step that the field was already

pushing toward. Based on the observations and data collection undertaken by the evaluators, it is clear that the presence of these demonstrations hastened the progress toward a more person-driven system of supports—especially in those states/sites where there was already a glimmer of understanding and a hunger to go further. (Bradley et al., 2001, p. 11)

Recent Developments

Two major federal regulatory changes have put the principles of self-direction front and center in federal Medicaid policy. In March 2014, the Centers for Medicare and Medicaid Services (CMS) issued a rule that laid out the characteristics that, in the future, must be present in any residential, day, and other services provided through Medicaid HCBS funding. The rule was the crystallization of many of the important historical forces noted above. It was premised on the general notion that people supported by Medicaid should have the same ability to make choices and participate in their communities as people who are not on Medicaid. A major criterion for judging whether service settings will be eligible for funding included whether they isolated the individual from the community and from people without disabilities. CMS laid out criteria by which to judge whether a setting meets the rule, including whether the setting

- Is integrated in and supports access to the greater community;
- Provides opportunities to seek employment and work in competitive integrated settings, engage in community life, and control personal resources; and
- Is selected by the individual from among setting options, including non-disability specific settings.

The rule also emphasizes the importance of employment and self-determination. States were given five years to bring their services and supports into compliance. Under the Trump administration, the deadline was extended by three years.

The issue of self-direction and individual choice was also addressed in Section 2402a of the Affordable Care Act of 2010.[1] This provision directed the Department of Health and Human Services (HHS) to develop guidelines to enhance person-centered practice through a process of improved planning and plan implementation and a more concrete emphasis on self-direction. A cross-agency work group at HHS spent two years developing the guidelines. With respect to planning, the guidelines noted that the process should

- Be driven by the individual and respect his/her preferences
- Include people chosen by the individual
- Provide necessary information and support to ensure that the individual directs the process to the maximum extent possible
- Provide discussions and information in plain language
- Reflect cultural considerations
- Identify strengths, preferences, needs and desired outcomes of the individual
- Include individually identified goals and preferences related to relationships, community participation, employment, income and savings, healthcare and wellness, education and others

With respect to self-direction, the HHS workgroup released comprehensive policy guidance. Some of the requirements are as follows:

- When offered within programs, self-direction should be available to all individuals regardless of age, disability, diagnosis, functional limitations, cognitive status, sex, sexual orientation, race, ethnicity, physical characteristics, national origin, religion, and other such factors.
- Individuals receiving Medicaid community services must have access to information and counseling and information on self-direction through a variety of sources as needed or desired, so they can make an informed decision when choosing a self-directed service delivery model.
- Case managers and administrative staff should have training in self-direction, recruitment and education of direct service workers, budget processing, how the plan relates to the self-direction budget, needed alternative supports, housing search, etc.

Consumer Uses Self-direction in Colorado to Meet Complex Personal Needs

CH is a woman in her thirties living with quadriplegia. She lives in Colorado and is supported by the Consumer Directed Attendant Supports and Services (CDASS) program. She had a spinal cord injury when she was 9 years old. Prior to CDASS, she was supported by her family and a professional home healthcare agency. She joined the self-direction program about 12 years ago, during its pilot phase, after experiencing frustrations with the agency service model—frustrations that centered around its lack of consistency, lack of responsiveness to her needs, and frequent staff turnover.

CH heard about CDASS from the advocacy community and from her home health agency, who understood her frustration. She thinks of the agency "firing" her, so she could move into self-direction to better meet her needs. She enjoys being able to recruit and hire her own staff, which she needs every day. She designed her own training program and developed a "culture of support" for those who provide her care.

She sees the self-direction program as a small business to meet her individual and changing needs. This includes recruiting staff, setting wage scales, managing staff, including promotions and terminations, and providing an orientation and training program. She has learned to perform these functions well and sees self-direction as the management function that has improved her life: CH noted, "Self-direction lets you be successful and work every day while getting the support you need. I couldn't have accomplished what I set out to do without it."

Once she was well supported and positioned in CDASS, CH worked with other advocates and the state Medicaid office to develop a spinal cord injury waiver that was designed more specifically to meet the needs of participants who required a wider range of services and supports. It was approved by the state legislature, submitted to CMS, and approved as a new Colorado waiver program in 2009, offering acupuncture, massage, and chiropractic care.

As a CDASS participant with a spinal cord injury, CH has learned to live with pain and manage her mobility. After many years of experience with different pain medications, including opioids, she learned how to use other services and therapies that could increase her independence and mobility. She used her experience and consultations to create a unique program for herself and others:

> I learned how to use a variety of approaches to manage my pain and increase my mobility. This included acupuncture, chiropractor services, massage therapy, and yoga. These services allowed me to eliminate or reduce the use of opioids and other pain medication. My movement improved as well.

Learning how to manage her support workers and services as a small business and developing her own program as an entrepreneur led her to think how to offer new approaches for other people with spinal cord injuries. This led her to develop a nonprofit organization that focuses on providing integrative service approaches that are not dependent upon medications. As CH said, "Our mission is to improve the quality of life for persons with physical disabilities through direct services and systemic change to access integrative therapies."

The organization has been successful as a provider of services and as a model for developing new service and therapeutic approaches. The state Medicaid program is still used as the payer where possible, but the organization develops its own priorities based on the needs of the people it serves and the budgets they need to meet those needs. From this approach, the organization has acquired its own building for service delivery and consultation. Organization members see it as part of the community of support they are growing. According to CH:

> At the end of 2013, we started identifying the needs of our clients that we couldn't meet in the facility we had at the time. We wanted to build a sense of community and a one-stop shop for those who need these kinds of services. It's important for us to take away the stigma many people with disabilit[ies] face in their daily lives. This is a place where participants can speak to anyone without fear or embarrassment.

They moved into a building that serves about 70 people daily. The program is now in the process of developing new funding sources to enable it to acquire specialized machinery and technology to provide primary care in conjunction with innovative long-term care services and supports.

Conclusion

This historical review suggests that self-direction has many forebearers and is the culmination of a mosaic of important movements supporting the rights and personhood of people with disabilities and older adults. It is a powerful movement that draws from many sources and that is rapidly becoming a cornerstone of public services systems.

Chapter 3

The Federal Role

Less Visible, Just as Important

Self-direction has become one of the few national innovations in the delivery of health and human services that was preceded by many years of research and analysis, much of it stimulated and financed by the federal government. Without this background work, it is doubtful that federal and state governments would have created opportunities for more than a million participants (so far) to participate in a new service delivery platform. Ben Bernanke (2011) sums up the importance of "evidence-based" policy making: "In the abstract, economists have identified some persuasive justifications for government policies to promote Research & Demonstration activities, especially those related to basic research. In practice, we know less than we would like about which policies work best" (p. 41).

All three branches of the federal government have played important but different roles in the development and normalization of self-direction and in the growth of opportunities for individuals to select the people who work for them and to manage their own services and supports. Often, as Knickman and Stone (2007) discuss in the special issue of *Health Services Research* that reported the findings from the Cash and Counseling randomized control experiment, the role of the federal government was not as obvious in the launch of the self-direction as the role of private foundations, but it was equally important.

To highlight the contributions of each branch of government, it is important to start with a timeline that shows how the roles of each branch were interrelated. Much of the growth in the number of federal agencies promoting the self-direction option can be attributed to the wide circulation of the research results from the Cash and Counseling–controlled experiment. Other federal agencies got involved as the implementation of self-direction necessitated new procedures, policies, and safeguards.

Timeline of Federal Government Actions Promoting Self-direction

The timeline below shows the sequence of events at the federal level that contributed to the recognition of self-direction as an important option for people with disabilities and older adults. These key milestones will be described in more detail later in the chapter.

- In 1989 the Office of the Assistant Secretary for Planning and Evaluation (ASPE) in the US Department of Health and Human Services (HHS) funded a study by the World Institute on Disability to catalogue numbers of self-direction programs for people with physical disabilities. This report was influential and led to the Health Care Financing Administration (now the Centers for Medicare and Medicaid Services) regulations under which family members who are not legally liable for the support of the person in need can serve as paid providers of personal care/home and community based services and supports.

- In the early 1990s, the Clinton Health Plan, at the urging of the World Institute on Disability, included the option for participants to direct their home and community based services. When the Clinton Health Plan failed, officials at ASPE remained interested in the efficacy of this option.

- In the mid-1990s, ASPE continued to use its research budget to examine participant-directed options. These efforts included an evaluation of California's In Home Supportive Services program, a naturally occurring experiment allowing the comparison of traditional and self-directed services and supports (Benjamin, Matthias, & Franke, 2000), and a comparison of outcomes from Michigan, Massachusetts, and Texas home-care programs which offered varying levels of opportunities for participants to select their own workers (Doty, Kasper, & Litvak, 1996).

- Federal agencies played vital roles in the Cash and Counseling Demonstration and Evaluation (1996–2003) and the replication of the model in 12 state Medicaid programs (2004–2008). ASPE, along with the Robert Wood Johnson Foundation, was a major funder of both efforts. The Administration on Aging (AoA) became a funding partner for Cash and Counseling and its replication in 2002. The CMS, although not a direct funder of Cash and Counseling, was a key member of weekly (later monthly) team meetings for more than 10 years to coordinate the demonstration and evaluation.

- The 1999 Supreme Court *Olmstead* decision—coupled with the CMS Real Choice Systems Change grants, which then helped states develop their home and community based services—was a game changer, and it continues to influence the commitment of states to community alternatives (described in chapter 2).

- From 2004 to November 2005, CMS revised the Section 1915(c) HCBS waiver application that most states use to provide HCBS under Medicaid. The revisions included self-direction options that mainstreamed both employer and budget authority programs. Many of the Cash and Counseling replication states were the first to be approved under the new waiver application process.

- In late 2005, Congress passed the Deficit Reduction Act, which created several new Medicaid statutory authorities for self-direction, including one—Section 1915(j)—that allows states to offer budget authority to Medicaid state plan personal care services participants. Self-direction was also explicitly mentioned as an available option for states electing the 1915(i) state plan optional HCBS benefit and the Money Follows the Person grant demonstration.

- The reauthorization of the Older Americans Act in 2006 authorized the Administration on Aging to implement participant-direction options in its programs.

- In 2009 the Veterans Health Administration (VHA), working with and through the aging and disability network, began to implement a Veteran-Directed Home and Community Based Services program that became a key driver in the VHA's efforts to rebalance its long-term care spending.

- Beginning in 1998 and spanning a 15-year period, officials at the Internal Revenue Service worked with self-direction program leaders and HHS officials to develop forms and processes—and to implement necessary changes to IT systems—to make the self-direction approach viable (where the participant is the employer but utilizes a financial management services agency to pay taxes).

- In 2010, the Affordable Care Act (ACA) included many options to improve self-direction in Medicaid. These included the Community First Choice (Section 1915(k)) provisions that gave states a 6% enhanced match if they included participant direction in their state plan options, and Section 2402a, which provided guidance on person-centered planning and participant direction that crossed all programs administered by HHS. ACA also created a Medicare-Medicaid Coordination Office that oversees pilot programs in states that serve individuals who are dually eligible for Medicare and Medicaid. In a State Medicaid Directors Letter dated May 20, 2013, to the states implementing these pilots, CMS spelled out requirements related to self-direction. If the state already had a self-direction option, it was required to continue that option. If the state had no such option, it was urged to adopt one.

- The Community Living Assistance Services and Supports Act (CLASS Act), signed into law in 2010 as part of the ACA, was a voluntary government program under which individuals could obtain long-term-care insurance. CLASS called for the creation of individual budgets to purchase services and supports to enable people to live independently in their communities. However, it was formally repealed in 2013 due to cost concerns.

- In 2014, the Substance Abuse and Mental Health Services Administration, in coordination with the Robert Wood Johnson Foundation and the New York State Health Foundation, started the Multi-State Demonstration and Evaluation of Self-direction in Behavioral Health. Under this experiment, people with serious mental illness can manage budgets to meet their recovery goals.

- In 2014, CMS issued new regulations governing HCBS waiver services. These regulations require a person-centered planning process that addresses health and long-term services and supports needs in a manner that reflects individual preferences and goals.

- In 2015, the Department of Labor's home care rule went into effect extending Fair Labor Standards Act protections to most home care workers.

- The 21st Century Cures Act of 2016 (Cures Act) contains a new Medicaid requirement for mandatory use of Electronic Visit Verification as part of an effort to mitigate possible fraud and abuse.

Roles and Individuals

Switching gears, let's examine the federal role by agency and function. Different agencies within the federal government have different functions and play different roles. In the discussion that follows, we examine four of these functions as they relate to self-direction: research, regulation, development for particular populations, and quality control. The role played by specific federal agencies and individuals with respect to each of these functions will be highlighted. Key individuals who were indispensable to launching and expanding self-direction will also be mentioned.

The research supported by ASPE paved the way and helped frame the issues for advancing self-direction. CMS also played a seminal role through their regulatory authority, Medicaid state plan and waiver approval authority, and initiation of projects including those integrating Medicare and Medicaid. The next agencies listed here—the Administration for Community Living (ACL), the VHA, and the Substance Abuse and Mental Health Services Administration (SAMHSA)—played vital roles in offering options for the populations under their jurisdictions and opening additional funding streams. The final grouping: the Internal Revenue Service (IRS), the federal Department of Labor (DOL), and the HHS Office of the Inspector General helped to integrate self-direction into existing delivery systems. But they have also played an important role in normalizing self-direction while increasing complexity and bureaucratization which may make self-direction harder for participants to negotiate.

As we recount the role of each of these agencies it is often necessary to highlight the role of one or two individuals who led the way. Organizations are made up of people, and we often miss the part a single person played in catalyzing action. Some may be surprised that a single person could make the difference in a large bureaucracy, but the authors were witnesses to the difference a single person can make. Put differently, without the individuals named in this chapter it is not clear that self-direction would have thrived. We make no pretense of covering all the actions these agencies took; instead we try to look at their functions and roles, using some important activities as examples.

Research

It would be difficult to describe all the ideas that emanated from ASPE regarding self-direction, but it is not difficult to identify the person behind those ideas: Pamela Doty. Doty had significant support for her work from the politically appointed leadership in ASPE—especially Robyn Stone, who secured the federal funding and negotiated the partnership with the Robert Wood Johnson Foundation. Pam Doty was the thought leader, the internal champion, the instigator of new ideas to improve implementation, and the one who worked incessantly to keep the self-direction option on the front burner. Even before the Cash and Counseling demonstration, ASPE, with Pam as the project leader, was funding studies that catalogued the growth of self-direction, compared the experiences of states that allowed participants to hire their own workers to states that did not provide that opportunity, and examined the naturally occurring demonstration of self-direction in California.

In addition to providing major funding for the evaluation of Cash and Counseling, ASPE helped coordinate efforts to get the necessary 1115 Medicaid waivers through the Office of Management and Budget, as well as SSI and Food Stamp waivers, so individuals could save part of their Medicaid budgets to make larger purchases without exceeding the asset limits of these latter two programs. ASPE also paid for ethnographic case studies examining how the Cash and Counseling option affected the lives of 76 participants in Arkansas, Florida, and New Jersey. After the original Cash and Counseling results were published, ASPE staff helped write *Developing and Implementing Self-direction Programs and Policies: A Handbook* (Crisp et al., 2010) laying out the distinctive elements of the model and describing promising implementation strategies. Later, ASPE played a key role with CMS in thinking through how to integrate budget authority into existing regulatory structures.

ASPE, again with Doty as the project officer, used its research budget to promote implementation research, examining key issues—from liability concerns and worker's compensation approaches to recent research on how DOL regulations on minimum wages and overtime affect the growth of self-direction. It was Pam Doty who first promoted the creation of a National Participant Network that provides a vehicle for program participants and their families to take an active role in the design, implementation, and ongoing evaluation of programs in their states. Recent ASPE-funded research showed that a commitment to self-direction was one of the factors correlated with a state's success in moving funds from institutions to community services. This finding has played an important role in the spread of the self-direction option. ASPE and the ACL played especially active roles in developing the guidelines for self-direction across all the HHS agencies as required under Section 2402(a) of the Patient Protection and Affordable Care Act.

Regulation

CMS played a very active role in the creation, and later adoption, of self-direction options. CMS (then known as the Health Care Financing Administration) played an active role in selecting the original Cash and Counseling sites, developing the Medicaid waiver applications, and performing readiness reviews before operations got underway. CMS staff also took part in all management team meetings for nearly 10 years. Once the Cash and Counseling demonstration had proven the value of the option, CMS developed templates to help states adopt authority options, and later in 2005, when the 1915(c) regulations were codified, CMS built self-direction into the very fabric of the waiver applications. CMS officials were very supportive of the provisions in the Deficit Reduction Act of 2005 that created the 1915(j) Medicaid state plan option, which allowed all states to set up programs like Cash and Counseling. In recent years, CMS has worked to expand person-centered planning and the self-direction option in all Medicaid authorities through its regulatory processes (e.g., for Community First Choice 1915(k)) and through State Medicaid Letters (e.g., directed at the demonstrations for individuals dually eligible for Medicaid and Medicare). More than any other agency, the staff at CMS operated in teams; whereas some individuals played heroic roles, many individuals across the whole Medicaid Disabled and Elderly Health Programs Group played important parts.

To limit the role of CMS solely to regulation would not be completely fair since that organization played a significant role as a grant maker, helping the states to carry out their obligation to expand home and community based services and supports in response to the *Olmstead* Supreme Court decision. As the Supreme Court gave states time to develop their home and community based options, what happened next was critical. The Bush administration implemented a special grant program, called Real Choice Systems Change, to help the states jumpstart the rebalancing of institutional versus community funding. Between FY 2001 and FY 2010, CMS awarded 352 grants in 39 categories for a total of approximately $288,586,710. (The use and impact of these Real Choice Systems Change grants are detailed in chapter 4.)

Development for Particular Populations

Older Adults and People with Disabilities. Starting in 2002, the Administration on Aging (now part of ACL) funded the Cash and Counseling demonstration and replication. ACL became an important advocate for self-direction. For example, Josefina Carbonnell, then assistant secretary on aging, worked hard to get authorization for the aging network to allow and promote budget authority options as the Older Americans Act was revised in 2006. As described below, it was ACL that planted the seeds for the VHA to start the Veterans Directed HCBS program, patterned after Cash and Counseling.

Veterans. In 2008, the VHA was struggling with how to meet the needs of disabled American veterans coming home from the battlefronts in Iraq and Afghanistan at the same time as numerous veterans from previous wars were aging and becoming frailer. Rather than try to create its own home and community care system overnight, the VHA, led by Dan Schoeps, who headed up Geriatric Purchased Services, decided to collaborate and utilize the aging and disability network, ably led by Lori Gerhard at the Administration for Community Living. In October 2008, officials from the VHA and the Administration on Aging met with staff from the National Resource Center for Participant-Directed Services, and by February 2009, the new VD-HCBS program was launched. VHA leadership has pioneered various mechanisms to simplify and standardize the option—including readiness reviews, an assessment tool that converts disability level to budgets, as well as standardized provider agreements and payment codes. In 2017, the incoming secretary of veterans' affairs (VA), David Shulkin, in his confirmation speech to Congress, committed to having the VD-HCBS option in all Veterans Medical Centers in three years. The evaluations of VD-HCBS done by various medical centers spurred interest across the country. Currently, the VA is funding its own evaluation of implementation approaches.

People with Serious Mental Illness. In 2007, the Retirement Research Foundation and SAMHSA funded re-analyses of the Cash and Counseling data. Not surprisingly, more than 20% of participants had mental health claims on their Medicaid billings. When compared to people with similar mental health needs in the control group, those who managed a budget had significantly better outcomes.

This led the Robert Wood Johnson Foundation to fund an Environmental Scan to see how state mental health and Medicaid directors, participants, and traditional and nontraditional providers perceived the advantages and barriers to people with serious mental illness (SMI) self-directing budgets for their recovery goals. This scan, in turn, has led to the Six-State Demonstration and Evaluation of Self Direction in Behavioral Health project, with SAMHSA providing the technical assistance and the Robert Wood Johnson Foundation paying for the process and systems level outcome evaluations.

Here again, the role of a single person is notable. Paolo del Vecchio, the former director of the Center for Mental Health Services at SAMHSA, shepherded this initiative and worked to include self-direction as a possible use for Mental Health Block Grant funds.

The National Institute on Disability, Independent Living, and Rehabilitation Research has funded complementary efforts through the University of Illinois-Chicago Center on Integrated Health Care and Self-directed Recovery and the Temple University Collaborative on Community Inclusion of Individuals with Psychiatric Disabilities.

Quality Control

Internal Revenue Service. Officials from ASPE, along with staff from the National Resource Center for Participant-Directed Services, worked for more than eight years with the IRS to perfect the processes that make it possible for participants to have a financial management services agency (FMSA) entity to handle the various tax-paying and record-keeping functions necessary for self-direction. In the early years of self-direction, IRS rules were somewhat contradictory and prevented the IRS from matching FICA (Social Security and Medicare) tax filings with FUTA/SUTA (federal and, where applicable, state unemployment insurance payments), which resulted in the IRS making mistaken determinations regarding the tax liabilities of self-directing participants. The task of ensuring the proper collection and crediting of these taxes when the FMSA filed and paid them as payroll agents for self-directing program participants required the development of new forms and major information system revisions at the IRS. Judy Davis was an instrumental federal employee without whom the whole taxes "thing" may have become a quagmire drowning self-direction in compliance issues.

Department of Labor. The salient role in self-direction of the DOL is more recent. The DOL issued the Home Care Final Rule on October 1, 2013. This Rule extended the federal minimum wage and overtime protections in the Fair Labor Standards Act to *almost 2 million* home care workers. After several court challenges, the US Supreme Court issued an order denying a request to review the Court of Appeals decision, meaning the new rule stood.

Whether the Home Care Rule will influence the growth of self-direction or the exercise of self-direction by program participants, only time, and additional research, will tell. Most home care workers employed by self-directing Medicaid or other public program participants now have to be paid at least minimum wage, and most will be entitled to overtime pay if they work more than 40 hours per week. Most states have responded by placing limits on the number of hours they can work per week for any one self-directing program participant. These limits may apply to the sum total of hours worked per week if the state is likely to be deemed a "joint employer." In such a case, states would have to set up systems to track overtime liability when a personal care attendant works for more than one client in the same or a related public program. Moreover, the attendant would be entitled to travel-time pay if such services are provided on the same day, and travel time between clients would also have to be included in the computation of hours potentially subject to overtime pay requirements.

The choice and control of self-directing participants may be compromised if states impose strict limits on worker hours to avoid paying overtime, and so on. In a worst-case scenario, limits on worker hours might not only adversely affect choice and control but also create worker shortages.

Office of the Inspector General. Finally, the Office of the Inspector General has raised concerns about mitigating the possibility of fraud and abuse in home care in general, and participant direction in particular. This attention has led to an interest in standards for financial management services agencies and, most recently, Electronic Visit Verification (EVV). Before the end of his second term, President Obama signed the Cures Act, which contains a new Medicaid requirement for mandatory use of EVV, allowing nurses, home health aides, and direct care workers to check in electronically through software apps or telephonic devices and record the exact date, time, and location of a visit.

This potentially makes billing and payroll processing much easier, with fewer pay delays or inaccurate paychecks. On the downside, however, this may decrease the role of the program participant as "employer" if s(he) no longer has to approve timesheets and that would increase the likelihood of the state or the FMSA being considered the "joint employer" of participant-directed workers under the DOL Home Care Rule.

Clearly, the regulatory role of these last three agencies can mitigate against fraud and abuse and affect the workers that participants hire, but these actions may represent an increase in bureaucratic rules requiring more management of the documentation and eroding person-centered care.

People as Well as Organizations

In concluding this chapter, we would like to reemphasize the role of individuals within organizations. The individuals listed in this chapter did not act alone, but without their leadership, we would not be telling the story of their organizations.

Personal Story of Pamela Doty, PhD

In the preceding narrative, we spoke often of the role of individuals within the bureaucracy; to complete this chapter, we interviewed Pamela Doty, PhD, a senior policy analyst in the office of the Assistant Secretary for Planning and Evaluation, to get some of her personal insights on how and why self-direction evolved as it did.[1] Pam, without a doubt, is the person with the longest interest in self-direction. Her influence has crossed issues and agencies. We are grateful to her for sharing her thoughts.

Clearly affecting policy from deep within a bureaucracy is not easy. Pam reported to an associate deputy assistant secretary in the HHS office of the assistant secretary for planning and evaluation (ASPE), a branch of government with broad influence, a research-and-policy-development mission, but no day-to-day program operational responsibilities.

When Pam first came to the federal government in the 1980s, she became interested in Medicaid programs in states like Michigan and New York that allowed participants to hire their own personal care workers. She told us that she "became concerned by efforts to promulgate Medicaid state plan personal care optional benefit regulations that would have required states to adopt what was referred to as a 'modified medical model' for delivery of personal care aide services." States rebelled against the Notice of Proposed Rulemaking. ASPE, with Pam acting as project officer, then sponsored the World Institute on Disability study to chart the prevalence and attributes of self-direction efforts around the country, and then advocated within the federal government for a regulation that would explicitly allow self-direction. With legislative changes to the personal care statute in 1993, and the eventual issuance of a final rule for PCS in 1997, the option of hiring one's own worker was ensconced in Medicaid regulation.

When Pam describes the conversations that led to the unique partnership between ASPE and the Robert Wood Johnson Foundation, she gives significant credit to her superior, Mary Harrahan, for interesting her boss, Robyn Stone (then the Deputy Assistant Secretary), in the topic, the need for a large, controlled experiment to sway policy makers, and the necessity of a prestigious partner who could also devote significant resources to this effort.

Pam admits, "Without me, Cash and Counseling never would have gotten the 1115 waivers and would have been dead in the water before it launched. I did battle with the Office of Management and Budget (OMB), nearly got myself fired; convinced Nancy-Ann Min DeParle that Cash and Counseling would not fall prey to fraud and abuse. I think it's fair to say—as you did—that I was and have been a thought leader with regard to self-direction generally, especially Cash and Counseling." It's fair to say that her leadership was far from limited to Cash and Counseling.

Pam's influence has continued to be important on every topic ranging from how to fit self-direction into the Medicaid waiver structure to fostering implementation research on topics such as legal liability and workers compensation. It was also Pam who pushed to add ethnographic studies to the Cash and Counseling evaluation so people could see not just the numbers but the people's faces. Examples of Pam's recent initiatives include research on the relationship between states successfully rebalancing their long-term-care funding and their commitment to self-direction options, and seminal research on how self-direction works in the private marketplace.

When asked how she was able to accomplish so much with so little actual power, Pam defers and points to such classics as the *Bureaucratic Entrepreneur* by Richard Haass (1999) and Arnold Meltsner's *Policy Analysts in Bureaucracy* (1976). She admits to having some disappointments along the way, including New York dropping out of the Cash and Counseling demonstration and various states not following through, when leadership at the top changed, on comprehensive plans that integrated self-direction into all HCBS programs (including Money Follows the Person) and applied the concept of an "individualized capitation" payment to create a self-directed managed care model. In addition to persistence, Pam has the virtue of perspective and a wry sense of humor. When asked about the role of the federal government in the future, she quoted the Hippocratic oath: "First do no harm."

Chapter 4

The Status of Self-direction across the Country

Though, nationally, large numbers of people are self-directing, the extent of self-direction varies widely from state to state and among groups of participants (e.g., people with intellectual disabilities, people with physical disabilities, aging adults, etc.). This chapter will explore the growth in self-direction across the country, differences in the use of the Medicaid State Plan and Home and Community Based waiver programs to support self-direction, and the specific experiences of four states that have made substantial investments in self-direction.

State Participation in Self-direction

Since the early 2000s, the number of self-directed programs and participants has grown considerably. In 2002, Doty and Flanagan identified 139 publicly funded self-direction programs. Subsequent changes in federal Medicaid policies in the next decade spurred additional growth in the self-direction option. In 2005, CMS revised the §1915(c) Home and Community Based Services waiver application to include a participant direction option. In early 2006, Congress passed the Deficit Reduction Act of 2005, which created several new Medicaid statutory authorities for participant direction, including §1915(j) that allows states to offer budget authority through their Medicaid state plan for participants using services. The 2010 Affordable Care Act (ACA) included several reforms supporting the development of self-direction including the Community First Choice (§1915(k)) option and a revision of the §1915(i) authority. These Medicaid waiver changes and additions expanded the ways in which states

> *Home and Community Based waivers provide opportunities for Medicaid beneficiaries to receive services and supports in their own home or community rather than in institutions or other isolated settings. There are a number of types of state-plan options and waivers, but the ones that are the most relevant to self-direction include 1915(c), Home and Community Based Waivers. 1915(i), State Plan Home and Community Based Services; 1915(j), State Plan Self-directed Personal Assistance; and 1915(k), Community First Choice. Medicaid programs serve people with intellectual and physical disabilities, mental illness, brain injury and older individuals.*

could offer self-direction. In addition, the launch of the Veteran-Directed Home and Community Based Services (VD-HCBS) program also increased opportunities for self-direction to veterans in states where it was offered.

Charting the growth and penetration of self-direction is challenging. The Office of the Assistant Secretary for Planning and Evaluation in the US Department of Health and Human Services supported a preliminary national survey in 2002 (Doty & Flanagan). However, ten years later, little was known about the populations served and the range of self-direction opportunities from state to state. To fill this gap, the National Resource Center for Participant-Directed Services (NRCPDS) at Boston College conducted an inventory of publicly funded self-direction programs in the United States in 2010–2011 and two follow-up surveys in 2013 (Sciegaj et al.) and 2015 (Sciegaj et al.). These surveys were based on contacts with state program managers and captured information on the number of programs, kinds of participants, and some of the program attributes.

From 139 programs in 2001–2002, the number of self-directed programs grew steadily. The 2010–2011 NRCPDS survey identified 212 programs, the 2013–2014 inventory recorded 277 programs, and the 2015–2016 survey identified 252 publicly funded programs. The net loss in 2015–2016 compared to previous NRCPDS inventories was the result of a change in definition. The 2015–2016 national inventory counted all "programs" operating under a single Medicaid 1915c waiver and all VD-HCBS programs operating in a state as a *single program*, whereas previous national inventories counted these programs separately. Since some states had as many as four different programs with self-direction under a single waiver, this change in definition had a significant downward impact. It is very likely that the number of individual programs continued to grow in 2015–2016.

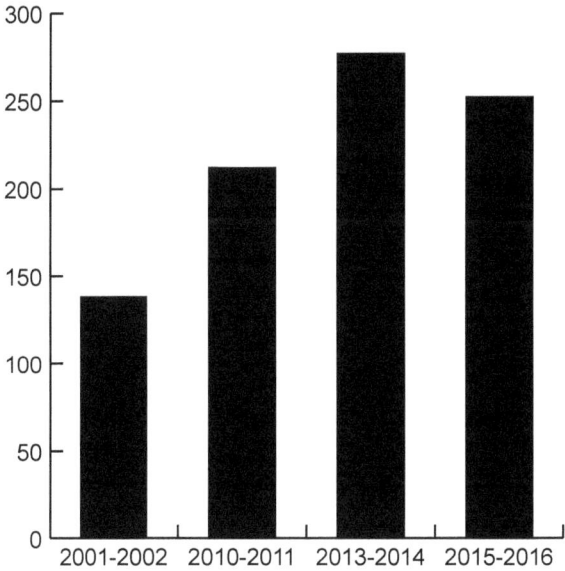

Figure 4.1. Number of self-direction programs in the United States. Adapted from "Highlights: Inventory of Consumer-Directed Support Programs" by P. Doty and S. Flanagan, 2002, U.S. Department of Health and Human Services, Office of the Assistant Secretary for Planning and Evaluation, and from National Inventories conducted by the National Resource Center for Participant-Directed Services in 2011, 2013, and 2016.

Growth in the Numbers of Individuals Who Are Self-directing

As programs grew, so did the number of participants. Doty and Flanagan (2002) reported 486,000 individuals were enrolled in self-direction in 2001–02. By 2016, the number of participants more than doubled to just over 1 million as documented by the state. In all the surveys, California accounted for more than half of the persons enrolled in self-direction.

Self-direction programs serve people of all ages with a wide range of needs, including adults with intellectual, developmental, and physical disabilities; older adults; and children with special needs. The number of programs serving Veterans has grown since 2007 with the expansion of the VD-HCBS in 36 states, DC, and Puerto Rico as of 2018. There has been

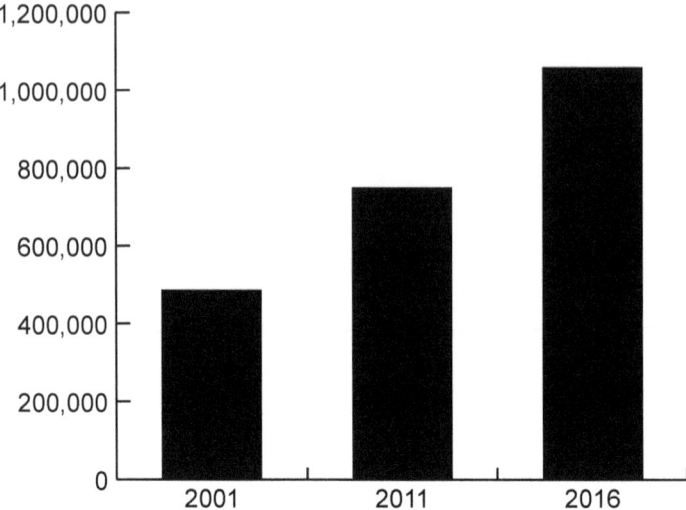

Figure 4.2. Number of participants in self-direction programs in the United States. Adapted from "Highlights: Inventory of Consumer-Directed Support Programs" by P. Doty and S. Flanagan, 2002, U.S. Department of Health and Human Services, Office of the Assistant Secretary for Planning and Evaluation, and from National Inventories conducted by the National Resource Center for Participant-Directed Services in 2011, 2013 and 2016.

little change in the number of programs that reported serving participants with other special needs, including people with traumatic brain injuries, people with HIV/AIDS, and people with autism. This may be a reflection of reluctance in some states to offer self-direction to people with more complex and lifelong needs. Self-direction for people with behavioral health issues is still nascent but is gaining traction (see chapter 9).

Medicaid remains the largest funding source for self-direction. The percentage of self-directed programs funded by Medicaid increased from 65% in 2001 to 78% in 2015–2016 (Sciegaj et al., in preparation). Other sources of funding for self-direction include the Veteran's Administration and state general revenues. Medicaid managed care for long-term services and supports has expanded, which has caused many advocates for self-direction to raise concerns regarding the ability and willingness of managed care companies to administer self-direction. The 2013–2014 inventory identified 18 states that contracted with managed care organizations (MCOs) (National

Resource Center for Participant-Directed Services, 2014) and by 2016, the number increased to 21 states (Sciegaj et al., in preparation). However, a comparison of state enrollments in self-direction in 2013 and 2016 did not show any negative change in those states that had managed care contracts (Edwards-Orr & Ujvari, 2018). Further, previous research by Sciegaj and colleagues (2013) did not find that managed care had any systemic negative impact on self-direction enrollments. Going forward, however, there is concern that the expansion of managed care will make it difficult to collect these data unless states require MCOs to report it.

Capturing the take-up rate (i.e., the percentage of participants choosing self-direction over all Medicaid HCBS recipients eligible for self-direction) is hard to document because it is very difficult to get precise information on the number of people eligible to self-direct in each Medicaid state plan or waiver. The American Association of Retired Persons (AARP, 2017) in its State Long-Term Care Scorecard, made an effort to present market penetration data as one of its measures of Consumer Choice. However, whereas the numerator—the number of people self-directing—comes from the national inventories published by the NRCPDS, the denominator is based on the estimated number of people with disabilities in that state. In other words, the measure only shows the estimated number self-directing per 1,000 people with disabilities, without regard to their Medicaid eligibility or the structure of the waiver programs.

This problem may be easier to address in the future if states provide timely and accurate data for the Transformed Medicaid Statistical Information System (T-MSIS). This reporting form is being revised by CMS to include fields that will require information at the individual client level for all Medicaid authorities on whether the individual was self-directing and whether they were using an "employer authority" or "budget authority" modality.

Participation of People with Intellectual and Developmental Disabilities in Self-direction

We have learned much about people with intellectual and developmental disabilities (I/DD) in self-direction due to continuous national research and the more than 20 years of data collection through the National Core Indicators (NCI). Carli Friedman (2018) from the Council on Quality and Leadership recently conducted a survey of state self-direction and participation by people with intellectual and developmental disabilities. The aim of this study was to examine if and how states permitted participant direction in Medicaid HCBS 1915(c) waivers for people with I/DD. Friedman analyzed HCBS waivers from across the country to determine frequency of participant direction, expenditures directed toward participant direction, and state goals for utilization of participant direction. The findings revealed a disconnect between the large number of waivers that allowed participant direction and extremely low state goals for actual utilization of participant direction. This indicates that for people with I/DD, enrollment in self-direction has been relatively slow despite research on the positive impact that self-direction has on quality of life and cost, as discussed in chapters 6 and 7.

Data from the National Core Indicators (2019) also indicate a relatively low proportion of I/DD participants who are self-directing. The data also indicate that for those participants who are self-directing, their outcomes are more positive than for those who do not self-direct. NCI is a collaborative effort between the National Association of State Directors of Developmental Disabilities Services (NASDDDS) and the Human Services Research Institute (HSRI). The purpose of NCI, which began in 1997, is to support NASDDDS member agencies to gather a standard set of performance and outcome measures that can be used to track performance over time, to compare results across states, and to establish national benchmarks. Currently 46 states administer NCI surveys.

The data on self-direction are drawn from the NCI In-Person Survey (IPS). The IPS is a face-to-face conversation completed with a minimum of 400 randomly selected individuals in each state who are 18 years of age or older and receiving at least one paid service from the state (in addition to case management). The data are from the 2018–2019 data cycle and show a wide range of participation in self-direction among states responding—from a high of 49% in Oregon to just 1% in Georgia and New York; notably, no one in the Alabama sample was self-directing.

The national NCI data show that the proportion of people self-directing has been relatively consistent at approximately 10% over the past five years. This in spite of the fact that the number of states collecting the data has grown over that same period.

NCI data also documented that among individuals with I/DD who are self-directing participation rates decline as people age: 63.1% are under 35 years old; 26.2% are between the ages of 35 and 54; and 10.2% are 55 and older. The smaller number of individuals in older age groups may

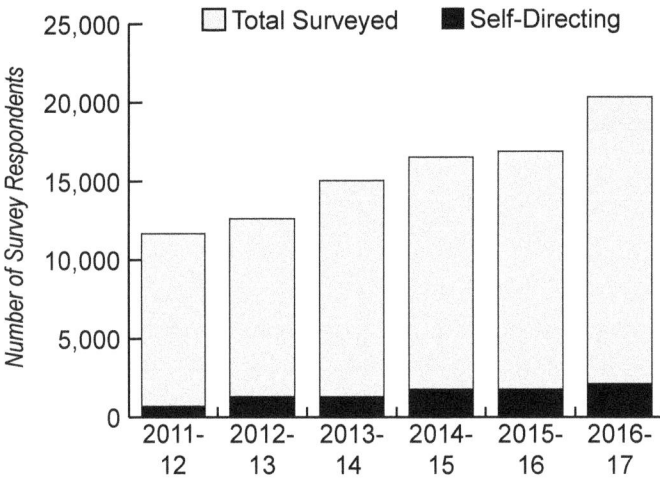

Figure 4.3. Number and proportion of National Core Indicators survey respondents (adults in the United States with intellectual and developmental disabilities) who are self-directing. Copyright 2018 by National Core Indicators.

be explained by the fact that when they entered the public-service system, the self-direction option was not available, and the new waivers focused on younger people and those entering the service system.

Individuals with autism are more likely to elect to self-direct their services than those with intellectual disabilities who are not on the autism spectrum (74.7% of individuals who are self-directing have a diagnosis of autism, compared to 25.3% who have a diagnosis of intellectual disability without autism). One reason that people with autism elect to self-direct may be explained by the fact that they are not satisfied with the traditional services offered in the I/DD systems. Self-direction allows people with autism to create their own supports to match their needs. Also, in many states, the waivers focused on children whose parents see self-direction as the only service option that met the need of children on the spectrum.

Further, individuals with I/DD who are self-directing are more likely to be described as having a mild or moderate disability (61.7%) than a severe, profound, or unspecified level of disability (38.3%). Whether this means that there is a ceiling on the growth of self-direction for this population given that people with more serious functional limitations tend not to self-direct remains to be seen. And, conversely, data from Michigan (chapter 6) suggests that those with serious needs are likely to choose self-direction to give them more service options. Most of the people with I/DD who are self-directing live at home with parents or a relative (21.2%); another 16.7% live in their own home or apartment; only 1.2% live in a group home.

State Implementation of Self-direction

Self-direction was initially developed as a federal policy innovation, well researched and documented, but it was up to the states to initiate, design, and implement it through Medicaid waivers and sometimes state funding. As we have seen, this has led to very different program models and penetration rates by states and population groups. For the remainder of this chapter, we will look at four different states with robust self-direction programs—California, Wisconsin, Virginia, and Tennessee—and the factors that contributed to their success. Each state has found unique ways to deploy self-direction to meet its specific needs and to expand and improve community-based services.

The penetration of self-direction in these four states is much higher than in most other states. In California's self-direction program, for example, 85% of eligible older adults and people with physical disabilities are enrolled. In Wisconsin, among individuals with intellectual and developmental disabilities, 47% of eligible individuals are participating in a self-direction waiver program. In Virginia, 45% of eligible older adults have enrolled. And in Tennessee, there is a 20% rate of eligible I/DD and aging participants.

California. California was the first state to initiate consumer-directed programs—before that appellation had been coined. The program, which serves two groups, people with physical disabilities and those who are aging, has grown rapidly and broadly across the state for seven decades. As of this writing, the state serves about 580,000 people statewide, representing about half of the people in the country who are self-directing. The historical events that shaped California's approach to self-direction played out in four significant phases, with a fifth ready to start soon.

The first phase began with a series of small initiatives aimed at individuals with disabilities living at home. Specifically, the state-funded Attendant Care program was created to serve survivors of polio who needed assistance to remain in their homes. It began in 1953 when Rancho Los Amigos Medical Center in Los Angeles hired personal assistants at a cost of $10 a day to care for 158 iron-lung users at home, thus avoiding the $37-a-day cost of providing nursing-facility care. The program provided grants to participants so they could hire aides to provide various domestic services. Funds came from the county and state government. The program eventually expanded to other interested counties.

In the 1960s and 1970s, activists in the independent-living movement helped to establish local self-directed service models. One successful program, launched by Ed Roberts, Judy Heumann, and other advocates, was the self-directed attendant-care program for students at the University of California at Berkeley. In 1972, Roberts and his allies launched the Center for Independent Living in Berkeley, which became a rallying point for the expansion of self-direction across the state. These early programs established the foundational principles that would govern the self-directed services in California and nationally.

The loosely organized programs created public awareness of the benefits of self-direction and ushered in the second phase of program expansion. In 1973, state legislation, called the Homemaker Chore Program, was passed. The new law enabled people with disabilities to receive home-based personal care services provided by county employees or home health agencies. The program gave participants who were elderly, blind, or disabled employment authority to hire, supervise, and fire staff, but did not provide budget authority for other services. The initiative was financed primarily by state funds with additional support from participating counties. It enabled consumers who could not hire or supervise their own providers the opportunity to receive supports from county employees or to contract with an outside agency.

One outgrowth of the program was the creation of a home care workers union that would later become the United Domestic Workers of America (UDWA). A second union, the Service Employees International Union (SEIU), a member of the national AFL/CIO, also began organizing direct care workers. The political clout of these two unions stimulated the continued growth of the program in counties across California.

During this phase, the program went through significant growth, which led to the development of a more formal structure and rules. Monthly caps were placed on service hours, which averaged 102 hours in 2018. Legislation was enacted that required the California Department of Social Services (CDSS) to develop and implement a standardized and equitable authorization and allocation process based on uniform statewide individual assessments. The care assessment that was administered by county staff used a functional scale that measured activities of daily living (ADLs), instrumental activities of daily living (IADLs), and measures of physical and mental capacity. The results of the assessment were used to determine the monthly hours of services required by each consumer. These care hours were then monetized using the county's rates to establish an annual individual budget.

Finally, CDSS enhanced a state payroll system for individual providers that incorporated a management information feature. Counties were then able to access real-time participant information, process eligibility documents, and calculate a participant's share-of-cost for services. Payroll checks were issued from the state comptroller's office.

The third phase began in 1993 when the California Medicaid (Medi-Cal) state plan was amended to include a new program, In Home Support Services (IHSS). To implement the new services, public IHSS Authorities were formed at the county level, enabling the local County Board of Supervisors to contract with a nonprofit consortium or establish a public authority for the delivery of IHSS. This led to the designation of the counties as the official employer of the direct care workers after a court battle initiated by the unions. The upgraded role of the counties stimulated continued program growth through expanded eligibility efforts for participants and collective bargaining with both unions to improve wages and benefits.

To fund the new Medi-Cal services, Medi-Cal paid for 50%, and the counties and the state paid the remainder. In addition, the new initiative included state funding for those individuals in need of services but not eligible for Medi-Cal.

Because counties were now the employer of record, they became active in collective bargaining and setting wages, although wage increases were limited to no more than three percentage points above the state-wide minimum wage. Employer of Record counties became responsible for screening providers and conducting background checks before placing workers on a registry to become available to work in the IHSS program. For counties that did not create a public authority, an advisory committee with a minimum of 51% consumer representation was established to make recommendations to the county supervisors on program development and structure and to ensure that the quantity and quality of providers met the expanding demand for IHSS.

In 2004, the state initiated an IHSS/Quality Assurance (QA) program that included social worker training, state/county monitoring, interagency collaboration to prevent/detect fraud and maximize overpayments recovery, and annual error-rate studies. In addition, the IHSS Independence Plus Waiver (IPW) Program became effective in August 2004 which funded services provided by family members, usually parents and spouses.

The fourth phase of the program began in March 2010 when the Affordable Care Act (ACA) was enacted nationally allowing for the establishment of a new Medi-Cal state plan option, the Community First Choice Option (CFCO). This option enhanced the ability of IHSS to provide community-based personal attendant care services to enrollees who would otherwise require institutional care. It also provided a 6% increase in federal funding for CFCO services and supports as of December 2012. Approximately 41% of IHSS consumers whose need and functional levels qualified them for the new waiver were transitioned to CFCO. To support the changes and the continued growth, the state created an enhanced state payroll and case management system. The updated state payroll system was more user friendly, provided a more efficient and centralized payment system, and made it possible to manage and track case activities.

Participants can choose between a consumer-directed model (CDM) or a professional agency—although only 12 counties offer the latter option. Clients in both programs are primarily older adults, many of whom have disabling or chronic health care conditions. Most participants require some daily assistance for meal preparation, cooking, cleaning, monitoring medications, transferring, dressing, toileting, bathing, and other activities of daily living. For some, this includes leaving the house when possible and enjoying the companionship of another adult in a community setting. Participants also receive Medicaid state plan services as well, including case management, home-delivered meals, in-home physical therapy, adaptive equipment, home modifications, and emergency call systems. In almost 70% of the cases statewide, the paid caregiver is a family member, with 50% living at the home of the member.

When the program grew to 200,000 in 2000, research was conducted by the UCLA School of Public Policy and Social Research on the efficacy of both self-directed and agency care models (Benjamin & Matthias, 2000). Research focused on the 12 counties where consumers could choose between the two models in order to compare the two approaches. The results were clear across all age groups: CDM clients reported being more empowered in their service relationship, more satisfied with the technical and interpersonal aspects of services, had workers who met their cultural and linguistic needs, and more positive about the quality of their lives. Equally important, they reported feeling no less safe than those using the agency model. The conclusions of the study clearly favored the expansion of CDM: ". . . statistically significant differences between the service models on client outcomes consistently favor the consumer-directed model" (p. 87).

There are several reasons that explain why California is leading the nation in self-direction for aging adults and people with disabilities. First, the state began to develop the initiative almost 60 years before the federal program model was developed. The initial program had no federal funding nor legislative mandate. It was built on a small, activist initiative that demonstrated the power and effectiveness of a self-directed model. The eventual shape of the publicly supported option retains the original values of independence and personal decision making.

Secondly, direct care worker unions—the United Domestic Workers Union (UDWU) and the Service Employees International Union (SEIU)—played a significant role throughout the history of self-direction in California: Since the program was officially recognized by state legislation in 1973, both unions saw it as an opportunity to organize service workers, influenced by the successful state organizing of low-wage farm workers in California by César Chávez. Early literature referred to IHSS as "the beginning of a movement" supporting both the "disability rights movement" and home care providers and clients "united for dignity and independence" (United Domestic Workers of America, 2017).

The California unions recognized that the usual ways of operating would not work in this context. Given that their clients were individuals with disabilities or individuals who were aging, they agreed that strikes were neither feasible nor humane. Also, they agreed that the IHSS participants could hire, supervise, and fire their workers. They understood their need to lobby the legislature for funds for services and benefits, and they understood their relationship to the public system to be very different from the traditional public-management/worker labor-union relationship.

Another important factor in the success of IHSS is its solid constituency of 580,000 participants and 498,000 support workers (P. Cervinka, personal communication, September 2018; D. Thompson, personal communication, September 2018),[1] not to mention many more tens of thousands of family members and friends of participants. This constituency is a powerful political force in the state. Budget meetings with the governor and legislative leadership regarding IHSS always involve IHSS users, often accompanied by union leaders and frequently supported by public marches and demonstrations.

Finally, IHSS has shown positive results for participants as illustrated in the results of the UCLA evaluation noted above. This success has led to another phase focusing on the I/DD population discussed in chapter 8. Legislation passed in 2013 has led to the creation of a new waiver that has gone into effect in 2019 requiring all the state's 22 regional I/DD service centers to begin offering self-direction to all people they serve. Considering that these centers serve a total population of approximately 300,000 clients, it is likely this new requirement will create tens of thousands of new self-direction participants.

Wisconsin. The development of self-direction in Wisconsin occurred in three phases, and a fourth phase has emerged recently. The first phase took place in 1984 in Dane County when a work group of administrators, stakeholders, and advocates created a vision for the future of the system providing developmental disabilities services and supports. The group committed to the following goals:

- Promote the inclusion of all persons served in the daily life of their communities

- Individualize all residential services

- End placements into institutions

- Focus on continuity, stability, and continuous learning of state-of-the-art approaches to respond to people's impairments or challenges

- Continue to work together to learn, improve, and adapt the system

The aspiration to individualize both traditional and nontraditional services led to a systemwide application of self-direction that affected all 1,400 persons across the county. By 1995, all but 35 of the 400 Dane County residents living in state institutions had been relocated to community residential settings and were directing their services with individual budgets. The remaining 35 had guardians who blocked movement to the community. Further, large group homes were replaced by smaller settings including homes owned by clients, and paid employment began to replace sheltered workshops. Services and supports were centered on the participant's goals and needs rather than on what providers were contracted to provide.

In 1996, a grant from the Robert Wood Johnson Foundation as part of a multistate self-direction demonstration enabled the county to further individualize services and supports. By 2004, about 1,100 individuals were in self-directed services with budgets that allowed both employment authority and budget authority. By 2016, 1,395 individuals—or 98%—of the 1,424 served in Dane County self-directed their supports and services with full budget authority. That rate was by far the highest in the country. This has led to extraordinary outcomes as documented by the Dane County Developmental Disabilities Coalition in a paper entitled "Building on the Dane County Difference" (2017):

- 785 people (55%) who are self-directing work in an integrated employment setting;
- 92% of Dane County students with developmental disabilities leave high school with paid employment;
- 808 people (57%) purchase their own supported living services that enable them to live where they want, with whom they want;
- Only four Dane County residents with developmental disabilities were admitted to one of Wisconsin's state mental health institutes, average length of stay was 12 days; and
- No Dane County residents with developmental disabilities were admitted to a state DD institution.

An important element of the county's self-directed system was that every participant had an independent support broker working for them. The support broker replaced the case manager for all participants in the county. The support broker helps the participant manage their budget, hire and supervise their staff, shop for goods and services, find jobs, or set up their own microbusinesses. In 2016, there were 92 support brokers assisting 1,424 participants, a ratio of 1:16. If a participant is not happy with his or her support broker, they can replace them.

The second phase took place at the state level. Participant choice and self-determination were embedded in Wisconsin's statewide Family Care–managed long-term services and supports waiver program that was phased in during the early 2000s. The Family Care program contracted with eight regional not-for-profit managed care organizations that in turn contracted with local agencies and nonprofit organizations to keep people in their homes by meeting their individual needs. This included giving all members the opportunity to self-direct some or all of their services.

After several years, it became clear that fewer participants than anticipated were taking advantage of self-direction in Family Care. A review of the reasons suggested that case managers were not good at explaining self-direction, and participants did not understand the option. When the Family Care program came up for renewal in 2007, CMS required, as a condition of waiver renewal, the state to establish a separate HCBS waiver program solely for qualified adults who elect to self-direct *all* their services and supports.

After renewing the Family Care Program, Wisconsin entered the third phase of self-direction with the launch of the Include, Respect, I Self-direct (IRIS) 1915c waiver on July 1, 2008. IRIS was designed to enhance opportunities for seniors and adults with physical and developmental disabilities who were eligible for Family Care to self-direct *all* their Medicaid-funded services. The program was available to qualified adults only in counties participating in the Family Care program—46 counties (of 72) at the time. The state Department of Health Services (DHS) retained an IRIS Consultant Agency to assist participants to select a qualified individual consultant to help them develop a budget and manage a person-centered plan that included employment authority and budget authority. Each county hired a local services agency to pay the bills, manage the payroll, and provide reports. DHS also contracted with Disability Rights Wisconsin to act as program ombudsman, assisting participants to file and settle grievances and appeals. The system of care remained county based.

The participant manages an individual budget based on an assessment of needs and chooses among allowable supports and services. The individual budget gives the individual family spending authority with the approval of a financial counselor. Based on Wisconsin law, the IRIS oversight agency provides a nurse who will help develop a care plan that is integrated with the participant's IRIS plan that includes a personal budget that meets their needs and preferences. This enabled the state to create two different programs for long-term care using self-direction, IRIS, and Family Care.

When the IRIS waiver was developed, the expectation was that it would serve a relatively small number of individuals who elected to self-direct all their services rather than receive them through one of the eight MCOs in the Family Care program. DHS officials initially projected that 1,500 individuals would be enrolled in IRIS by 2011. In fact, almost 6,000 individuals were participating in the program by early 2012 with demand increasing in all the counties (Hagopian, 2013).

The unexpected surge in enrollment in the IRIS program posed problems for the counties that were not prepared for the unexpected demand, including an inadequate management infrastructure and an inequitable process of establishing individual budget allocations. These operational issues constrained the ability of IRIS participants to make choices as well as to receive supports to direct their own services. These problems were documented in a 2011 evaluation of the Family Care program conducted by the nonpartisan Legislative Audit Bureau (Wisconsin Department of Health Services, 2018). In response to the Audit Bureau's findings and growing concerns from the legislature and the governor about the growing cost of the Family Care program, the Wisconsin DHS developed a plan for the long-range sustainability of both programs. The plan included action steps to improve ". . . the ability of consumers to choose the most integrated, community-based and cost-effective services." IRIS is now seen as the premiere program for self-direction in the state.

As of 2016, the Family Care and IRIS programs served about 55,000 people in long-term care in 65 of the state's 72 counties. This included about 15,000 people enrolled in IRIS. Of all participants in both programs, 27% were self-directing some or all of their services. That included people with developmental disabilities, fragile health conditions, physical disabilities and problems of aging. This is a participation rate far higher than most states for similar populations.

In 2015, Wisconsin Act 55 directed DHS to make a variety of changes to the Family Care program to make it more efficient and provide a wider range of services. In response, the governor proposed to create one large statewide program under the auspices of for-profit managed care programs to administer both Family Care and IRIS, as well as acute care. The two programs accounted for about $2 billion of the $3.4 billion that the state and federal government were spending on long-term care per fiscal year. The merger under statewide for-profit MCOs was expected to create economies that would save the state money. In addition, the plan would replace the legacy waivers for long-term care in the remaining 7 counties for an estimated 3,000 people, and serve, at a minimum, an additional 500 people who were previously waitlisted.

Advocates worked against the proposal, arguing that it would undermine very successful long-term care programs and self-direction. Statewide savings were projected at only 1.7% of current expenditures. After robust public discussions and hearings across the state, the proposal to consolidate and privatize all the state's programs was dropped by the administration. In a letter to the Joint Finance Committee, published in the *Milwaukee Journal-Sentinel* on June 10, 2016, Kitty Rhoades, secretary of the Department of Health Services, said the administration was no longer pursuing consolidation under for-profit MCOs. Instead the administration proposed Family Care/IRIS 2.0 which would include the following:

- An Integrated Health Agency (IHA) to develop an individual's IRIS budget for self-direction based on assessment of the member's care needs

- An IRIS specialist to perform the same functions as the current IRIS consultant agency and assist IRIS members to identify long-term care needs and develop an individualized plan to meet those needs

- Continued ability of members to have budget authority and full employer authority

- Continuation of the ability of individuals to self-direct under Family Care/IRIS 2.0

The plan included adding the remaining 7 counties and an estimated 3,500 members by the first quarter of 2018. The state agreed to continue to use local not-for-profit MCOs to administer the program. All eligible adults were slated to have access to coordinated primary, acute, and behavioral health services, in addition to long-term care services and self-direction. These changes are designed to preserve the community-based service system for Wisconsin's frail elders and adults with disabilities by coordinating necessary health care services and long-term care, while managing the expenditure growth of an aging population.

Virginia. Virginia currently has five Medicaid waivers that provide the opportunity for self-direction using employment authority. Eligible individuals include people with physical disabilities, older adults, those with developmental disabilities including intellectual disabilities, children with mental health issues, and children in need of early periodic screening and diagnostic services. As of 2017 more than 23,000 individuals enrolled in the waivers have opted to self-direct; the majority are older adults and those with physical, intellectual, and developmental disabilities. In total, participants employ approximately 26,500 direct workers who provide personal care, companion care, and respite care (K. Kimsey, personal communication, March 2017; T. Smith, personal communication, April 2017).[2]

The movement to self-direction in Virginia began in 1995 when the Virginia General Assembly passed House Joint Resolution 539 that required the state's Medicaid agency, the Department of Medical Assistance Services (DMAS), to conduct a study of consumer direction with recommendations for implementation in Virginia. The resolution grew out of an intense public debate in a series of open meetings and hearings attended by consumers, family members, advocates, providers, and state staff pressing for the opportunity for individuals to have choice and control over how and by whom their services were provided. Local Centers for Independent Living, Area Agencies on Aging, and Community Services Boards overseeing local health and developmental disabilities services all supported the legislation.

In 1996, DMAS completed a report that strongly recommended that the state adopt self-direction as a platform for service delivery (Virginia Department of Medical Assistive Services, 1996). While initially the program aimed to serve people with spinal cord injuries, it soon expanded to individuals with physical disabilities and aging adults. Based on a review of models in other states, the Commonwealth adopted an approach that stressed personal empowerment, control, and flexibility. Significantly, the DMAS recommendations included giving participants a clear choice between an agency-based or participant-directed model.

The new initiative did not include the cash budgets that were part of the Cash and Counseling model but instead focused on hiring in-home staff at the direction of the participant. Designers of the plan wanted to build on conservative elements of self-direction and reduce any inherent risks that might flow from a cash benefit. The desire to create new opportunities to expand the workforce by including family members and friends drove the design. The benefit provided up to 42 hours a week of personal care services for older adults and individuals with physical disabilities with no cognitive impairment who met the level of care required for nursing-home facilities. The benefit also included up to 200 hours of respite care per year.

Staff wages were set by the Virginia General Assembly, and regulations and policies were developed by DMAS, subject to review by the Virginia Department of Labor. DMAS was designated as the fiscal agent and call center, and the Centers for Independent Living served as service facilitators/support brokers, assisting people with the enrollment process and helping participants to find, hire, and manage their staff.

The program was launched in 1997, and several hundred participants were enrolled. In 2000, it was expanded to include people with intellectual and developmental disabilities. The concept of an "authorized representative" to support participants was included to ensure that adults with limited cognitive ability could participate. This feature was very popular, and enrollment continued to climb.

Fueled mainly by word-of-mouth among families and participants, enrollment in the waivers continued to grow to about 1,450 consumers by 2006. To promote and manage this fast-growing program, DMAS applied for and received a CMS System Transformation Grant in 2005. This enabled DMAS to contract with Virginia Commonwealth University to develop a detailed handbook for participants, family members, and service facilitators on how to apply for, receive, and manage their own services. The workbook was published in 2007 and was designed to be practical and supportive, written by experienced program managers and consultants.

The continued demand for consumer direction led DMAS to seek expanded financial-management services and additional service coordination agencies. After a national public procurement process, Public Partnerships, LLC (PPL) was chosen to serve as the Fiscal Employment Agent and customer service center while requirements for service facilitators were updated to encourage local social service agencies across the Commonwealth to participate and support self-direction. A statewide Advisory Board for Consumer Direction was established that included participants, family members, service providers, direct care workers, state staff, and PPL.

In 2011, a large group of consumers in the program, led by Keith Kessler, a long-time self-advocate with a widespread network of stakeholders and participants, drafted "Your Guide to Directing Your Own Supports in Virginia." Written by participants for participants, the guide was funded under another Systems Transformation Grant awarded by CMS. The enrollment continued to grow until it reached more than 23,000 participants and 26,500 direct care workers in 2017, a sixteen-fold increase in 13 years. I/DD participants represented a 50% utilization rate among those eligible to enroll in the waivers, and older adults and physically disabled participants represented a 45% utilization rate among those eligible. These rates of voluntary participation are among the highest in the country.

There are several reasons for this growth in participation rates. First, there was a consistent network of advocates and families interested in participant direction from the start. The network received support from the local

Centers for Independent Living and Area Agencies on Aging, who provided repeated and effective testimony to the legislature and the Medicaid agency regarding expansion of choices for consumers. Their collective advocacy led to expanded legislation, waivers, and program improvements. Arguments to create and expand the consumer-direction model were usually preceded by studies that reviewed successful models in other states and made cautious projections on financial savings to the Commonwealth. Though expansion was seen by the industry as a threat to their market, their objections were overcome since self-direction was presented as a choice for consumers, not a requirement.

Second, the leaders of DMAS and other state agencies were uniformly committed to improving and expanding the opportunity to self-direct. To make good on this commitment, the state successfully applied for two CMS-funded System Transformation Grants—in 2005 and 2010—aimed at supporting individuals, families and providers to implement the self-direction reform. Additionally, DMAS put in place program documentation and accountability processes including quarterly audits by an outside accounting firm to assure the legislature that self-direction was a good financial decision. Lastly, DMAS contracted for the technology needed to enable the program to grow in a systematic fashion.

The next challenge for self-direction in Virginia is the introduction of managed care programs for people requiring long-term services and supports. After a national public procurement process, DMAS chose six MCOs and began in late 2017 to transfer responsibility for the provision of services and supports for people requiring long-term care. This will only affect people served under the current waivers for the elderly and disabled—about three-quarters of all self-directing participants. MCOs will be required to offer self-direction but will be able to make certain changes such as requiring more training for staff or monitoring of services with DMAS approval. Interviews with DMAS staff suggest that the agency expects continued growth in self-direction under managed care.

Tennessee. The Tennessee program, unlike California and Virginia, was designed to rebalance the institutional system to community support, a goal that was broadly embraced by stakeholders and state agencies. Additionally, TennCare (the state's Medicaid agency) was the plaintiff in several lawsuits filed by or on behalf of individuals residing in state institutions based on the 1999 Supreme Court *Olmstead* decision. Self-direction was a way to address the mandated community options in the court orders. Unlike other states, Tennessee included nursing home care in MCO contracts which created financial incentives to offer self-directed options for those who wanted to leave nursing homes.

TennCare began self-direction with options for aging adults and people with physical disabilities in 2009 following the approval of a 1915c CHOICES waiver that was designed to reduce reliance on institutional care. Under the new waiver, TennCare created employment authority for participants to hire staff to provide attendant care, personal care, and respite care. Consumer-directed care options included the ability to hire friends, neighbors, or family members who have not lived in the participant's home for the last five years. This allowed participants to broaden their community residential care choices, including companion care, community living supports, and adult "foster" family living arrangements.

At the time that the CHOICES waiver went into effect, Tennessee had one of the highest rates of institutional care in the country. In the 2009 calendar year, only 14% of all aging and disabled enrollees in long-term care were in community-based services, and 86% were in nursing facilities. Seven years later, in 2016, after implementation of the CHOICES waiver, individuals living in community settings tripled to 43%, the national median rate, and the number continues to increase (Tennessee Health Care Finance and Administration, 2016).

The implementation of the CHOICES waiver also served to rebalance resources between community and institutional care. Tennessee's ranking for HCBS spending as of 2014 was 21st in the country, and for aging and disabilities, 22nd. Both of these rankings were slightly higher than the national average but represented a vast improvement from the state's ranking in the bottom 10 in the country when CHOICES went into effect. Moreover, in 2012 and 2013, Tennessee was recognized by CMS as among the top 10 states for progress in increasing the percentage of funding for long-term community services and supports (Mattson & Bergfeld, 2017).

The CHOICES waiver also has contributed to the resolution of issues arising from litigation. Patti Killingsworth, the Director of Long-Term Care for TennCare observed:

> We have used the flexibilities of consumer direction to aid in the resolution of civil rights litigation, including the ability to receive services in the community using a consumer direction model, and to allow individuals to also self-direct health care tasks, training and supervising their consumer directed workers to assist them with health care tasks that would otherwise have

to be performed by a nurse, often in an institutional setting (personal communication, June 2017).[3]

Tennessee made its expectations for participant-direction clear to all MCOs. The contracts covering participant direction include 35 pages detailing all policies, procedures, forms, processes, and reports that are required. In addition, each MCO had specific targets for participant-direction enrollment for each year of its five-year contract. In a 2013 review of five states that required that MCOs provide participant-direction, the US Department of Health and Human Services Office of the Assistant Secretary for Planning and Evaluation found that only Tennessee had enrollment requirements, quality benchmarks, and training requirements for participant-direction. The report concluded that "Tennessee has the most extensive set of performance indicators" for participant-direction—a major reason TennCare was able to reach its rebalancing performance goals.

To improve consistency and meet performance goals, TennCare used a single financial management agency to work with all four MCOs. This was helpful in rolling out the waivers statewide and increasing self-direction usage for all the MCOs. The relationship between the MCOs and the single financial management agency has been important to continued program growth and minimization of disruption as several thousand people have changed their primary residences and had to learn how to recruit, hire, and employ their workers.

The importance of reducing nursing home and institutional utilization prompted the state to carry out two major studies documenting the changes in quality and the impact on their costs: (1) Tennessee Health Care Finance and Administration, Bureau of TennCare, *2016 Quality Assessment and Performance Improvement Strategy*, and (2) the Tennessee Comptroller of the Treasury, Office of Research and Accountability, *Senior Long-Term Care in Tennessee: Trends and Options 2017*. These two studies indicated that the CHOICES waiver was responsible for shifting resources from institutional to community services and supports. The data for 2011 through 2013 showed a substantial decrease in member months in nursing facilities and an increase in member months in community services. MCO member months for nursing facility care as a percentage of all CHOICES member months decreased by 16% and member months for community services increased by 41%. Total expenditures for nursing care decreased 11% while those for community services increased 77%.

The CHOICES program expanded access to community services in a system that had previously offered few alternatives to nursing home care. Once more cost-effective community services, including self-direction, were made widely available to TennCare members, participation in and expenditures for community services increased, resulting in an overall decrease of $120 in monthly spending on each individual CHOICES member, including nursing home residents who were identified as a population needing community-based services. This decrease occurred despite an increase in the average per member per month cost of providing nursing home services. The savings were achieved not by reducing the amount of services that people received but rather by serving more people in more cost-effective settings that aligned with participant choice.

In addition to the CHOICES waiver, enrollment in Tennessee's first IDD 1915(c) consumer-direction waiver has grown steadily since it started in 2005 with strong support from advocates and families. As noted above, self-direction for I/DD was initially developed to respond to mandates from the federal class-action suits in two state institutions. It provided an opportunity to residents who wanted to leave the facilities with a range of choices regarding life in the community. In 2017, the program, which includes employment authority only, served about 25% (or 300) of the 1,200 individuals who were initially eligible. To encourage participants to enroll, case managers are required to present and explain the option. Unlike the CHOICES waiver, the program is administered by the state with state case managers, not by private MCOs.

A new Employment and First Choice IDD 1915 (c) waiver was implemented in 2016 and has broad goals and expectations. It focuses on supports that assist participants to learn how to live in the community and to find employment. It includes employment authority as well as budget authority to purchase services identified in individual assessments. Services to be purchased include local transportation and job coaching to gain the skills and sustain employment. Implemented in 2016, 2,400 participants have been enrolled, and about 328 have requested participant direction. The state's expectation is that at least 35% of those in the waiver will elect to self-direct given the emphasis on employment and community inclusion. The waiver is managed by the MCOs, who are urged to recognize participant independence as in their financial interest. MCOs have hired staff to introduce the option to participants and to help them see self-direction as a positive way to make the changes in their lives.

TennCare CHOICES Participant Interview

GPS is a 77-year-old member of the TennCare CHOICES program and has been a member since it started in 2010. He moved to Tennessee in 2007 and as a retired army veteran received health care through the Veteran's Administration. GPS had become a functional quadriplegic from a rare form of muscular dystrophy that started in his thirties. It took many years before he was seriously impaired and had to rely on the services of others. He had served in the army and then became a personal injury lawyer for approximately 15 years. Eventually, the disease debilitated him to the point that it became too much for him to continue his law practice.

When he moved to Tennessee, he began receiving services from a private home health care agency but was unhappy with their practices and their services. He was not able to fully supervise his worker, did not always receive the personal care he requested, and had to go back to the agency whenever he wanted to make a change or create a different service to meet his personal and changing needs. The home health care agency presented a layer of rules and bureaucracy that created more difficulty for him and wasted time in getting the care he needed.

He heard about the CHOICES program from a doctor at the Veteran's Administration in Nashville. Since he was looking for ways to get the support he needed without giving up the control he wanted, he thought it was worth a try. He qualified as a functional quadriplegic who needed assistance in all activities of daily living. He thought that consumer-direction provided exactly what he wanted and joined the entry class of CHOICES. The fact that the Tennessee managed care companies provided both long-term health care and consumer direction made it an easy choice:

> I wanted to gain more independence and gain some relief from the burdens on my life that I experience every day. CHOICES offered that opportunity to me. I didn't know quite what to expect since the program was brand new and the start was somewhat confusing and messy. After a few years in the program, I realized that the difficult start was primarily due to the program's newness and the unfamiliarity of those working to implement it.

GPS has been in the program for seven years and has gone through many changes from the beginning, some technology and policy changes and its continued growth. His view of it is very clear:

> Consumer-direction is the best thing that could have happened to me. It is the best service for the long-term care community. It gave me the greatest flexibility and control over my life and what I do every day. The Tennessee program is the best. The leaders and the staff are excellent, and they are constantly striving to make things better.

GPS is most appreciative of the opportunity to be the employer, deciding who to hire, providing the training, and supervising his staff. Being in charge gives him control and a sense of dignity that he was never able to get from working with home health care agencies.

> It lets me ease my burdens and plan my life, something most people can do every day. I have enough burdens on my life already. Consumer-direction puts me in charge so I can get things done the way I want to.

There have been some issues in the program that he believes have been fixed or could be fixed to improve it for all users. The major failure was the use of an Electronic Visit and Verification (EVV) system required at the start of the program. It required workers to call in when they arrived and call out when they left GPS's home and provide detailed information on the services they provided over the phone. It created rigid requirements that not all direct care workers were good at meeting continuously. And it didn't allow for the normal changes of schedules and activities, nor did it recognize that some services occurred in the community. GPS found that correcting the problems the EVV system created was time consuming and annoying. The system was replaced by an electronic time sheet that could be used by computer or smartphone, creating more flexibility and security in entering information.

GPS has also identified some policies and processes that could improve the program, particularly for the direct care workers. He believes the salaries of workers are too low, and "since you get what you pay for, higher salaries will bring in a better quality of worker who is more likely to stay." He sees that worker retention not only would improve continuity of care, but it would also reduce the costs associated with recruiting and training new workers.

He has also observed that most workers live paycheck to paycheck and need to have better cash flow when entering the program. The startup process for hiring new workers takes too long, about two months from a hiring decision to the time when the worker gets their first paycheck. And if there are paperwork problems, it could take longer. Also, direct care employees need to have First Aid/CPR training completed and personally paid for before they can start. This creates another financial burden for most of them.

He would recommend the program to anyone eligible for in-home care. Giving consumers flexibility and control provides a much better option than agency care. He would tell interested consumers:

> It helps you ease the burdens of daily living and get the things *you* want to get done rather than operating from someone else's schedule. In terms of in-home care, I could not recommend it more highly. You are in charge!

He thinks the consumer-direction option will grow faster in Tennessee because of the opportunity it gives people to live their lives the way they want while saving the state funds for services, particularly when compared to the cost of agency and institutional services. GPS frequently speaks at conferences and workshops with this message. He thinks the state needs to market consumer-direction better to people eligible for services and make it easier for people to get started. This includes providing training and assistance to consumers in recruiting and hiring staff and a faster paperwork process, including criminal background checks for workers, to get people started and workers paid promptly. He remains upbeat about CHOICES. "I can live my life the way I want with all the limitations I have. Other people need to have the same opportunity."

Conclusion

Although broad federal guidelines are in place, the way that self-direction is implemented, and its success, is determined at the state level. There is wide latitude for state managers to design a participant purchasing authority flexible enough to meet a range of individual and state needs while improving the lives of those receiving services and supports. Together, the four states highlighted have taken advantage of five different HCBS waivers. Because of the flexibility of the self-direction model, these states have been able to design unique approaches that maximize personal choice and control to address local problems and issues for different populations. This includes the option of self-directing some services and having either employment authority or full budget authority.

Participation rates vary widely by type of disability, but where self-direction has been properly designed and managed, the results show significant enrollment—as evidenced by the high proportion of individuals from all disability groups who are self-directing, particularly in California and Wisconsin.

There are four factors that enable these programs to continually grow and thrive:

1. Strong policy leadership from the state's Medicaid agency. This includes innovative planning, widespread involvement with the stakeholder community, strong contract management, and use of MCOs to use self-direction to achieve specific state goals.

2. Continued documentation and publication of the costs, results, and outcomes by the state Medicaid agency. Even where the results lag, the studies are used to document the issues and improve the programs.

3. Active political involvement and promotion at the legislative level from those served by the program—including participants, family members, advocates, and workers, including unions that represent them. Sometimes this includes designing successful substate pilot programs and moving them to statewide implementation.

4. State commitment at the executive level to build an infrastructure that supports self-direction. This includes the use of well-trained support brokers or case managers and specialized payroll services and the use of financial management services and technology designed specifically for self-direction and customer services. Although California designed its own in-house technology, for most states, this means contracting for these services from organizations built to implement and manage self-direction.

In chapter 8, we will look at how these and other factors can influence the growth of self-direction.

Chapter 5

Setting Individualized Budgets to Support Self-direction

The advent of self-direction has resulted in challenges to the traditional ways in which services are planned and delivered. Among aspects of the service delivery infrastructure, self-direction has highlighted a specific mismatch between conventional budgeting methods and individual control over the distribution of resources. Consequently, states have developed a variety of methods tailored to self-direction that link funding to each individual's needs and aspirations. The development of individualized funding methodologies can potentially offer all participants the opportunity to manage their own budgets and exercise greater control over the supports they receive, and so their lives (Edwards-Orr & Ujvari, 2018). In other words, an individual budget is critical to the success of self-direction.

While policy makers increasingly favor granting decision-making authority to service recipients, they are challenged by a rising demand for services, tight budgets, shifting support preferences, and serious workforce shortages. As a result, individual authority over a personal budget has to be reconciled with the need to serve thousands of people across a jurisdiction (Kimmich et al., 2009; Agosta et al., 2010; Petner-Arrey et al., 2019). Inevitably, within a context favoring self-direction, policy makers are pressed to decide "who gets what and how much." In this chapter, we provide a framework for categorizing the various means that states have adopted to set individualized budgets. Finally, we discuss a series of complementing considerations and offer concluding remarks.

Framework for Categorizing Individualized Funding Methodologies

The individualized budgets used in self-direction may be defined as *a targeted amount of money, or other allocation, such as support hours, that an individual is assigned and has authority over to acquire the services they need and prefer.* These budgets may be applied narrowly to fund a single service, such as personal assistance, or they may be applied broadly, covering multiple services spanning an individual's full day. When narrowly defined, often modest budget amounts, say $5,000 to $10,000 annually, are tied to the targeted service(s) and placed under the control of the individual, so that the budget may be applied more flexibly to address support needs. This could include exerting greater authority over a targeted service (e.g., personal assistance) and/or applying the funds for acquiring different goods or services. When more broadly applied to address wider aspects of a person's life, individualized budgets range extensively in amount, with some budgets exceeding $100,000 a year. This is because for some people with significant disabilities, direct supervision and assistance are needed for longer periods of the day, if not the entire day. Consequently, their budget might cover the services they receive at home, in their community, or at their job.

There are several approaches for computing individualized budgets. The simplest is based on a review of past service use and costs to determine what a person needs for a future budget. In this manner, individuals are tied to their historical patterns and budgets since what was offered in the past is carried forward to guide future spending. This is troubling if past spending was insufficient or otherwise not reflective of the person's needs. It may also perpetuate ill-advised past spending biases. Moreover, this approach cannot be used with new program enrollees because there is no service history on which to draw.

An alternative approach uses past service patterns to anchor projections so that spending may be anticipated, but it primarily relies on each individual's *present* support needs and expectations *going forward*. Consensus has yet to emerge as to how best to gather, organize, and interpret these projections to develop rational means for computing a budget. Policy makers, however, tend to favor one of two methods. The first relies on conversations with the person with disabilities (that is, the service recipient) and others to build a support plan that details the types of services needed, including their frequency and duration. In this way, the plan is used to compute the budget. The second uses a systematic assessment of support needs that is later linked to a budget.

Conversational Method

The conversational method is associated with person-centered planning approaches, whereby a planning facilitator, such as a case manager or support broker, engages with the service recipient and commonly members of the recipient's circle of support (for example, family, friends, staff). Through discussion, the planner aims to identify:

- *Aspirational goals* that reflect longer term intentions—such as marriage, getting a job, taking a desired vacation—or more immediate goals that require dedicated focus and attention like selecting new furniture for a home

- *Learning or skill-building objectives* for skills that the person decides to learn, such as being more assertive, taking the bus to work, playing a musical instrument, cooking meals, paying bills, or getting in and out of a chair when mobility is impacted

- *Community participation activities* that the individual wants to join, such as a civic club or religious organization, volunteering for a food drive, or simply spending time with friends and family

- *Day-to-day support needs* are to help a person to complete necessary daily activities, such as eating, dressing, showering, using public transportation, crossing streets, shopping for food, or attending to medical needs

The individual's dreams, aspirations, objectives, and day-to-day support needs are considered, as well as their connections with family and their community. The purpose is to identify the services and supports that will further individual preferences, all while considering what is important *to* the person and *for* the person to live a healthy and safe life.[1]

The discussion process results in a plan that is unique to each person and identifies the full spectrum of supports available to that person. As the discussion unfolds, the planning facilitator notes the direct services that the person is expected to use in the coming year. Once identified, estimated services may be tallied up, and when considered in relation to the rates for the planned services, a total annual budget may be computed. In this way, conversation—and individual judgment—is used to detail service needs and a budget allocation is a direct output of this conversation.

Later, individual budget amounts, and their associated service plans, are reviewed by program supervisors who consider whether each plan is fitted to the person's needs and who help ensure that budgets fall within reasonable ranges. Here, past service use patterns and spending might be examined to guide the reviews, and budgets may be approved outright, or the service amounts may be lowered in accordance with presumed support needs.

For many, this approach seems maximally "person-centered" because it relies heavily on conversation among those most affected by the impacts of the budget. After all, who knows better about what is needed than the individual and his or her circle of support? Yet, when this method is applied to thousands of people over time, a great deal of time on the part of well-trained social workers is required to determine how best to support individual needs. Inevitably, inequalities in judgments are likely to emerge as differences in training and experience among the planning facilitators may lead to discrepancies among service recipients with varying needs. As Nerney (2001) points out, while the approach may satisfy many, those that advocate for their needs most strongly may well end up with greater budget amounts than those who more modestly assert their needs. He concludes:

> As the prime determinant of an allocation, [this approach] lacks the precision needed by policymakers and funders who have the fiscal obligation to manage finite appropriations for services . . . It is unrealistic to suppose that the attainment of personal goals, on a highly individual basis, can serve as the sole foundation for allocating scarce resources. (p. 8)

Assessment-Based Methods

An underlying premise of assessment-based methods is that information may be collected systematically on each person and his or her support needs. To start, an assessment tool (or tools) is used to gather sufficient information to identify the service recipient and to gather other essential data—such as their age, residence type (since cost varies dramatically by residential setting), and other identifying information that can be used to tie assessment scores to other important data.

Regarding the actual assessment, the tool must be valid for assessing support needs across essential life domains, including:

- Support needed for *Activities of Daily Living* (ADLs). ADLs include skills such as bathing, maintaining personal hygiene, dressing, mobility inside and outside the home, using the toilet, and communicating with others. The assessment should measure the amount and frequency of support that a person needs to complete ADLs.

- Support Needed for *Instrumental Activities of Daily Living* (IADLs). IADLs are an additional set of life functions necessary for maintaining a person's immediate environment, including paying bills, shopping, preparing meals, or using public transit. Again, the assessment should measure the amount and frequency of support needed.

- *Cognition/Memory Support Needs*. These include noted difficulties maintaining attention or concentration, learning, perception, task completion, awareness, communication, decision making, memory, planning or problem-solving, and the supports required to manage cognition/memory issues.

- *Medical Support Needs*. This category includes medical conditions or diagnoses that affect an individual's daily functioning and the support that they require to manage those needs, including any support required to manage mental health needs.

- *Behavioral Support Needs*. These include support needed for behaviors that are self-injurious, hurtful to others, destructive to property, disruptive, uncooperative or withdrawn, or inattentive. The assessment should also measure the type and amount of supports required to manage such behaviors.

Importantly, the assessment tool must provide a measurable score to distinguish relative need, low to high, across targeted domains and among those assessed. It must also produce scores that are consistently accurate and reliable. To ensure that the instrument does indeed test what it purports to test (validity) and does so regardless of the interviewer/rater/respondent (reliability), it is critical that the tool have documented validity and reliability. Standardization of the assessment is imperative as results must be compiled and used to contrast support need across a population. To further ensure accuracy and reliability, comprehensive formal training programs should be provided to those conducting the assessments.

Numerous instruments exist for assessing support needs, with varying strengths and shortcomings (Taylor et al., 2015). Some—such as the *Supports Intensity Scale*,[2] *Inventory for Client Agency and Planning*,[3] or the *interRAI* suite[4]—are used in multiple jurisdictions and are well documented. Others—such as Florida's *Questionnaire for Situational Information*,[5] Wisconsin's *Functional Screen*,[6] or Minnesota's *MNChoices*[7]—are locally developed and not used across jurisdictions. All cover the general topic of "support needs"; however, they do so in different ways and with varying levels of documented psychometric testing.

A recent review of 260 Medicaid-financed community programs across the United States yielded 41 initiatives in 31 states where standardized assessment outputs are directly linked to a resulting individualized budget amount (Petner-Arrey et al., 2019). In fact, this review suggests two distinct approaches to setting these budgets: individual-based approaches that result in everyone having a unique budget and level-based approaches where a group of individuals, having similarly assessed needs, is allocated the same budget amount.

Individual-Based Approaches. Individual-based approaches can result in a unique and distinct budget for each person, meaning if a state serves 20,000 people in each program, theoretically, there could be 20,000 unique budgets. Petner-Arrey and colleagues (2018) illustrate two means for computing such budgets: item based and formula based.

Item Based involves selecting items within a measure and associating responses to these items with a unit of support (e.g., hours or dollars). These units are added together to yield a total amount of support or budget. The amount might be stated in support hours or dollars. For instance, consider the support needed for dressing. An item may probe the amount of support needed to dress. Depending on the response to the item (e.g., low, medium, or high), a unit of support (i.e., time, money) is associated with the response. This approach is repeated for each item included in the model. A final tally across all the selected items and responses yields the individual budget amount. The amount of support associated with each item and response might be set based on professional judgement and/or an analysis of previous service use and expenditure patterns. The state of Oregon provides an example of this type of approach. Beginning in 2011, two locally developed tools, the Adult Needs Assessment (ANA) and Children's Needs Assessment (CNA), were used to assess the support needs of service recipients with intellectual and developmental disabilities (Oregon Department of Human Services, Office of Developmental Disabilities Services, 2019). Both assessments cover similar information pertaining to demographics, need for support in ADLs, and medical/nursing needs, as well as other exceptional needs. The assessment is used to identify precise units of support that are associated with completing various life activities.

To determine an individual budget, an assessor transfers information and responses from the assessment into a spreadsheet where all the results are tallied to yield specific hour amounts of support. For instance, consider an individual who requires a two-person lift six times per day and that each instance of such support takes approximately 10 minutes. This effort, in the Oregon model, equates to one hour of needed support per day (6 instances times 10 minutes equals 60 minutes). This hour amount is summed together with results of other items to compute allowable monthly service hours that may be eventually associated with a dollar amount.

A primary benefit of an item-based approach is transparency. This approach directly associates responses to specific assessment items with a unit of support and reimbursement rate, so it may be appealing to many who directly observe the relationship between identified need and a resulting budget amount. One drawback of item-based modeling is that it relies on only the specific support needs asked about in the items included. Resources that are needed to complete life activities outside of the prespecified set of life tasks are not addressed, so they are not measured or included in the model. As a result, the approach may underestimate overall support needs and limit a budget's applicability to addressing needs in other life domains.

Formula Based means involve statistical analyses of the support needs of individuals in relation to historical costs. Items from the assessment are examined statistically to determine what combinations of variables best explain items such as annual costs and/or service hours used. Ideally, the analysis reveals a good correlation between assessed needs and variables depicting costs or past service use. Eventually, the analysis yields a formula that assigns each person a budget amount based on his or her personal scores on the assessment, sometimes in combination with the person's past expenses.

The state of Florida uses a formula-based approach within its *i-Budgets* initiative within its home and community based program for people with autism or intellectual and developmental disabilities. The instrument used to assess support needs, the Questionnaire for Situational Information (QSI) was designed and tested in 2007 (Havercamp, 2009a, b, c, d) and is occasionally updated. Subsequently, Niu and Bell (2010) applied regression-based statistics to develop a first-generation algorithm for setting individualized budget amounts tied to assessment outputs.

The base elements composing the independent variables of the regression model include the individual's age, living setting, and five summary and individual item scores from the QSI. These variables were regressed against historical costs with several modifying factors accounted for (e.g., spending outliers). The regression model yields a series of weights that are associated with each of the independent variables. To calculate a person's individual budget, the score on each variable is multiplied by the variable weight. The resulting values are summed and squared to determine a final dollar amount.

This dollar amount produced by the algorithm serves as a starting point for a final budget determination in what is referred to as the *EZ i-Budget Calculator*. This figure is subsequently adjusted to an amount that is consistent with the overall legislative appropriation, resulting in an *Allocation Algorithm Amount*. Finally, a support coordinator meets with each recipient to review these results and explore if there are other significant needs that must be addressed outside the designated budget amount. When this process is complete, a final budget amount is approved and authorized.

Another example of the formula-based approach is Wisconsin's self-direction initiative, established in 2008 as an alternative to the state's mainstay managed care effort, Family Care. Wisconsin's self-direction initiative is known as *Include, Respect, I Self-direct (IRIS)* and is described further in chapter 4 (Wisconsin Department of Health Services, n.d.a). IRIS is meant for seniors as well as for people with physical disabilities, intellectual and developmental disabilities, and behavioral challenges. Individuals who select IRIS for their long-term supports work with an IRIS Consultant to develop a service plan that meets their individual needs and a financial services agency to assist them to hire workers and pay for their supports (e.g., in-home supports, day and employment services, respite support). The allocation is based on an assessment of need using the states locally developed "Functional Screen" (Wisconsin Department of Health Services, n.d.b) with amounts arrived at through systematic analyses correlating assessment scores with historical spending patterns.

A benefit of using a formula-based approach is that the results of analyses may yield a statistically sound and defensible model. This potential strength may turn to a shortcoming, however, if the relationship between assessment scores and historical service use is not strong. Moreover, the approach may result in complex statistical formulae that are not easily understood by service recipients and their families, making it difficult for them to file a grievance or appeal any decisions that they believe are not reflective of their support needs. Finally, another risk of a formula-based approach is that it is anchored to historical costs. Historical costs have embedded within them influences from past policy and practice that may be inconsistent with progressive ideals driving the system forward. As a result, this approach may reinforce past, unwanted practice because the funds allocated to individuals are tied to those practices.

Level-Based Approaches include those where groups are established that are characterized by the amount of support common to members of each group. Level-based approaches recognize that when large numbers of service recipients are assessed, their measured support needs will distribute from low to high. People with the least need may require periodic, drop-in assistance. People with the greatest need may require constant physical assistance and/or oversight, with a range of support needs falling between the two ends of the spectrum. These approaches often begin with statistical analysis on an assessment to understand the groups that can be formed with the data. Next, the type and amount of public services that, on average, should be made available to individuals within each of these categories are considered. Once agreed upon, the type and amount of services allocated to each group are tied to the unit cost for delivering the specified services so that a budget amount for each group can be computed. In general, these budgets increase from low to high in accordance with assessed needs.

Of the 41 initiatives reviewed by Petner-Arrey, Kardell, and Kidney (2019), more than three-quarters use a level-based approach. Typically, levels are arranged to depict support need, say from low to high. Separate levels may also be established and dedicated to extraordinary needs, such as medical, behavioral, or other unique support needs. Figure 5.1 displays a five-level support-needs framework. Levels 1, 2, and 3, respectively, depict low, moderate, and high general support-needs groups. The levels "M" and "B" include individuals with extraordinary medical and behavioral needs. Given this general construct, many differing iterations are possible, but the principal idea is to separate individuals into a reasonable number of groupings based on their assessment scores, and to compute budgets for each level.

West Virginia provides an example of this type of approach within its system for people with intellectual and developmental disabilities. The state

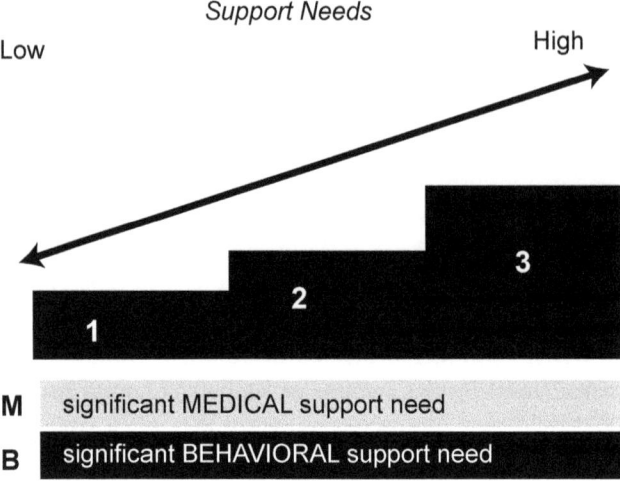

Figure 5.1. Five-level support needs framework. Adapted from "Moving from seven to five support levels for determining personal supports budgets" by J. Agosta, C. Kidney and A. Vazquez, 2018, Human Services Research Institute. Copyright 2018 by the Human Services Research Institute.

uses the Inventory for Client Agency and Planning (ICAP) (Wikoff, 1989) to assess support needs. First, a base budget is set for each person, which is a dollar amount ranging from low to high and varying by age group and living setting. These base budgets are derived via statistical analyses. Next, additional amounts are "added on" to the base budget associated with one of five levels that are derived from scores on two assessment domains. Subsequently, additional funds are added based upon scores related to observed behavioral challenges (moderate to extremely serious).

Another approach, applied in some states (e.g., Hawaii,[8] North Carolina[9]) builds an individualized budget tied to level assignment, age, residence type, and the projected "service mixes" associated with each level. A service mix illustrates the type and amount of service that may typically be needed by individuals in each level. The mixes are informed by historical service use and professional judgment but may also reflect emphasis on new trends in services or innovative approaches, such as anticipated use of employment or remote technologies. Service mixes are often reviewed by stakeholders and revised as a result.

As an example, individuals in "Level 1" may be very capable and living in their own residence, so their service mix may be composed primarily of periodic, drop-in assistance. People with this level designation will have assessment scores revealing as much, but they eventually will be assigned budgets to match their need for such modest support. In contrast, those assigned to "Level 3" living with their family may require significant support and oversight. The associated service mix should reflect such needs and be composed of significant access to in-home supports, resulting in a higher individualized budget than that associated with Level 1.

This approach yields a model where budgets per level are tied to anticipated service use for all those assigned to the level by age group and residence type. As a result, while offering a ceiling allocation associated with each level, this approach allows for flexibility in how each person applies the budget to meet his or her own needs.

A drawback to a levels-based approach, as with any method based on assessment, is that outputs—that is, the level assignments and budget allocations—are tied to the reliability and accuracy of the assessment. Further, some individuals, depending on their assessment score, straddle between support levels where a single point or two either way could result in a level assignment that is higher or lower, the outcome being a different budget assignment.

Regardless of the overall strategy applied, numerous possibilities are conceivable within each approach, and hybrid strategies are also possible. For instance, an item-based approach may be applied to identify and fund services keyed to ADLs, but a level-based approach might be taken to allocate resources for daytime supports (e.g., employment services).

Complementing Considerations

Whatever the approach is to generate individualized budgets, these budgets and their utility for promoting self-direction and addressing personal support needs rests within the larger context of systems serving thousands of people. To assure equity and to avoid perverse incentives, the budget amount that a person who is self-directing receives should fund a level of supports comparable to the level of support the individual would have received in the traditional delivery system. No matter the model of service delivery, policy makers must decide what their state is able and willing to spend to meet the identified needs of people with disabilties. This sometimes results in different states allocating very different amounts of money for people with similar needs. It is therefore important to have a continous quality-improvement process that periodically examines whether the money being spent is adequate to achieve the goal of helping people to remain safe and independent in the community.

A variety of considerations must be accounted for in establishing budgets, including the following: (a) policy intentions consistent with the ideals of community inclusion, self-direction, operational efficiency, and allocative equity; (b) supportive systems elements aligned with these policy intentions; and (c) operational practices to support self-direction.

Complementing Policy Considerations. While individualized budget methodologies are meant to help advance person-centered ideals, it is essential that these methodologies not be designed to reinforce historical service use and spending but to advance emerging preferences for service delivery. Building a *methodology* exclusively on these patterns ties the future to the past and makes forward progress difficult. It is more effective to fashion the methodology that takes into consideration new and preferred ways of supporting people to live the most inclusive lives possible within their communities. For example, some states, recognizing that the majority of the support people with disabilities receive comes from family members, are paying increased attention to the needs of these caregivers and allowing Medicaid to pay for family assessments and defined services for the caregiver. Whether and how to build these supports into budgets will be a topic for future consideration.

Additionally, individualized budget methodologies must be true to each individual but in aggregate must account for the collective well-being of all. Person-centered thought stresses regard for individual needs and preferences, and inevitably on promoting favorable outcomes consistent with each person's goals and objectives. Such thinking, however, fosters the idea of individualized budgets built within an exclusive focus on one's own life and without awareness of the great many others also needing public support. Yet, policy makers must account for *all* those receiving services.

While seeking to ensure that individuals have the support they need, resources must be distributed in ways that are efficient yet equitable to all. Efficiency gains come from understanding exactly what it costs to provide a service at a given level of quality to meet a specific person's needs. Equity requires understanding what supports individuals need and a fair allocation of resources to address personal needs. Individual budgeting methodologies, especially those informed by systematic assessment of individual needs, offer an opportunity for using available public resources most effectively to serve both the individual and the collective well-being of all those in need.

Complementing System Elements. Having a means to allocate individualized budgets is fundamental to a self-directed service system. Having such means, however, while necessary, is not enough. When budgets are applied to multiple aspects of life, other system elements must be fashioned to accommodate individual needs in ways that promote system policy intentions consistent with community inclusion and self-determination.

Complementary system elements, for example, include an ample *service array* or meaningful allowable purchases that allow for individuals to apply their budgets to acquire the actual services or goods they prefer with reasonable *reimbursement rates that attract staff and providers*. By example, consider circumstances where individuals seek community-integrated employment and are assigned an individualized budget to apply to this objective. In planning, it may be discovered that needed employment services (e.g., job find, job coaching, transportation assistance) are not available within the service array and/or that reimbursement rates for these services are so low that the individual cannot readily acquire such services. Likewise, others may live at home with their families and seek greater opportunities to participate in community events but discover that needed support is not available or the rates are too low to attract qualified direct support workers. Even when participants in self-directed programs can set their own rate of pay for providers, if the budget allocation itself was based on insufficient rates in the traditional program, there may not be enough money to purchase all needed supports and services.

No state Medicaid program is prepared to finance all of the functional assistance all individuals eligible for Medicaid HCBS require to meet all of their needs "at home." States are only required to ensure that the supports provided protect "health and safety." This applies to both self-directed and traditional options. Meeting all need regardless of setting would require spending far more, on average, per individual served than it would cost to provide paid care in residential care facilities. Providing supports in the individual's home is only less costly because most recipients of paid home support rely primarily on unpaid help from family, friends, and neighbors. To the extent budgets do not meet all needs, support brokers need to help participants gain access to other resources and integrate their work with acute-care providers and chronic-disease-management and health-promotion programs (Mahoney, K., Mahoney, E. et al., 2019). According to CMS instructions for 1915c HCBS waivers, service plans need to be more comprehensive than the spending plan which stipulates how the Medicaid budget will be used, and states need to provide support services to help participants locate needed resources even if they are non-Medicaid.

Finally, systems creating individualized budgets must be prepared to support people to make choices about their funding. That is, systems must be easily navigated by service recipients; must have clear expectations about how money can be spent, including detailing any specific limits on funding; and must have people knowledgeable enough to help service recipients to spend their individualized budgets according to their needs and preferences. There must also be publicized means for individuals to request exceptions to their budget when the funding cannot accommodate their needs or to assist individuals to find additional support. Most important, there must be a robust means of educating people about their funding so that they can responsibly use their allocated budgets to get what they need when they need it.

Complementing Operational Practice. Given an individual budget, several companion issues must be resolved to guide day-to-day practice. These include the following:

The Services That Individualized Budgets May Be Used to Acquire. The premise underlying individualized budgeting methodologies is that funds will be allocated to individuals so that they can apply them in ways they see fit. But are there limits to how the funds might be spent? Generally, given that public funds are in question, limits to individual spending authority ought to be anticipated. Yet, depending on the funding source and the amount of money in question, great amounts of personal authority and responsibility might be offered. People might, for example, use funds to hire staff to provide support and/or to purchase needed goods (e.g., a microwave oven or a specialized adaptive device). Cash and Counseling initiatives in the United States are designed in this way and offer great opportunity for individuals to exert considerable authority over their budgets with good effect (Carlson et al., 2007).

In contrast, when individualized budget methodologies are used more broadly to cover multiple aspects of an individuals' life, larger budget amounts per person are generally at stake, so greater scrutiny may be given to how the money is spent. Consider that some services, like daily supports needed to complete ADLs and IADLs, are used by individuals each day. These base supports can be figured into everyone's individual budget. Other services, however, may be seldom used or used once only (e.g., adaptive technology purchases or housing design, or single-event or time-limited behavioral consultation). These types of services should not be built into everyone's individual allocation but provided exclusively to those who need such support as warranted. Other expensive and not regularly used services, such as skilled nursing, therapies, or behavioral consultation, may also be held out of the budget and offered per person as needed.

In addition, two other factors should be considered. First, regardless of how a budget is computed, individuals will want to apply the budget in ways to satisfy their own preferences. State funders, however, will need to decide what goods or services the budget may be used for and which are not permissible. For instance, funders may not approve of applying budgets toward unproven practices (e.g., new, untested therapies) or to purchase items or services deemed inappropriate or even illegal.

Funders may also place limits on the amounts of services that may be secured. For example, funders may not approve a preference for using an entire allocation on a single service, such as respite support or personal assistance; instead, they may require greater balance to the support plan. It may be decided, for instance, that some amount of respite is appropriate but that funding should also be used to support the person to explore job opportunities or participate in various facets of community life. All along, the funder will want to ensure that the budget is spent in ways consistent with its overall policy intentions and at a pace that will last through the allocation period.

The funder may also elect to exclude some services altogether from the budget methodology—for example, paid residential services such as group homes. This type of service presumes that a service provider will offer residence and support throughout an agreed-to period. During this time, the provider has fixed costs for operating the residence (e.g., staffing) and keeping a room with support available regardless of whether a service recipient is in attendance on a given day. Also, because the cost and the funder's expectation of quality standards are fixed, service recipients are often not free to negotiate with the provider over what amount of his or her budget will be applied toward the residential service. As a result, funders commonly set aside these residential costs and manage them separately from the individualized budget amount.

Overall, whatever the individualized budgeting strategy in use, funders always retain responsibility, and therefore some level of authority, over how the budget is applied. As a result, individualized budgets, because they root back to the public treasury, inevitably come with some amount of restriction to govern what goods or services may be purchased.

Supporting People with Exceptional Needs with a Budget. Individualized budget methodologies are generally designed to accommodate most people satisfactorily. That is, these approaches provide for a "best fit" means for meeting the needs of most people. There will be exceptions, however, when someone's needs are extraordinary and must be accommodated on a per person basis. Often, these individuals will have specialty support needs tied to medical and/or behavioral challenges. This is particularly true for people with chronic illnesses whose needs may change. Regardless of the causes, an *exceptions process* should be in place to help identify these individuals systematically across the jurisdiction early on to ensure that their needs are satisfactorily addressed. Without such a process, policy makers risk misidentifying certain people as having less need than they do, perhaps placing their health and well-being in jeopardy. Later in the service planning and delivery process, inadvertent oversights like these will likely come to light, resulting in stakeholders voicing need for additional support to be added to the plan.

Always, it is best for individuals and overall system workings for these instances to be avoided to the extent they can be by addressing this issue upstream in the process through a systematic exceptions protocol that offers an individual the opportunity to request additional services and associated funding when it is needed.

Making Individuals Aware of Their Budget in Advance of Their Supports Planning Meeting. A common approach, described previously, to arriving at a budget appropriation involves a conversation during an annual service planning meeting. The individual's support needs are decided on, leading to an assignment of services and then an associated budget appropriation. Often, this conversation and resulting appropriation are tied tightly to what the individual previously received, and individuals will not necessarily know how to get what they need going forward.

Individualized budget methodologies carry promise for significantly altering this dynamic. In the United States, the Centers for Medicare and Medicaid Management, the primary funder of disability services, indicates that an individual budget amount is *prospectively determined*—that is, determined before the planning meeting and that the individual is told what amount is allocated *before* developing a service plan (Crisp et al., 2010). In this way, the individual, knowing the budget amount, has the opportunity to apply the budget as they most prefer. They also have the opportunity to understand associated costs and place relative value on the services they receive as a result of this transparent process.

This change is significant. Knowledge of a budget changes the planning process and requires new actions from all involved. For *individuals with disabilities*, knowing one's budget means having greater control over the supports one receives. It also means the service recipient will have greater responsibility to make decisions about what is needed and preferred but to do so within the limits of the assigned budget.

Similarly, *for family members*, the introduction of a budget amount to the planning process also brings opportunity and responsibility. Family members should be prepared to help their loved ones understand their budget, to identify choices they may make in selecting both paid and unpaid supports to meet their needs, and to support the decisions they make. An individualized budget may also help family members to consider the available options and divert funding to the most needed services. Likewise, *case managers and support brokers* will also now have greater opportunity to help individuals take charge of their lives but must do so within a preset budget amount for paid services.

Conclusion

Since the 1970s, the disabilities field has grappled over the best means for establishing and managing community service systems for people with disabilities. Initially, people were treated as passive recipients of services whereby the services available and how they were delivered were decided by others. Systems are changing, however, to more definitively reflect ideals that promote community inclusion and self-direction. People, after all, want to direct their own lives and want a say over the disability policies that affect them.

Still, this continual evolution of thought and practice plays out within the context of the funds available and the obligations policy makers have to ensure that resources are used wisely and in accordance with their policy intentions. How exactly should dollars be distributed? What amount per person is adequate? How can policy makers be fair about it? What might these dollars buy? How much should be paid for the services delivered or goods purchased? How much control over resources should service recipients have? To what ends? These questions pose a complicated policy puzzle that becomes more intricate as increasing numbers of people seek services, available public budgets grow leaner, and concerns over the availability of direct support workers become more pronounced.

Embedded within these many policy choices are decisions regarding how individualized budget amounts are arrived at. Some support conversational methods for arriving at a budget amount, but this approach may lead to allocative inefficiencies and inequities across a jurisdiction. Others prefer assessment-driven methods, but people do not easily trust algorithms for addressing human need, preferring their own personal judgments instead (Frick, 2015).

To address this issue effectively, it is essential that policy makers, people with disabilities, and their families all be involved in conversations about redesigning systems and offering individualized budgets. There needs to be a clear understanding that all those choosing self-direction will have the opportunity within available funds. Doing so, however, will require an agreement that reform will simultaneously ensure efficiencies, value, and equity across all users while also granting individuals the authority to direct their own lives.

Chapter 6

The Impact of Self-direction

Results for Participants

Although self-direction is relatively new as a vehicle for delivering human services, researchers have conducted several major studies to examine the quality-of-life outcomes of self-direction for participants. There are also emerging findings regarding the impact of self-direction on the workers who support participants. This chapter will provide an overview of the results of those studies and will reflect on what the findings mean for the sustainability of self-direction.

Early Models of Self-direction

Flexible Family Support. Shumway has argued (1999) that the first systematic application of the principles of self-direction was the introduction of flexible supports for families with family members with developmental disabilities. Those early programs were based on a recognition that to maintain people with disabilities in their communities, public systems needed to do a better job of supporting their families. Families advocating for increased support were clear that supports should be tailored to the distinctive needs of individual families and should respect the knowledge and expertise of families. One of the first programs of this type—and ultimately the most flexible—was the family subsidy program in Michigan, which began in 1983. Eligible families in that state were given a yearly stipend of $2,600 that they could use at their own discretion to support their family, with no strings attached.

In the 1980s, family advocates around the country approached their state legislators and urged them to create flexible family support programs that allowed families to decide what was best for their family member. States such as New Hampshire, Massachusetts, New Jersey, Iowa, Illinois, and Oregon all adopted programs based on the emerging family support movement. The Human Services Research Institute evaluated two of those programs, Iowa and Illinois, to determine the efficacy of the more flexible and family-centered approach.

In Iowa, the legislature passed legislation granting eligible families a monthly stipend calibrated to the SSI payment amount for an adult living in the home of another minus room and board. The stated purpose of the legislation was "to reduce the number of placements in public or private facilities by defraying the special costs of caring for a child who requires certain special education services" (Iowa Legislative Statute 225C.36, 1988). The evaluation canvassed approximately 140 families who had been receiving the subsidy for most of the fiscal year prior to June 1990 to determine what had or had not changed in their lives. The results showed that some families could bring children home from residential settings because of the subsidy, and others no longer saw a reason to place a family member. In terms of outcomes, most of the families reported, among other things, that their quality of life had improved, that they felt more capable of caring for their family member, and that the whole family was now able to do things together (Bradley et al., 1992).

In Illinois, the Developmental Disabilities Council funded four pilot family support programs that combined services and cash assistance. Satisfaction with the program among families was high and four important features contributed to the success of the program (Bradley et al., 1992):

- Maximization of family control over the services and supports they received
- Minimization of the emotional "cost" of securing services
- Recognition of the importance of the family caregiving role
- Flexibility to accommodate the unique needs of the family

Bonnie Schoultz (1993), at the Center for Human Policy at Syracuse University, conducted a qualitative evaluation of the New Hampshire family support program, which grew out of a well-orchestrated statewide campaign by families that resulted in family support legislation based on the principles of flexibility and services and supports tailored to individual families. Schoultz found that, because of this grassroots legislation, the state created a program that recognized the unique needs of each family, kept children from out-of-home placements, and capitalized on local in-kind contributions and other resources to maximize the impact of family support.

Self-direction Pilot. In 1993, the Robert Wood Johnson Foundation awarded a three-year grant to Monadnock Developmental Services of Keene, New Hampshire, to demonstrate how a system of supports would look if people with disabilities and their circle of friends, or network, were truly in charge of their own services—that is, if they achieved self-determination (Nerney et al., 1995). The pilot program aimed to achieve three goals: (a) to enable individuals and their families to control dollars without dealing with cash; (b) to change the role of case management to a "personal agent" chosen by the participant and not aligned with a service provider agency; and (c) to demonstrate how a person-centered approach could be embedded in a "capitated" or managed care payment system. An evaluation of the outcomes for the 38 individuals who participated in the pilot from 1993 to 1996 was also funded.

Using a structured interview protocol, researchers surveyed the participants twice: early in their program participation in 1994 and again in 1995 (Conroy & Yuskauskas, 1996). The survey covered a variety of areas, including choice, quality of life, and satisfaction. The two researchers found important changes between the first and second surveys. Scores increased on most indicators of choice and control, reflecting more control over schedules, personal finances, schools, community activities, and so on. Scores also increased across all dimensions on the quality-of-life scales, including seeing friends, health, nutrition, happiness, and comfort. Notably, peoples' circles of friends also increased.

Cash and Counseling: Twenty Years of Research

As mentioned in preceding chapters, Cash and Counseling was a 19-year series of related grants to test on a large scale, and later replicate, the self-direction paradigm as a way of delivering supports and services for people with disabilities and older adults. The grants supported an efficacy trial, an effectiveness trial (for replication efforts), and a national resource center to engage in research to improve implementation and to assist states and other organizations working to customize the model for their own purposes.

Cash and Counseling marked a large-scale test and a true randomized control experiment of self-direction: of those who were interested in self-direction, half got to manage their own services and supports, while the other half remained in the traditional system. The comprehensive evaluation effort examined the outcomes of 6,700 people from three states. The initial groups served were older adults and people with physical and developmental disabilities. People with serious mental illness were added in later demonstrations and analyses.

The experiment tested an advanced model of self-direction where the participant (with the assistance of a representative if desired) had the opportunity to manage a budget similar in size to what an agency would have received to serve them. The participant developed an individualized spending plan and could choose to hire the worker of their choice and/or make renovations to their home or purchase assistive devices and goods and services that would help them remain independent in the community. The only test for the spending plan was if it helped the person remain independent in the community.

Finally, the model was quite robust. Each state served the elderly and adults with disabilities; Florida chose to also serve adults and children with developmental disabilities.

The Preference Study. While the states were developing the federal waivers necessary to implement the Cash and Counseling demonstration and creating the infrastructure that people would need to self-direct, the Robert Wood Johnson Foundation funded a series of focus groups in each demonstration state, followed by a survey of a representative sample of home care clients, followed by more focus groups to understand the earlier findings. The most surprising finding was that, by and large, people did not want the cash; they wanted control without the necessity of handling the taxes and paperwork associated with hiring workers and managing budgets. Other findings led to the creation of the role of support broker who, unlike a case manager in the medical or "professional knows best" model, acts more as a coach—helping the person to think creatively about how to meet their needs, develop back-up plans, arrange training, and sometimes tackle various employer tasks (up to and including terminating workers).

Results from the Controlled Experiment. The controlled experiment funded by the Robert Wood Johnson Foundation (RWJF) and the US

Department of Health and Human Services Office of the Assistant Secretary for Planning and Evaluation (ASPE) began in December 1998, when Arkansas accepted its first participants, and ended when the last data were collected in the summer of 2003. The findings fell into three categories: individual-level outcomes, caregiver and paid-worker outcomes, and costs.

The effect on access to care was remarkable and unanticipated. People in both the treatment and control groups were asked, nine months after they had been assessed for participation, if they had received any care services in the last two weeks. In Arkansas, 95% of the adults with disabilities in the treatment group (those self-directing) answered "yes," while only 66% of the control group (those receiving traditional agency services) answered "yes." Of the elderly in Arkansas, 95% who self-directed said they had received personal care in the previous two weeks, compared to only 80% in the comparison group. Whether these differences were due to worker shortages, the difficulty agencies were having in recruiting workers in rural or urban areas, or the self-directing participants' ability to attract new people to the labor market is unclear. What is clear is that access to supports increased dramatically.

The study examined four additional quality measures for individuals: (a) satisfaction with distinct elements of how the services were delivered; (b) unmet need; (c) 11 health outcomes ranging from bedsores/decubitus ulcers and contractures to falls and burns; and (d) overall life satisfaction. Notably, when participants were asked questions such as, "Does your worker treat you with respect?" or "Does your worker come on time?," the differences between the treatment and control groups were so dramatic (in every case favoring those who self-directed) that the lead evaluator, from Mathematica Policy Research, remarked that he had never seen such strong results. Similarly, those who managed their own budgets and individualized their spending plan had dramatic reductions in unmet need.

The effect of self-direction on health outcomes was unexpected. For the 11 health-outcome indicators (measured over seven subgroups), those who remained with traditional agencies never did better in a statistically significant way, while those who managed their own budgets did 20% to 50% better than their peers, who remained in the traditional system on 30% of the measures (Carlson et al., 2007).

Finally, overall life satisfaction increased dramatically for those who self-directed. This was particularly surprising given that prior research had shown this as a hard measure on which to show an impact and that the average monthly budget in a state like Arkansas was only $340 a month![1] In other words, a modest investment of resources had a significant impact on participant satisfaction.

Primary informal caregivers (family and special friends) reported experiencing far less physical, financial, and emotional strain, and, whether they were paid for their services or had the increased peace of mind to know that capable, consistent others were providing the care, caregivers' overall satisfaction with the supports and services also improved in a major way.

The costs associated with self-direction are discussed at greater length in chapter 7. However, the treatment-group members generally had higher expenditures for home and community services and lower costs for institutional care than control-group members. This is not surprising considering the large percentage of control-group members who reported they had not received any care in the prior two weeks. In Arkansas, this amounted to a breakeven proposition. In fact, looking at three years of Medicare and Medicaid costs, the treatment group had an 18% reduction in nursing facility usage (Dale & Brown, 2006). In New Jersey and Florida, those who managed their own budgets had costs that were 5% to 8% higher, but the evaluators noted that an important part of these cost increases was due to the administrative supports that states were just learning how to purchase. Another factor to keep in mind is that Cash and Counseling measured the total costs of the treatment group compared to the total costs of the control group, regardless of whether people got the prescribed treatment. When one looks at per-member per-month costs, the way insurers do, the costs of the self-direction option are quite promising.

The Ethnographic Study and the Process Evaluation. Another component of the evaluation of Cash and Counseling was an ethnographic study that followed 76 participants, their family members, and their support brokers. This study examined, through real-life stories, how lives were changed, what it meant to self-direct, and how the option allowed participants to adapt to changing lives and changing environments. These case studies provided insight into how and why self-direction worked and what self-direction meant to peoples' lives (San Antonio et al., 2007). The case studies showed that program participation had enhanced the consumer's ability to communicate with their caregiver, provided increased continuity of care, increased reliability of care, increased the ability to change care arrangements according to needs, and increased the ability to change hours of care. This resulted in more satisfaction with the ways in which the work was done and with the quality of care (San Antonio et al., 2007).

The Five-Part Dissemination Strategy. The fifth and final step in intervention research is the dissemination and sharing of results to obtain care that meets these criteria (Fraser et al., 2009). In this respect, the Cash and Counseling Demonstration and Evaluation was especially successful at finding ways to reach national and state policy leaders, researchers, program administrators, and the public at large.

Results from the Twelve-State Replication in Medicaid. The story of how Cash and Counseling went from a controlled experiment to a 12-state replication under the auspices of Medicaid is a combination of serendipity and opportunism. On September 11, 2001—the day the Twin Towers came down—Dr. Kevin Mahoney, the national program director for Cash and Counseling, was addressing a group of state and local leaders in Lincoln, Nebraska. Since air travel had halted, Mahoney drove back to the East Coast to keep his scheduled meetings at the Robert Wood Johnson Foundation that Friday. Foundation leaders, who would have been spread across the country, were all at the headquarters given that all planes were grounded. Mahoney learned that the foundation was considering declaring the Cash and Counseling demonstration a success and phasing it out. Instead, Mahoney facilitated an exploration of how the foundation could move past a "demonstration" to establish the concept as a routine practice.

Following on the success of Cash and Counseling's demonstration phase, RWJF and ASPE—along with the federal Administration on Aging and the Retirement Research Foundation—moved to select 12 states to replicate the demonstration model. In this new stage, termed the effectiveness stage, the model was tested on a large scale in less constrained circumstances. This phase lasted from 2004 to 2008, and the evaluation, led by Janet O'Keeffe of the Research Triangle Institute (O'Keeffe, 2009), showed how the model was successfully implemented across the nation—from western states such as Washington and New Mexico, to southern states like Alabama and Kentucky, to the Midwest (Iowa/Minnesota/Illinois/Michigan), and from the Appalachian Mountains (West Virginia/Pennsylvania) to the New England states of Vermont and Rhode Island. The O'Keeffe report—which was an implementation analysis, not an individual outcome study—showed how states adapted and innovated but were still able to maintain fidelity to the original framework.

Subgroup Analyses and Implementation Research. In the years that followed, research results focused on new populations and so-called implementation research issues. With funding from the Retirement Research Foundation and the federal Substance Abuse and Mental Health Services

Administration (SAMHSA), researchers reanalyzed the Cash and Counseling data looking at older people who had mental health claims on their Medicaid billings in Arkansas (Shen et al., 2008a) and for nonelderly adults in New Jersey (Shen et al., 2008b). When the research showed how much better the outcomes for these group were (compared to their peers served by traditional agency approaches), a whole new line of inquiry was launched looking at how people with serious mental illnesses would fare if given the option of managing a budget for their recovery goals.

Another line of inquiry showed that people with various ethnic and racial backgrounds used the budget in very different ways (Meiners et al., 2003). Other subgroups, including youth in transition and veterans, also saw positive outcomes from self-direction (Harry et al., 2017; Mahoney & Kayala, 2013).

Glasgow's widely respected RE-AIM model (Glasgow et al., 1999), which insists that research on external validity—including reach, adoption, implementation, and maintenance—can be as important as research on internal validity (i.e., efficacy) reminds us that findings from research on implementation contribute to the sustainability of an innovation. In the years following the controlled experiment, ASPE funded research on issues ranging from legal liability and workers' compensation to support broker roles and training.

A National Resource Center. Finally, as the replication phase of Cash and Counseling ended, there was another turning point when Atlantic Philanthropies joined with the Robert Wood Johnson Foundation to fund a business planning process and a National Resource Center for Participant-Directed Services (NRCPDS) built on the assumption that self-direction would become an accepted part of the human-services system. Since its inception in 2009, the NRCPDS has been conducting periodic inventories of the growth of self-direction and the numbers of individuals served (2010, 2013, 2017) and research on new and emerging issues such as case studies on how self-direction fared as states turned to managed care (Crisp et al., 2013).

This chapter has devoted significant attention to the Cash and Counseling Demonstration as it is the only large scale, randomized controlled experiment showing the effectiveness of the budget authority model and because the Centers for Medicare and Medicaid Services was so closely involved in the testing and implementation and then used this experience to craft funding templates for future states to replicate this approach. In addition, the attention drawn to the favorable results of this work was important to Congress as they passed legislation as part of the 2005 Budget Reduction Act allowing all states to replicate this model.

But Cash and Counseling was not the only evaluation that tested this approach. There were several important demonstrations for persons with developmental disabilities. In addition, some states have undertaken their own evaluations.

Evaluation of Robert Wood Johnson Pilot Demonstrations for Self-Determination for People with Developmental Disabilities

In 1997, one year after the Cash and Counseling program began, the Robert Wood Johnson Foundation (RWJF) invested in a broad range of demonstration activities around the country aimed at exploring the ways in which people with developmental disabilities could influence the character and configuration of the supports they receive through increased self-determination. The emphasis on the choices and preferences of people, which formed the heart of each of the 19 demonstrations, represented a significant departure from conventional practice.

In addition to New Hampshire—which had received a grant for a self-direction pilot three years earlier (the Monadnock Developmental Services pilot program described previously)—RWJF made grants to 18 states to further the self-determination agenda. These projects promoted new configurations of services and the empowerment of individuals with developmental disabilities to gain control over the shape and content of needed supports. The foundation allocated over $5 million in support of the demonstrations. Allocations for each project ranged from $400,000 for a 3-year period, to $200,000 for a 2-year period, and to $100,000 for a 1-year period.

The Human Services Research Institute (HSRI) and the Center for Outcome Analysis were designated as the external evaluators. HSRI had the responsibility to review the implementation of the pilots and to assess the fidelity of the efforts to the governing principles and to conduct an implementation analysis to determine what factors contributed to success and what factors presented barriers to the initiation of self-direction. The Center for Outcome Analysis assessed the outcomes of program participants.

Implementation Analysis. One of the overarching findings of the implementation analysis was that self-direction strategies should "fit" within the context and culture of the state and/or region where services are provided and that there are many different models that work, depending on the local service system (Bradley et al., 2001). There were successful efforts in both urban and rural areas, in statewide projects, and in individual counties. The recommendation was that if the principles of self-direction are followed, program elements can vary depending on the service context. For instance, the flexibility of the self-direction initiative depended on the extent of regulation and formal rules. In New Hampshire, flexibility was valued given the history of family support in the state as well as minimal regulations. In other states, such as Massachusetts, flexibility was more difficult to achieve given that the system was more regimented. The structure of the state system also played a role in the shape and content of the demonstration. In county-based systems, like Ohio, Wisconsin, and Pennsylvania, implementation varied within the state.

Another general theme was that success in embedding self-direction in a system was dependent on whether the principles were adopted across the system or whether the initiative was seen as one program option on a spectrum of services. The evaluators also found that leadership at the state or regional level was crucial to the adoption of self-direction. Where there was buy-in and commitment at the highest level, self-direction was more likely to gain traction. This lesson was borne out years later in the success of self-direction in Virginia, Tennessee, California, and Wisconsin—as described in chapter 4.

The prominence of self-advocates in the implementation of self-direction was also seen as key to successful implementation. To ensure that self-advocates are supported to make contributions, the evaluators recommended the following (Bradley et al., 2001, pp. 74–75):

- Ensure self-advocate representation at all meetings where major policy decisions about self-direction are being made

- Support statewide self-advocacy councils (drawn from self-advocacy groups within that state) that can make recommendations on an ongoing basis

- Hold meetings in accessible places and provide transportation

- Support meaningful self-advocate participation by providing training and technical assistance

Although the evaluation did not focus on the direct support workforce *per se*, the evaluators recommended that public managers take a close look at where the workforce will come from, what training will be required, and how to infuse person-centered "doing" into worker orientation. They stressed that it will be necessary to look at job design, salary, benefits, and retention issues and how they differ when services are delivered within a framework of self-determination.

Additional recommendations included a suggestion to keep financial and administrative processes as simple and transparent as possible; to develop fair and accurate means of creating individual budgets; to create digital resources that service brokers as well as participants can use to track budgets; and to separate support brokerage and administrative case management into two different roles. Finally, the evaluators recommended that the Centers for Medicare and Medicaid Services should develop clear guidelines on the use of home and community based services waivers (HCBS Waivers) to fund self-direction.

Evaluation of Participant Outcomes

The Center for Outcome Analysis conducted a quantitative analysis of the outcomes of participants in five of the original demonstration sites plus a later demonstration in California (Conroy et al., 2002). The evaluators used a variety of tools to measure decision-making power, quality of life, person-centered planning, adaptive behavior, and family perceptions. The evaluators trained interviewers in the six states to conduct face-to-face interviews at Time 1 (as early in the self-determination process as possible) and Time 2 (anywhere from one to three years later). The number of participants tracked during the analysis was 426.

All six states showed statistically significant increases in the average Decision Control Inventory (Conroy, 1995) scores from Time 1 to Time 2. In California, the overall scale score on the DCI increased from 80.9 at Time 1 to 88.9 at Time 2, an increase of 8 points on a 100-point scale. The top five areas of decision making that showed the greatest gains from Time 1 to Time 2 in California were in "choice of agency support personnel," "time spent at work/day program," "option to hire/fire support personnel," "choice of people to live with," and "whether to have pets in the home." All five of these areas were statistically significant (Conroy et al., 2002, p. 93).

In all six states, participants showed statistically significant increases on the Quality of Life Changes Scale from Time 1 to Time 2. California self-determination participants showed the largest increase on this scale: they gained an average of more than 18 points from Time 1 to Time 2. In

California, the five areas that showed the greatest increases were "running my own life," "overall quality of life," "getting out and getting around," "happiness," and "treatment by staff" (Conroy et al., 2002, p. 98). The evaluators also found increases in the "person centeredness" of the planning process as well as modest gains in community inclusion.

In 13 of the demonstration sites, Conroy and colleagues also conducted a mailed survey of families who had family members who were participants in self-direction. Of the 760 surveys sent to valid addresses, 248 surveys were returned. Families were asked about their family member's items on the Quality of Life Changes Scale since opting for self-direction; all items showed statistically significant increases. All items increased in perceived quality from before individuals began to self-direct to one year later. Life areas in which perceived quality increased the most were "getting out and getting around," "running own life and making choices," "seeing friends and socializing," "happiness," and "overall quality of life." Gains in these areas were consistent with self-determination principles in so far as they reflect more attention to integration and the development of personal relationships. Life areas in which perceived quality increased the least were "safety," "health care including dental," "health," "food," and "family relationships" (Conroy et al., 2002, p. 97).

Individual State Studies

In addition to the two national evaluation studies that were funded by RWJF, evaluations were conducted of individual states that participated in the demonstration; these included evaluations in Maryland, Massachusetts, and Michigan.

Maryland. In Maryland, the Developmental Disabilities Council funded an evaluation of self-direction that included individual outcomes and a systemic critique. The Human Services Research Institute was chosen to conduct the study (Kimmich & Becker-Green, 2000). HSRI interview data, which functioned as a supplement to the state's consumer interview—the Arc Maryland's "Ask Me!" study—indicated that participants in self-determination were treated with more dignity and respect, were making more decisions about the direction of their lives through the planning process, had more choice and received more flexible services. HSRI noted that "the dramatic increases in the use of nontraditional supports presage the movement toward a service delivery system that truly meets the unique needs of an individual" (Kimmich & Becker-Green, 2000, p. 3).

Massachusetts. In Massachusetts, Public Partnerships (then categorized as an intermediary service organization, or ISO, but now labelled a fiscal intermediary) commissioned a study of a demonstration project in which it was involved in Metro Boston. The study (Taub et al., 2004) covered two years of implementation and employed the National Core Indicators (NCI) Adult Consumer Survey to assess the characteristics and outcomes of participants in self-direction. The survey results were compared to results of the statewide NCI Adult Consumer Survey administered to a sample of individuals across the I/DD system.

The results of the two-year assessment were somewhat mixed. Individuals enrolled with the fiscal intermediary had the following characteristics compared to the state NCI sample:

- A higher percentage lived in independent homes or apartments

- A higher percentage had a label of mild or moderate intellectual disability (as opposed to a label of severe or profound)

- More participants indicated higher privacy outcomes (such as using the phone and being alone with guests) and had a greater familiarity with their service coordinator

- Fewer participants indicated they participated in community activities such as eating out, going out for entertainment, or participating in exercise or sports

- More participants made choices—including where they live, their support staff, housemates, and service coordinators—and were more likely to see friends.

- Participants were less likely to feel safe in their neighborhood (which may have been a function of living in urban Boston)

Michigan. A third state evaluation was conducted in Michigan to assess the impact of self-direction (Head & Conroy, 2005). Data were collected on 70 individuals who participated in the state's self-direction pilot. The data were collected at two time points: before 1998 and after 2001. According to the evaluators, the elapsed time between the first and second set of interviews was stretched as far as possible in order to ensure the maximum amount of time to detect significant effects.

Quality-of-life and individual budget information were collected. According to the authors, the study showed that the 70 individuals who were self-directing experienced positive outcomes in a variety of areas. Specifically, over the period of the study, they made more decisions and had more control over their lives; additionally, their quality of life increased significantly, as did their community participation.

Impact on Workers

Other than the three studies discussed later in this work, there are very few studies of the impact of self-direction on workers who provide supports.

The Cash and Counseling evaluation also examined the experiences of the workers that participants hired, contrasting their experience with the agency-hired workers assisting the control group. The full findings can be found in the dedicated issue of *Health Services Research* (San Antonio et al., 2007). In short, though, the workers whom participants hired were far happier, reported similar levels of accidents and incidents, and, in two out of three states, reported receiving higher hourly wages, although fewer benefits.

Conroy and colleagues (2002) included a survey of workers in six demonstration sites as part of their review of the RWJF demonstration. In three of the six states (Hawaii, Ohio, and Wisconsin), staff saw a statistically significant increase in the quality of their work life. In the remaining three states (California, Maryland, and Michigan), staff indicated that their work lives had improved but not at a statistically significant level. The authors pointed out that direct care staff in all six states started out with relatively high ratings for the quality of their work lives.

A recent study by Swaine and colleagues (2016) looked at the impact of self-direction on direct support workers. In their study in Virginia, they interviewed 15 workers who provided support to HCBS Waiver participants with physical and developmental disabilities who were self-directing in addition to 20 individuals who were self-directing. Their findings with respect to consumer satisfaction showed that participants experienced greater control over their services and supports in addition to increased access to health care compared to their previous experiences in the traditional system.

Workers interviewed expressed concern about the lack of training they received prior to providing support and voiced concern about the inability to make a living on the low wages paid—which were constrained by the caps on individual budgets. On the positive side, workers said they were satisfied with their experience and felt substantial pleasure working in the self-directed environment. One of the interviewees made the following comment:

> I like the fact that I feel like I'm helping somebody else. I like being able to make something easier for an individual . . . I like the fact that I can use compassion in this job [in contrast to my other] job where there's such restrictions. At least here if a person needs a hug, it's not sexual harassment. If they need somebody to cry to, you can sit there and be that shoulder for them. I take that responsibility very seriously. (Swaine et al., 2016, p. 469)

Conclusion

The evidence presented in this chapter clearly suggests that the budget authority and Cash and Counseling models are robust. Further, the efficacy and positive outcomes of these models were proven regardless of the type and strength of the evaluation approach and regardless of the auspices of those evaluations. That being said, the fact that the largest of these evaluations was a random controlled experiment involving 6,700 individuals followed by a replication in 12 state Medicaid programs across the country provides incontrovertible evidence of the efficacy of this model.

These findings have been reinforced by recent studies (Harry et al., 2016b; Harry et al., 2016a)—conducted using a participatory action research approach—that showed that over the five years that for people who were self-directing, the program was sufficiently flexible to adapt to their changing needs. Further, the study found that their personal staff helped participants to connect to their communities.

Over the years, skeptics of self-direction have feared that the option would lead to a decline in the quality of services for vulnerable individuals, but the evaluation results to date do not support such skepticism. It led to positive results for older people, younger people with physical disabilities, and people of all ages with intellectual/developmental disabilities. As will be shown in chapter 9, self-direction also works for people with serious mental illness and for veterans. As noted above, the studies reviewed in this chapter provide evidence for the efficacy of self-direction across a range of individuals who rely on public services and supports. They also include important caveats such as the pivotal role of leadership, the challenges to self-direction posed by an overly burdensome regulatory structure, the variations in the prominence of self-direction in decentralized service systems, and evidence that people who are self-directing may be less involved in their communities.

However, regardless of the auspices of the initiatives or the nature of the populations participating, the results largely show enhanced quality of life, satisfaction, and choice and control.

Chapter 7

The Impact of Self-direction

Financial Results

Cost: An Important Outcome

In addition to assessing participant outcomes of self-direction, research on self-direction has also included analyses of costs. Cost studies have ranged from an early analysis of self-direction among polio survivors in California to the major Cash and Counseling research to ongoing studies of self-direction in Medicaid waivers. If self-direction is to expand as a significant service delivery option, documenting costs and cost savings will be important, especially given the rising cost of health care and human services.

As an introduction to this chapter, it is important to begin by defining key terms including "cost benefit," "cost effectiveness," and "budget neutrality" since they are prone to multiple interpretations. Additionally, cost analyses require explicit definitions of the methods employed, including the following:

- what costs are counted
- how costs are measured
- the level at which the measurement is conducted (system or individual)
- the nature of the comparison group and how closely it aligns with the intervention group

The term "cost benefit" is rarely used in human services research as it implies that the costs and benefits of human service interventions can be measured in dollars—and it is rarely feasible to put an acceptable dollar figure on human lives or outcomes. Still, cost-benefit analyses could be useful when costs and benefits *can* be quantified, and researchers are able to compare interventions, even interventions with different goals, to see which group has the highest ratio of benefits to costs. Unfortunately, no cost-benefit analyses linking participant outcomes with costs were identified.

More typical is cost-effectiveness analysis, which involves a comparison of interventions that have very similar goals and outcomes to determine which yields a greater benefit for the same dollar amount or the same benefit but at a lower cost. Most of the studies in this chapter can be classified as cost-effectiveness studies.

Finally, "budget neutrality," a term that is often misunderstood, means the services delivered in the intervention cannot cost a dollar more than would have been spent in the absence of the intervention. This is the most rigorous test of costs, and it is the test to which federal Medicaid 1115 Research and Demonstration waivers like Cash and Counseling were held. If applied tightly, it not only means that the costs for the treatment group cannot be higher than the costs for the control group, but it also means there was no "woodwork effect"—that few if any people came into the program who would not have applied if the intervention option had not been in place. The original Cash and Counseling states had to meet this test.

These terms will be used in the discussion that follows to show how they are applied and how a misunderstanding of these approaches can confuse policy makers as well as the average citizen.

The evaluation of costs can take place before the program is underway (*a priori*) or after the program has been in operation long enough to have worked out any major implementation issues. If you evaluate a program too early, you can miss many of the effects that take time to mature. For some, the notion of an *a priori* examination of costs may seem strange, but it is appropriate to examine the logic model of a major intervention before investing large dollar amounts. For example, when the Congressional Budget Office puts a price tag on proposed legislation, of necessity, they must examine the logic and proposed cost of an intervention. In the case of Cash and Counseling, the "a priori" logic model evaluation was straightforward. If participants' budgets were always the same or less than what an agency would have received, and the costs of the supportive services (support brokers and financial management services) to assist participants manage their budgets were lower than agency overhead, the model would be cost effective if it could reduce unmet needs and address other quality improvement goals.

How This Chapter Is Organized

This chapter will cover the lessons learned from a number of published studies that document the cost impact of self-direction from different perspectives and for different populations. The first study is the Cash and Counseling research conducted by Mathematica Policy Research with funding through the Robert Wood Johnson Foundation (RWJF) and the US Department of Health and Human Services Office of the assistant secretary for planning and evaluation. This is the largest and most sophisticated economic analysis of self-direction to date. Next will be a look at the outcomes of the smaller-scale evaluations conducted in states that mounted self-direction pilot programs for people with intellectual and developmental disabilities in New Hampshire, Michigan, Massachusetts, and California. Following that will be a discussion of the cost outcomes of self-direction from studies funded by state agencies in Tennessee and Colorado. The cost evaluations recently completed on the emerging self-direction programs for people with serious mental illness will be discussed in chapter 9 in the discussion of self-direction participants. We conclude the chapter with an interview with a mother of a son with developmental disabilities and autism, illustrating the cost effectiveness of self-direction from the participant's family's perspective.

Cash and Counseling Cost Studies

The Cash and Counseling Demonstration and Evaluation provides the richest and most complex cost analyses in self-direction. The Cash and Counseling experiment was governed by the requirements of Medicaid Section 1115 waiver demonstrations that require strict standards of budget neutrality.

The evaluation conducted by Mathematica Policy Research (MPR) was a randomized control experiment with well over 6,500 individuals in three states. The evaluation was limited to people who had at least some interest in self-directing since self-direction is an option that the individual chooses, and not a requirement. Therefore, policy makers needed to know whether self-direction worked for people who specifically chose to manage their own supports and services. Half of the people were randomized to self-direct and half to receive their services through the traditional agency model. Mathematica used state-of-the-art statistical techniques to conduct their analysis (Dale & Brown, 2007). To gain the full value from random assignment, MPR used an "intent-to-treat" approach; that is, anyone assigned to the treatment group was kept in the treatment group, even if they did not follow through and manage a budget. Conversely, everyone assigned to the control group was always considered in the control group, even if they did not receive agency services. This approach preserved the full power of a randomized control experiment even as the numbers of those actively participating changed over time.

In order to control for the "woodwork effect"—in this case, any large number of people seeking the self-direction benefit who would not have been interested in traditional long-term supports and services—the evaluators limited the ratio of new to existing clients to the average of that ratio over the previous three years. This constraint to program access was not problematic for the states involved in the original demonstration.

The controlled experiment looked at all individual Medicaid and Medicare costs (for acute, chronic, and long-term care) for both the treatment and control groups for at least one year. Since it generally took states up to two years to enroll the thousands of individuals in the study, a substantial number of people had two years of comprehensive cost data, thus allowing researchers to compare early and more mature results.

In each state, expenditures for home and community based services were higher for those choosing the cash-and-counseling option in both years. As the MPR study points out, this is because large numbers of people served in the traditional agency model never received many of the prescribed personal care services; in fact, some received none of the personal care services in their state-approved care plans. When the people in the control group did not get care, their costs were zero. The higher initial costs were the result of the success of the self-direction model to provide timely services. Notably, every study participant, nine months after entering the demonstration, was asked whether they received any personal care supports in the last two weeks. The results are shown in figure 7.1: Percentages of Participants Receiving Paid Assistance at 9 Months. Every Cash and Counseling group in every state reported receiving more prescribed services than those served by traditional agencies in the control group. In Arkansas, the percentage of those receiving

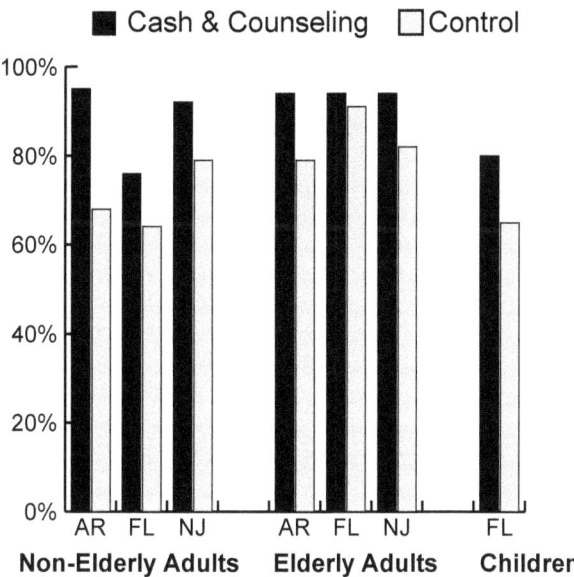

Figure 7.1. Percentage of participants receiving paid assistance after 9 months. With the exception of the Elderly Adults in Florida category, results for the Cash & Counseling (treatment) group were significantly different from the control group at the level of .01. Adapted from "How does Cash and Counseling affect costs?" by S. Dale and R. Brown, 2007, Health Services Research, 42, pp. 488–509. Copyright 2007 by Health Research and Education Trust.

prescribed care assistance in the self-directing group compared to the traditional agency group was most striking: 95% compared to 68% for persons with disabilities and 94% compared to 79% for elderly participants. Similar but less dramatic results were found in New Jersey and Florida. In Florida, the only state serving children, 80% of those in the Cash and Counseling program received prescribed services compared to only 65% of those served in traditional agencies—a 15% difference.

The availability of community supports reduced the need for institutional services. In all three states, expenditures for nursing home and hospital services were below the control group in all categories in the first year, and most groups were below the control group in the second year. The lower institutional costs for both years in Arkansas for adults and elderly, and for Florida children, were particularly significant.

Table 7.1. Non-Personal Care (Institutional) Medicaid Costs—Year One Differences per Person

Arkansas	Treatment	Control	Impact
Adult	$ 8,689	$10,432	−$1,743
Elderly	$ 7,211	$ 7,530	−$320
Children			
New Jersey	Treatment	Control	Impact
Adult	$15,697	$16,829	−$1,132
Elderly	$ 8,345	$ 8,757	−$413
Children			
Florida	Treatment	Control	Impact
Adult	$ 5,416	$ 5,785	−$369
Elderly	$ 5,475	$ 5,771	−$296
Children	$14,008	$16,447	−$2,439

Adapted from "How does Cash and Counseling affect costs?" by S. Dale and R. Brown, 2007, *Health Services Research*, *42*, p. 501. Copyright 2007 Health Research and Education Trust.

Table 7.2. Non-Personal Care (Institutional) Medicaid Costs—Year Two Differences per Person

Arkansas	Treatment	Control	Impact
Adult	$ 8,998	$11,460	−$2,462
Elderly	$ 6,425	$ 7,704	−$1,279
Children			
New Jersey	Treatment	Control	Impact
Adult	$12,653	$13,411	−$758
Elderly	$ 9,077	$ 8,579	$458
Children			
Florida	Treatment	Control	Impact
Adult	$ 5,312	$ 5,145	$158
Elderly	$ 6,970	$ 6,558	$412
Children	$14,559	$16,830	−$2,231

Adapted from "How does Cash and Counseling affect costs?" by S. Dale and R. Brown, 2007, *Health Services Research*, *42*, p. 502. Copyright 2007 Health Research and Education Trust.

In Arkansas, the increased home care costs were fully offset by the decreased nursing facility and hospital costs. Florida and New Jersey saw slight cost increases, but, as the MPR researchers pointed out, this was the first time that states could offer a cash and counseling "budget authority" option, so all states were learning to manage the new costs for financial management and support brokers. Furthermore, there were dramatic improvements documented in access and quality across the states, an argument for cost effectiveness.

These results were so promising that the research team from MPR decided to capture a third year of Medicare and Medicaid cost data in Arkansas. The results showed that nursing facility and hospital costs were 18% lower for the treatment group than for the control group during the 3-year period for adults and elderly. For those who had received personal care services before the demonstration, nursing facility savings, together with savings in other long-term care costs, fully offset the higher use of agency-based services (Dale & Brown, 2007). The experience of those who managed their own budgets was cost effective compared to those served by traditional agencies. Very few interventions have demonstrated similar reductions in nursing home and institutional usage, particularly at this level. MPR's extension of the study to a third year highlights the importance of following interventions for long enough for effects to fully materialize.

It is interesting to note that the cost evaluations mandated by CMS (Dale & Brown, 2007) carried out by Mathematica used a very different approach, one more akin to the types of per member per month analyses used by MCOs. These analyses looked only at actual expenditures for a select list of home and community based service costs over a five-year period. The costs for those enrolled in Cash and Counseling were compared to the costs of the randomized control group home care population. In any given month, the analysis excluded people who had no spending on HCBS or who were receiving only services that weren't being counted (e.g., hospital care). This approach prevented "zero spending" from lowering the average cost for the control group members and ensured that the control group included individuals who had service expenditures during the relevant period.

Each of the three Cash and Counseling states met the CMS requirement. The official 1115 waiver closeout budget-neutrality cost report for Arkansas credited the Cash and Counseling experiment with $5.6 million in savings, even without including the savings resulting from reduced nursing home use (Arkansas Department of Human Services, 2008).

Follow-up study in Arkansas. After the controlled experiment ended, Arkansas state staff continued to document and compare expenditures and service utilization for Cash and Counseling recipients to those of people receiving traditional services as shown in table 7.3.[1] The Cash and Counseling model was continued under the Independent Choices (IC) waiver, and the control group was called Agency Based (AB) care. The continuation of the data collected by the state over these five years demonstrated the cost effectiveness of the self-direction model as it matures.

Over the period running from state fiscal years 2005 through 2009, the total Medicaid expenditures for IC participants were consistently lower than those receiving AB services, growing from about $1,000 less per year per participant to more than $2,000 less per year. The total cost of Medicaid services for the control group increased from about 10% more per year to about 20% more per year during the five-year period. This was the result of the higher cost of community services ("core services") and the increased utilization of nursing home services ("institutional services"). This led to the total IC Medicaid expenditures growing more slowly than agency expenditures over five years, 23% vs. 31%. Despite the lower cost, more hours of personal care services were purchased by IC participants, about twice as many hours per week, leading to a significant increase in the cost effectiveness of the IC model. These results were compounded as participants choosing IC nearly doubled during the five years while enrollment by participants in the traditional agency model declined by 16%.

There were some limitations to the available data: the Cash and Counseling participants in the study were self-selected and theoretically differed from agency PCS users, and the state did not have universal assessment data that would permit a case-mix adjustment. Still, the results are consistent with earlier results from the controlled experiment and show that savings continued, and that Cash and Counseling was a more cost-effective system for an increasing number of participants.

Future Cost Analyses of Self-direction in Integrated Care. Some policy analysts, including some in senior positions in MCOs, have reasoned that the MPR cost evaluation results alone are not sufficient to justify a large investment in self-direction. Despite major improvements in participant and caregiver quality and satisfaction measures, they argue that additional work is needed to demonstrate the costs of self-direction in managed care where attempts are made to integrate acute, chronic, behavioral, and long-term care. The authors of this book look forward to the day such additional studies can be completed. Certainly, early demonstrations of self-direction in behav-

Table 7.3. Arkansas Medicaid Expenditures Per User Per State Fiscal Year: Agency and Independent Choices

Agency Model

	2005	2006	2007	2008	2009	Change	Change
Total users	15,309	15,303	14,134	13,830	12,797	(2,512)	–16%
Agency PC $ per user	$3,962	$3,951	$4,055	$4,104	$4,187	225	6%
Agency PC hours per user	7.9	7.9	8	8.2	7	–0.9	–11%
Core services $ per user	4,081	4,576	4,999	5,691	6,991	2,910	71%
Institutional $ per user	3,018	3,168	3,382	3,476	3,486	468	16%
Total $ per user	11,061	11,695	12,436	13,271	14,664	3,603	33%

Independent Choices

	2005	2006	2007	2008	2009	Change	Change
Total users	1,433	1,766	1,958	2,330	2,678	1,245	87%
Agency PC $ per user	$4,269	$4,222	$4,406	$4,688	$5,925	$1,656	39%
Agency PC hours per user	14.7	14.6	15.2	16.2	16.9	2.2	15%
Core services $ per user	$3,628	$3,809	$3,689	$3,601	$4,031	$403	11%
Institutional $ per user	$2,232	$2,211	$2,371	$2,799	$2,466	$234	10%
Total $ per user	$10,129	$10,242	$10,466	$11,088	$12,422	$2,293	23%
Agency/waiver total user cost $	*$932*	*$1,453*	*$1,970*	*$2,183*	*$2,222*		
Agency/waiver total user cost %	*109%*	*114%*	*119%*	*120%*	*118%*		

Source: Personal communications with Arkansas Department of Human Services officials 2008–2009.

ioral health show promise (as described in chapter 9) as does the concept of integrating long-term care unless it takes an overly medicalized bent.

The Cash and Counseling Demonstration and Evaluation had a tremendous effect on the policy community; a randomized control experiment of this size is hard to ignore. But, as the reader will see in the sections that follow, these types of results have been supported in different states, with different populations, using varied types of analysis. The overwhelming body of research indicates the self-direction approach passes virtually any cost test, especially if benefits as well as costs are taken into consideration.

Cost Studies of Self-direction for People with Intellectual and Developmental Disabilities

The second wave of self-direction cost studies came in part from the 19 pilots funded by the Robert Wood Johnson Foundation focusing on persons with intellectual and developmental disabilities. It should be noted that these pilots were originally known as "self-determination" programs, but we will refer to them as self-direction in this chapter since that is how their budgets and purchasing process was designed. There are published studies in three of the demonstration states: New Hampshire, Michigan, and Massachusetts. Another published study of self-direction for people with intellectual disabilities was carried out in California. The cost-study methodologies differed markedly in each state. Although one compared cost to another group without self-direction, no study had a randomized control group. The studies were relatively small, ranging from about 60 to 90 participants, over two or three years of program expenditures. One study focused on how people managed their budgets over two five-year time periods.

Monadnock, New Hampshire. In Monadnock, New Hampshire, 62 participants opted for self-directed budgets and the ability to make purchasing decisions with help from a case manager and a local financial management agency. This pilot was designed to test the notion that movement of power and control toward service recipients could lead to enhanced quality of life and satisfaction while simultaneously reducing expenditures (Conroy & Yuskauskas, 1996).

The study was divided into two groups, one whose needs were substantially the same during the two-year study (n=40) and one who experienced major changes in need, both increased and decreased, during the same time (n=22). The analysis of expenditures for the first 40 people showed an average annual savings of $7,698 per person compared to previous expenditures for these same individuals. This meant that service costs were reduced to 87.6% of what they had been at the start of the two-year study. Among the second group, there was an average savings of $10,594, or a reduction to 84.5% from the baseline costs, inflation included. The steady-need-group costs were reduced by 12.4%, the costs for the group who needs increased or decreased were reduced by 15.5%. As discussed in chapter 6, the participants in this study expressed continuous satisfaction with their services, leading to the conclusion that while costs declined significantly, individual autonomy and satisfaction increased. The success of the project provided impetus for the 1997 RWJF National Program for Self Determination for Persons with Developmental Disabilities in pilots across the country.

Michigan. The evaluation of Michigan's Self-direction Initiative was carried out by the Michigan Department of Community Health (Head & Conroy, 2005). The Michigan pilot had four local project sites administered by the county Community Mental Health Services Programs (CMHSP). At each site, people were enrolled voluntarily in self-direction and received individual budgets and purchasing authority. The study concentrated on 70 of the 329 individuals enrolled in self-determination. The 70 were chosen because there was complete budget, expenditure, and outcome data available for them throughout the study period. The researchers reviewed the variables describing the 70 studied against the 329 choosing self-direction and concluded that ". . . these participants were not substantially different . . . what was found for the 70 participants is probably generalizable to the 329 people visited" (Head & Conroy, 2005, p. 227).

The pilot research was designed to test a basic hypothesis: "If people gain control, their lives will improve, and the costs will not increase." Each participant engaged in a person-centered planning process to develop his or her plan for services and supports. The plan was translated into an individual budget designed to pay the full cost of the needed services and supports. The plan and budget were compiled in a document agreed to by the participant and the local CMHSP administrative entity.

Costs were measured by comparing the total baseline costs used for everyone in 1998, the year before beginning self-direction, to the total budgeted costs used three years later in 2001. The results were corrected for inflation. The mean public cost per participant in 1998 was $61,788. At the end of the third year, it was reduced to a $56,788 budget, a reduction of 8%. Adjusting for inflation using the Consumer Price Index, the total reduction doubled to a 16% savings, from $67,322 to $56,788 average cost per year (Head & Conroy, 2005 p. 233).

Previous expenditure levels per participant varied widely, ranging from only $1,000 per year to $160,000 per year. As in New Hampshire, the study documented "a tendency for the people with high initial costs to show greater savings" (Head & Conroy, p. 234). People with small initial budgets sometimes saw expenditures increase since many people whose needs had not been fully met were able to use self-determination to increase services and expenditures. The program allowed costs to increase when the personal budgeting process determined that a participant was not getting what she or he needed. Despite this "no cap" policy, overall costs were reduced substantially for the group of 70 participants over the three-year period.

In analyzing these cost results, several factors were determined to influence the changes. First, in establishing the level of the budget, coordinators used an initial funding target that could be less, and sometimes was less, than the current expenditure rate. However, there were no caps on the budgets, and some budgets moved higher than 1998 expenditures, while some were reduced. Using a budget target in the process often led to more creative and individualistic approaches to service delivery, since some participants had to do more with fewer resources. Second, participants were not required to accept unwanted services. They could choose arrangements that fit their personal preferences and values, including considering their need for privacy and not allowing providers into their home. Third, participants could negotiate prices with providers in the marketplace and shop for lower rates. Last, by employing care workers directly, participants could eliminate the agency cost of administration, which was higher than the cost of financial management. In some cases, participants planned for annual increases in the hourly rates for direct care services to retain staff while managing their budgets. The authors concluded that "the results in Michigan show not only that self-direction is a fiscally conservative approach to service delivery, but also that participants in self-determination perceive themselves as having more choice, less professional domination, and higher overall quality in their lives" (Head & Conroy, 2005, p. 238).

Although the groups were small and not chosen randomly, the reports of increased personal empowerment and quality discussed in chapter 6 strongly suggest that the self-direction pilots in New Hampshire and Michigan were cost effective when compared to earlier participant expenditures.

Massachusetts. Massachusetts was one of 19 states chosen to pilot self-direction for people with intellectual and developmental disabilities by the Robert Wood Johnson Self-Determination program. This permitted the development of a pilot program where all participants exercised both employer and budget authority. The pilot took place in the Greater Boston area. After

RWJF funding ended, the Massachusetts Department of Mental Retardation (DMR) used state funds to continue the program, and, in 2005, the state amended its Medicaid 1915(c) waiver to expand self-direction statewide. Approximately 100 participants enrolled in the original pilot.

In 2007 and again in 2015, the agency's financial services manager, Public Partnerships LLC (PPL), conducted studies with DMR to determine how participants managed their budgets. One topic covered in both studies was the amount that participants spent compared to their approved budget. The studies sought to identify whether participants overspent or underspent their budgets and how they used the freedom they acquired through self-direction. Both studies focused on participants who were enrolled and active in the program for five consecutive years.

In the first study, researchers documented spending for 51 individuals from FY2001 to FY2006 (Fenton, 2008). Annual spending was measured against individual budgets which increased about 3% per year allowing for inflation. Across all five years, participants spent an annual average of 85% to 89% of their budget, with a five-year average of 87%. No participant overspent their budget. It was noted that although participants were given assistance to manage their funds and purchase all their budgeted services and supports, they chose to spend 13% less than they could.

In 2015, a similar study (Fenton, 2015) was conducted with 87 participants who were in the program from FY2011 to FY2015. By then the statewide program had about 300 participants. The age range and gender mix of the participants was similar to the earlier study. In this case, participants spent 98% of their budgets on average each year, with about half spending 100% of their budget. As in the previous study, no one overspent their budget. The increase in individual expenditures was explained by the fact that over the 15 years the program had been in place, service coordinators had become proficient in helping participants to make more purchases and fully use their budgets. In addition, all participants received training and assistance to review their monthly budgets and review their expenditures online, and the availability of services had been enhanced through the 1915(c) waivers. Neither overspending nor underspending was a problem.

California. The California Legislature, in 1998, mandated that the Department of Developmental Services create three self-determination pilots. The three sites selected for the pilots were the East Los Angeles Regional Center, Tri-Counties Regional Center, and Redwood Coast Regional Center. Unlike the pre/post expenditures comparison approach used in New Hampshire and Michigan, researchers in the California study (Conroy et al., 2002) looked at the expenditures of the self-determination participants in the pilot sites over three years, comparing them to nonparticipants in the same county sites. Participants in the study were not selected at random; however, a review of the demographic characteristics (age, gender, and ethnicity) of those in the pilot and those who were not participants showed no significant differences between the two groups.

The results were significant. Over a three-year period, annual costs increased for the self-determination participants, but they increased substantially less than for the comparison group of non-participants. The evidence further supports the inference that self-determination held back cost increases that might otherwise have occurred in the same system. Table 7.4 shows the combined expenditures for California's three self-determination pilot sites, serving a total of 91 participants, compared to the expenditures of the non-participant comparison group served in the same pilot sites. The monthly costs for the comparison group rose almost twice as fast as the costs for the participants.

The researchers concluded:

> These data lead rather inescapably to the inference that self-determination as it has evolved in California has not only been cost neutral, it has been fiscally conservative. The increases in costs that might have been expected in the absence of self-determination were slowed, perhaps even cut in half, by Self-Determination for Persons with Developmental Disabilities. (Conroy et al., 2002. p. 116)

When linked with improvements in quality of life and decision making outlined in chapter 6, this study again suggests that self-direction led to clear improvements in cost effectiveness.

Table 7.4. California Monthly Expenditures by Group

	July 1998	June 2001	Total change	Annual change
Self Determination Participants	$978	$1,571	62%	21%
Comparison Group	$632	$1,378	118%	39%

Adapted from "Outcomes of the Robert Wood Johnson Foundation's National Initiative on Self-Determination For Persons With Developmental Disabilities " by J. Conroy, A. Y. Fullerton, M. Brown, and J. Garrow, 2002, Center for Outcome Analysis.

State Studies in Tennessee and Colorado

The following two studies in Tennessee and Colorado are the work of state agency staff documenting the financial impact of self-direction.[2] Both states made considerable investments in self-direction using Medicaid waivers. Whereas state research efforts may not be based on more sophisticated methodologies employed by more academic researchers, states are able to access substantial local data and reflect the priority concerns of public managers. Importantly, these studies were used to determine a "proof of concept" to guide the future direction of state self-direction policy and Medicaid waivers.

Tennessee. Tennessee designed a Medicaid waiver to rebalance their long-term care system from nursing home dependent to community based services. When the CHOICES waiver went into effect, Tennessee had one of the highest rates of institutional care in the country. In calendar year 2009, 86% of elderly and disabled individuals enrolled in long-term care were in nursing facilities, only 14% were in community based services. This resulted in about 90% of the long-term care budget going to higher cost nursing facilities. The impact of the waiver is summarized below.

During the five period of the study about 10,000 individuals—a 164% increase—were added to home and community based services. Of this group about 3000 chose self-direction. This was accompanied by a 22% reduction in nursing home utilization. This change in utilization brought about substantial changes in costs. Over five years nursing home costs per person increased by 28% while community services costs per person decreased by 13%. The reduction in bed use created higher costs for nursing homes while the expansion of community based services created efficiencies and lower costs. The impact of both changes created remarkable results. Over a five-year period, the number of people served in long-term care increased by 9% while the increase for expenditures went up only 12%. This resulted in a substantial rebalancing of the system with inflation adjusted costs increasing only *2% over 6 years* for the total Medicaid program for long-term care. Unlike the other studies discussed in this chapter, the Tennessee evaluation included the use of a waiver for self-direction in a managed care system to specifically reduce the use of nursing facility care for the elderly and persons with disabilities.

The study conducted by staff of the Medicaid agency TennCare provided a well-documented analysis of Tennessee's Medicaid expenditures for these services over six years, using it for ongoing CHOICES waiver applications.

Colorado. In 2016, the Colorado Department of Health Care Policy and Financing conducted and published a study on the costs of the CDASS program in response to a report by the state auditor that expressed concern about the continued growth of the program and the increased cost (Colorado Department of Health Care Policy and Financing, 2016). State agency staff studied the cost impact of 2,300 clients who had recently moved into the state's consumer direction waiver. Costs increased substantially when compared to costs the year before the waiver began. Three different groups were analyzed showing an increase of 58% to 86%, not adjusted for inflation, during the first year of the waiver.

The study did not include random selection of clients but reviewed three HCBS population subsets:

- Clients who never participated in CDASS
- Clients who were not in CDASS originally, but then selected and received CDASS
- Clients who were in CDASS throughout the study period

According to a staff member of CDASS, after much internal discussion, the Colorado study staff suggested the following reasons for the increased cost:

- Prior to consumer direction, needs were not being met for many years; services were not fully provided and therefore service costs were low.
- CDASS responded to a long-standing unmet demand by creating new service opportunities for many participants without clear limitations.
- Previously, many caregivers did not have access to payments or had limited access to payments—self-direction presented a new income opportunity for them.

The results were presented to the office of the state auditor, the program's advocates, and the agency service providers to better understand how the program works and whether the state should continue to invest. The conclusion was that the program worked well for those in need, often creating services for those who had received little, but it needed better management, and the state continued to invest in the program and manage its growth.

Case Study: A Parent's Insights on Cost

In this interview, a parent of a young man with multiple serious disabilities explains how self-direction created opportunities for him to remain at home and in the community while increasing his abilities and happiness. This parent used the flexibility of the program to get what her son needs while spending substantially less public funding in agency-based services.

V is a professor of special education with a 38-year-old son with autism, cerebral palsy, and other disabilities. He had been in a self-directed state-run program for 18 years, since 2000. V and her husband adopted R when he was five years old, born prematurely with no prenatal care. He had cerebral palsy, couldn't walk or talk, was hydrocephalic, and was visually impaired. His autism wasn't diagnosed until after the adoption. V was told that he would never walk or talk. She never accepted these limitations, and R has learned to be mobile, talk, read pictures, take directions, and engage with others.

R entered the state's self-direction program when it began in 2000, when he was 21 years old, one of the program's first enrollees. V enrolled him because although he was in an integrated high school setting, his health issues made him miss school 20% of the time and he needed staff availability at home to help him through his illnesses, keep up with his school work, and be involved in ongoing community activities when he was well.

Initially, R received 30 hours of staff assistance per week, 6 hours per day for 5 days per week. His early years in self-direction went very well both at home and in developing volunteer work in the community. He worked at the local college in the student lounge, cleaning tables and vacuuming. R was always involved in staff interviews and participated in the staff training that was overseen by his mother.

Self-direction worked well for R after high school as well, as he became more independent at home and more sociable in the community. Staff stayed an average of 2 to 3 years and developed long-term relationships with R. One staff member stayed 11 years.

Beginning in 2005, R had his own apartment in a home downstairs from where his parents live. Over time, however, his health issues—as well as those of his parents—became more dominant. His mobility declined, and he began using a walker. His autism continued, sometimes leading to outbursts and yelling, and he needed increased help with pain management. This led to revisions in his care plan and substantial increases in his budget. R has staff come in to assist him at home or in the community two shifts a day, every day of the week.

In 2012, his parents started to use an agency to provide staff after several years of self-direction in the hope that he might be able to move out of the family home into supported living.

> We tried two different agencies over two years, but we gave up because the agency staff was inconsistent, had high turnover and didn't meaningfully engage him. His care plan for an agency budget was $50,000 more than his care plan for self-direction, but the quality of his life was lower. We moved back to self-direction and R's quality of life increased immediately. We don't ever plan on going back to agency services.

R's staff tend to be young, often students in the local college, and are encouraged to bring their friends to R's apartment, which has become somewhat of a social center for his staff. They help him with meal preparation, laundry, and apartment chores. His care plan aspires for him to have 10 meaningful activities per day that can happen at home or in the community. He continues with some volunteer work at the college and enjoys being in the community, including music and art activities. Since most of the staff are part-time, a total of 12 different staff assist him during the week, all of whom are interviewed by R. His mother continues to oversee the training. "R is pretty happy most of the time and very interactive with his staff and the social situation they create," his mom says.

In recent years, it was decided that R needed overnight staff who didn't need to be awake but could respond to issues in the night. Her state's program doesn't allow overnight sleeping staff, so V recruited students to be roommates. This has been a helpful innovation and there have been no problems recruiting students as roommates.

> Self-direction works well but there needs to be more support for parents who do most of the training. Also, since most participants live with their parents, their parents need more support and assistance to design the care plan and manage the staff. I am involved in a

> working group with families of participants who don't have the background in disabilities that I do. Many of them could benefit from the services of a community support specialist to create more community opportunities and to help in designing training programs.

Conclusion

While cost reduction was not the primary goal of self-direction, when methods for documenting costs were built into the self-direction initiative, the results showed cost reductions. The research shows that well-designed self-direction programs can lead to cost savings compared to costs incurred for long-term care for comparable populations. Cost savings might even be higher for those with more complex needs. Further costs may increase at the beginning of a program because participants, who previously did not have needed supports, were given funds hire and train their own staff. Once these initial expenditures are taken into consideration, costs in the subsequent years come into control.

To provide a more holistic picture of the impact of self-direction, it is important to measure other costs and savings not directly related to home and community long-term care services, including a decrease in utilization of more expensive institutional care including nursing homes, hospitals, or other residential care. Overall, most of these studies showed that cost reductions are accompanied by much higher participant and worker satisfaction and improved social and clinical outcomes as documented in chapter 6.

This summary of cost studies makes it reasonably clear that a self-direction program can reduce the annual costs of long-term care, either when measured against a comparable group in agency-based services or the cost of care in the previous year of agency-based services. The Cash and Counseling randomized control experiment, with its 6,700 participants, shows that self-direction can even meet the harsh test of budget neutrality while producing marked increases in quality and access to care.

There are many factors that seemed to contribute to these positive economic outcomes:

- People purchase primarily what they need and want; they are not inclined to use all the resources simply because they are available in their budget.

- Creating individual budgets with flexible services and supports enables users to make cost effective and innovative decisions that improve outcomes that are often less expensive than agency-based services.

- Individual budgets can reduce the use of other more expensive Medicaid services—including nursing facilities, hospitals, and institutional care—because they give participants more opportunities to avoid inpatient care and meet their needs in their home community, their primary choice of place.

- The additional costs for counselors and financial management can be established to assure they are the same or less than the cost of agency-based service administration.

These findings are a strong argument to allay the fears of public managers and legislators who worry that given increased freedom, relaxation of certain payment rules, possible mismanagement by participants, and the possibility of opportunistic providers, self-direction will result in rising costs. The large number of studies reviewed here in fact show the contrary. Increased freedom and participant-management resulted in creative purchasing and more person-centered services; they did not result in overspending or rising costs.

Chapter 8

Factors That Can Influence the Growth of Self-direction

There are many factors currently at play that may contribute to the expansion of self-direction in the future. These include changing population demographics and service preferences, workforce shortages, increased interest in self-direction among state legislators, a federal regulatory environment mandating person-centered planning, greater citizen involvement in changes to state Medicaid waivers and plans, and increased support for self-direction among national membership groups and professional associations. It remains to be seen whether other trends—such as the complex infrastructure of self-direction and negative attitudes among some case managers, the growth of managed care for long-term services and supports, the move to integrated care in behavioral health, changes in federal labor and oversight rules, and workforce shortages—will slow the adoption of self-direction.

Demographic Trends That Will Impact Self-direction

Two major demographic changes—a dramatic growth in the number of older individuals needing long-term care (including people with disabilities who are living longer) and the increasing diversity of the US population—will continue to result in changes in the delivery of human services. Two other factors—worker shortages and the desires of many baby boomers for community rather than nursing home options—may increase the prominence of self-direction as a service delivery option.

In 2010, the proportion of the US population over 65 was 13% (US Census Bureau, 2011). That percentage is expected to grow to 20%—or one in five Americans—by 2030 (Grayson & Velkoff, 2010). The Administration for Community Living estimates that someone turning age 65 today has almost a 70% chance of needing some type of long-term care services and supports in their remaining years. Further, individuals needing long-term care, including older adults and individuals with disabilities, increasingly want to be supported in communities rather than more institutional settings. "Aging at home" has become the catchphrase for supports that enable people to avoid nursing home admission. To accommodate the preferences of this growing segment of the population, it will be necessary to build a more flexible infrastructure for long-term community based services and supports.

In 2003, AARP surveyed a representative group of members over the age of 50 regarding how they would like to be supported if, in the future, they needed help with basic activities of daily living like bathing, dressing, or getting out of bed. The results showed that 75% of respondents preferred managing their own supports and services rather than receiving care from an agency. These responses suggest that the large baby boomer population will continue to want choice and flexibility as they age.

Over the past decades, the US population—including those needing long-term services and supports—is becoming more diverse. Between 1990 and 2030, the number of older people in four ethnic groups (Hispanics, African Americans, Native Americans, and Asians and Pacific Islanders) is expected to grow from 14% to 25% of the over-65 population (Ortman et al., 2014, p. 12). The nation is diverse in terms of race, gender, ethnicity, sexual orientation, and functional and cognitive ability, to name but a few dimensions. The long-term care system will have to become more flexible to respond to individual situations and needs. One size does not fit all.

With respect to accommodating diversity, the self-direction model offers some unique lessons regarding how to handle a wide range of needs. The photos below appeared in brochures created in Arkansas as part of the Cash and Counseling Demonstration Program funded by the Robert Wood Johnson Foundation and the assistant secretary for planning and evaluation.

In discussion groups with several Area Agency on Aging directors, care managers and their supervisors, one of those directors, Lou Swan from the Worcester, Massachusetts, Elderly Services Agency, emphasized the strengths of self-direction in a private conversation with one of the authors. He noted that his agency tries to serve participants from heritages ranging from Albanian and Ethiopian to Brazilian (to name a few). According to

Figure 8.1. Faces of participant direction. Photo of Mrs. Lillie Brannon, Arkansas Division of Aging and Adult Services (2001) Independent Choices, p. 5, Kelly Quinn, photographer. Photos of Mrs. Janice Maddox and The Cruz Family, Cash and Counseling Program (2002), pp. 6 & 9. Kelly Quinn, photographer.

Swan, allowing participants to shape their own spending plans tailored to their cultural preferences is the only way he can support such diverse clients.

As noted in chapter 6, data from the original Cash and Counseling states confirm this assumption. Different ethnic groups spend their budgets in very different ways. The experiences of the participants shown in the photos above make this point. Mrs. Janice Maddox of Pine Bluff, Arkansas (on the left), used her $413 monthly allowance to pay her adult granddaughter, Keisha Long, to spend at least two hours a day, seven days a week attending to Mrs. Maddox's personal assistance needs. Her allowance was also used to pay her grandson $10 a week to do odd jobs around the house. And the allowance helped pay for over-the-counter medications and new dentures. The Cruz family of Zephyrhills, Florida (center photo), asked their daughter to serve as their representative to help them manage their combined budget of $1,062 a month. Their budget went toward personal care supplies, respite care, home improvements, transportation, and medication management. Finally (on the right), Mrs. Lillie Brannon of North Little Rock, Arkansas, rejoiced in the fact that she was "the boss." Even though she never left her home except to go to the doctor or the hospital, she rejoiced in having "escaped from a nursing home" and hiring her own workers.

It is not surprising that the 2008 Commonwealth Fund Opinion Leader's Survey (Miller et al., 2009) found that 61% of the 1,147 leaders from across the long-term care spectrum (including legislators, people from the business community, nonprofit agencies, academia, and national membership and advocacy organizations) who responded to the survey favored expansion of self-direction efforts like the Cash and Counseling program as a potential strategy for reform of publicly funded services.

Impending Worker Shortages

According to estimates from the National Center for Health Workforce Analysis (2004) within the US Health Resources and Services Administration Bureau of Health Professions, an additional 1.2 million nursing aides, home health aides, and people in similar occupations will be needed in the next 10 years to cover the projected growth in the number of people needing long-term care, especially given the high turnover among staff. Looking at the projections above, this suggests that 3.6 million additional nursing aides will be needed by 2049, a growth of about 120,000 per year. This comes at a time when the pool from which such workers have traditionally been drawn—largely women between the ages of 25 and 50 without postsecondary education—continues to shrink. This worker shortage has been one of the primary reasons that some states have turned to self-direction because the workers that participants hire are typically *not* already working in the long-term care arena. Further, many of these workers remain in the workforce even after they leave the employ of their original employer (Benjamin et al., 2008). Allowing participants to hire family, friends, and neighbors adds to the workforce and increases the chances that older people can get care from people who know them and love them as individuals. Under Cash and Counseling, most participants in every state hired people they knew.

The changes described above should fuel an expansion of self-direction over the next several years. That is assuming that federal and state policy makers continue to build the infrastructure for self-direction and embrace policies that make self-direction a prominent feature of long-term services and supports systems.

Facilitating Self-direction through Public Policy

As we have seen in chapter 4, there is a wide variation in access to and utilization of self-direction across the country. Within states, there is also variation in which groups of individuals (e.g., older adults, people with intellectual disabilities, etc.) are enrolled in self-direction. Some state legislatures are taking a leadership role in encouraging the use of self-direction for eligible participants. Regulatory changes at the federal level are also fostering the take up of self-direction. The following are some recent examples.

State Legislation. Several states, with pressure from families and advocates, and recognizing the cost effectiveness of self-direction, have passed legislation to expand the self-directed option.

Massachusetts Real Lives Legislation and Autism Initiative. One of the most comprehensive legislative initiatives is the "Real Lives" legislation that passed in Massachusetts in 2014 (Massachusetts Real Lives Bill-H4237, 2014). The act requires that *all* individuals who are eligible for services from the Massachusetts Department of Developmental Services (DDS) be afforded the option of self-directing all or part of their services and supports based on their choices and their individualized budgets. This represents a very different approach for the state where the self-direction option was not always introduced to potential participants. Representative Thomas Sannicandro, the coauthor of the legislation, described the intent of the bill as follows (Vennochi, 2012):

> At its heart, the Real Lives bill isn't about money. It's about recognizing the rights of people with disabilities to make choices about how and where to live—and not limiting them to choices made by someone else . . . Everybody has some idea of what they think is best for them . . . some might need more help in making their decisions. But those decisions should be theirs to make.

The act directed DDS to establish policies and training programs regarding the self-direction option and to convene a statewide advisory board that would monitor progress and submit annual reports to the legislature.

In addition, Massachusetts passed state legislation in 2008 (Massachusetts Department of Developmental Services, n.d.) creating a home-based program for children with autism up to the age of eight and their families.

Each enrolled family receives a budget calculated individually to support a wide range of home-based services, including behavior training and consultation, a variety of therapeutic services, homemaker services, home modifications, and respite care. Families are assisted by "system navigators" from local autism centers to recruit and hire staff and manage their budgets. From 2014 to 2017, the program has served 180 families. It is now part of a new Medicaid waiver and is expected to grow *continuously* until it reaches the estimated statewide need of about 1,000 families.

Hawaii Legislation Supports Caregivers for Older Adults. Hawaii passed legislation in 2017 to support working caregivers helping to sustain people 60 years and older, who are not Medicaid eligible, in their homes. Hawaii's Kupuna Care (KC) is a state program designed to assist families by providing a variety of home-based caregiving and support services. The legislation is designed to create individual budgets calculated to provide enough assistance to keep people at home and out of a nursing facility. It includes the ability to hire a family member or friend who otherwise would be providing services at home with no pay. The program is designed to pay working caregivers in the program who provide services to support their *kupuna* (relative) up to $70 per day to cover the cost of providing adult day care, chore services, home-delivered meals, homemaker services, personal care, respite, or transportation. In 2017, Governor David Ige of Hawaii noted that the program reflected Hawaiian cultural traditions:

> The landmark initiative is a first step in recognizing the significant contributions and sacrifices of Hawaii's working caregivers as they celebrate and honor their kupuna. Support for our caregivers is critically needed as Hawaii's population is aging more rapidly than the national average and our seniors live longer than seniors in any other state.

It is important to note that this is a state-funded program that does not rely on any federal funds and expects to continually grow to meet the demands of the state's aging population.

Washington's Long-Term Care Trust Act. In April 2019, Washington created the first public long-term care insurance program in the country enabling qualified participants to purchase long-term care services and supports to maintain their independence and eliminate the requirement of spending down their resources to become eligible for Medicaid. The Long-Term Care Trust Act will provide up to $36,500 per participant to directly purchase a wide range of flexible services and supports that include supportive care in the home, home-based equipment, and training and pay for family members and other individuals providing caregiving duties, community transportation, and care coordination. Participants can become employers and employ and train family members and other caregivers as in the self-directed model. As Jason McGill, the assistant director of the Washington State Medicaid program noted: "This model will work, and it could be used almost off-the-shelf by every state" (Weisman, 2019).

The program will be financed through a payroll tax of $0.58 per $100 of income for all workers earning W-2 income. It will require an initial three-year vesting period to establish sufficient funds in the trust and will be overseen by a new public trust commission effective January 2021. The commission is responsible for establishing and monitoring standards of quality care as well as the long-term financing of the program.

Oregon Legislation on Worker Issues and Private Payers. Oregon passed legislation in 2010 to create a new public authority called the Oregon Home Care Commission. It was designed to support and expand self-directed care. The commission has four primary responsibilities:

- To define the qualifications of homecare and personal support workers;

- To create a statewide registry of homecare and personal support workers;

- To provide training opportunities and training certifications for homecare and personal support workers; and

- To serve as the "employer of record," including the purchase of worker's compensation, for purposes of collective bargaining for homecare and personal support workers who receive service payments from public funds.

In 2014 the legislation was amended to allow private pay consumers to purchase homecare services from the commission through its registry, making it the first state self-direction program to be open to use by the private sector.

California Legislation Expands Self-direction for People with Intellectual Disabilities. In 2013, the California state legislature crafted a bill requiring the Department of Disability Services to implement a new statewide program establishing a Medicaid waiver funded "self-determination" program. The program covers all the state's 22 regional centers, which serve more than 300,000 individuals and provides an individual budget for all interested participants and their families. It has very specific goals and phase-in requirements:

> The Self-Determination Program will provide increased flexibility and choice, and greater control over decisions, resources, and needed and desired services and supports to implement their IPP (Individual Program Plan) . . . Following the phase-in period, the program shall be available on a voluntary basis to all regional center consumers, including residents in developmental centers who are moving to the community, who are eligible for the Self-Determination Program. (California Welfare and Institutions Code, 2013)

Centers for Medicare and Medicaid Services (CMS) Policies. After several months of public comment in 2013, CMS issued new rules regarding those services and supports that would be eligible for Medicaid waiver services. The new rules, which aligned with the Americans with Disabilities Act and the Supreme Court *Olmstead* decision, stressed that people receiving Medicaid HCBS long-term services and supports should have full access to the benefits of community living and the opportunity to receive services in the most integrated setting appropriate. Given the breadth of the new rules—and the impact on existing services—states were given five years to comply. That deadline was subsequently expanded to seven years from the date of official promulgation in March 2014.

The new rules, termed the "HCBS Settings Rule," stressed the importance of person-centered planning in addition to other guidelines regarding community inclusion, privacy, and choice. The new planning guidelines highlighted the importance of the active involvement of the participant and a singular focus on the goals and preferences of that individual. Rather than assessing needs in order to refer the individual to an agency, person-centered planning starts with the desires and aspirations of the person and builds supports around that vision. Case managers are therefore challenged to think more broadly about resources and supports. These national planning requirements have the potential to result in an expansion of enrollment in self-direction since all HCBS waiver participants must be given the option to direct their services. With the new CMS rule, the self-direction option is no longer solely dependent on individual state initiatives.

Self-direction was also encouraged in a governmentwide guideline regarding the ways in which each cabinet agency would advance self-direction within their specific agency. The guideline, which was developed as part of the Community First Choice provisions of the Affordable Care Act (Section 2402), provides a roadmap to a national focus on self-direction.

Initiatives by National Membership Groups and Professional Associations

Nonprofit membership, advocacy, and other organizations have also made contributions to the movement to increased choice and self-direction.

American Association of Retired Persons Scorecard. The American Association of Retired Persons (AARP) conducts regular surveys on the quality and availability of long-term care in all states. The surveys create a "scorecard" that measures and compares states in five main categories on 25 specific indicators. The main categories include the following:

- Affordability and access
- Choice of setting and provider
- Quality of life and quality of care
- Support for family caregivers
- Effective transitions between nursing homes, hospitals, and homes

Starting in 2014, AARP included self-direction as a major quality indicator. In the 2017 survey (Reinhard, Accius, et al., 2017), AARP added several specific indicators and concluded that the presence of self-direction improves the choice of setting and provider and increases the quality of long-term care:

> In a high-performing system, consumers should have the right to decide how and where those services are delivered, and who provides them. Consumer direction, self-direction, or participant direction are used interchangeably to describe a model that allows individuals to hire and fire service providers, set their hours, and, in some cases, determine their rate of pay. (Edwards-Orr & Ujvari, 2018, p. 12)

The AARP survey determined that although the number of self-directed programs reported was stable between 2013 and 2016—at about 250—program enrollment grew considerably from 740,000 to 1,060,000, an increase of 143% (Edwards-Orr & Ujvari, 2018).

National Advocacy to Reform Guardianship and Encourage Alternatives. Many individuals are constrained from self-direction because they are under guardianship. Data from the National Core Indicators suggest that as many as 46% of individuals in the ID/DD service system have guardians (National Core Indicators, 2016–2017). As a substitute to guardianship, there is an emerging alternative called Supported Decision Making (SDM). SDM relies on the creation of circles of support to assist the individual with a disability to make important life decisions such as agreeing to a medical procedure, getting married, or entering into a contract.

The American Association on Intellectual and Developmental Disability (AAIDD) in conjunction with the national ARC issued a joint policy statement on guardianship in 2016. An excerpt from the statement follows:

> Regardless of their guardianship status, all individuals with I/DD retain their fundamental civil and human rights (such as the right to vote and the right to make decisions related to sexual activity, marriage and divorce, birth control, and sterilization) unless the specific right is explicitly limited by court order.

Because of advocacy to reduce the routine use of guardianship, states such as Texas have passed legislation that requires courts to explore SDM prior to granting guardianship. Further, the National Guardianship Association revised its standards of practice in 2013:

> The Guardian **shall** encourage the person to participate . . . in all decisions that affect him or her, to act on his or her own behalf in all matters in which person is able to do so, and to develop or regain his or her own capacity to the maximum extent. (p. 9)

Finally, the American Bar Association produced a *Practical Guide to Guardianship* in 2016 that emphasized that all alternatives to guardianship should be explored, that lawyers should start with the assumption that guardianship is not required and that prior to guardianship, the individual's strengths and capabilities should be explored as well as his or her deficits. Reducing the use of guardianship, the possibilities of self-direction may be enhanced. Further, by expanding opportunities such as SDM, many can play a more active role in making choices about significant aspects of their lives.

Trends That May Constrain the Growth of Self-direction

The discussion above highlights many factors, including population dynamics, public policies, and the growing advocacy by national membership and professional associations that have, or potentially will, facilitate the growth of self-direction. There are several trends that have developed that could increase or decrease the demand for self-direction.

Case Management. Service coordinators and support brokers are seen as a key to the success of self-direction. A recent study canvassed 58 state developmental disabilities program administrators in 34 states with self-direction programs regarding the strengths and challenges of self-direction (DeCarlo et al., 2018). The findings reinforce the centrality of case management/support brokers in the success of the program. Given their pivotal role, it is important to clarify the roles of case managers/supports brokers in support of self-direction and to provide training on the benefits and mechanisms of self-direction.

> Administrators in this study emphasized how critical well-trained and engaged case managers were to successful implementation of self-direction . . . administrators echo the importance of having "buy-in" from case managers, and that dissatisfied or negatively disposed case managers can limit access to self-direction by simply not mentioning it to potential participants. Moreover, case managers who harbor concerns or misconceptions about self-direction may not present accurate information out of fear for their clients' safety. (p. 8)

In addition to clarifying the roles of case managers, states need to develop comprehensive training programs and to identify case managers with an interest in self-direction to serve as support brokers or recruit new staff, including peers, to fill this role. Separating traditional case management from support brokerage may provide a more focused emphasis on the desires of the individual given the multiple program and fiscal responsibilities vested in traditional case managers. It can be argued that case managers are not the most appropriate individuals to guide self-direction. As stated in the Centers for Medicare and Medicaid Services guidance on self-direction:

> A supports broker/consultant/counselor must be available to each individual who elects the self-direction option. The supports broker/consultant/counselor supports the individual in directing their services and serves as a liaison between the individual and the program, assisting individuals with whatever is needed to identify potential personnel requirements, resources to meet those requirements, and the services and supports to sustain individuals as they direct their own services and supports. The supports broker/consultant/counselor acts as an agent of the individual and takes direction from the individual. (Medicaid.gov, 2018)

Strictly speaking, service coordinators are not "agents" of the individual, nor do they take direction from the individual. Service coordinators with individuals who are self-directing on their caseloads are therefore both carrying out their required administrative functions and attempting to live up to the aspirations in the above guidance. It is possible to conclude that there is a conflict between those two functions.

Further, traditional case management has some built-in constraints with respect to self-direction. Many case managers around the country have high caseloads. In Massachusetts, for instance, caseloads can be as high as 60 individuals per case manager. Supporting people to self-direct—especially at the beginning of the process—can be labor intensive for the case managers. With large caseloads, finding the time to assist participants to master the various aspects of self-direction can be problematic. Finally, training for case managers does not always include the fine points of self-direction.

Managed Care and Integrated Care. Several states are turning to MCOs to run their long-term service and supports programs. This may presage a possible move toward a more medical model in long-term care. A recent study (2013) by the National Council on Disability included the following cautionary observation:

> In several important ways, the basic concepts underlying managed care conflict with the principles of consumer choice and control . . . Managed care attempts to achieve system wide efficiencies by consolidating decision-making authority in a single management entity, restricting consumer choice to network-ap-

proved providers, and substituting lower-cost interventions for higher-cost interventions wherever possible. The self-direction model, in contrast, vests decision-making authority with the individual receiving supports, with or without the assistance of a designated representative(s). (p. 37)

The Council study goes on to note the threat that advocates see in the expansion of managed care including the inherent conflict between the medically oriented care management model used by many MCOs and the overarching goals of self-direction (independence, personal control, and improved quality of life). Advocates also worry that the MCOs will be responsible for determining who can and cannot self-direct their services. Finally, advocates fear that the MCO care managers—with little experience of self-direction—will be solely responsible for introducing the concept to participants. This is not different from public care management systems and both will benefit from care managers with interest and training in self-direction.

That is not to say that self-direction cannot be successfully embedded in a managed care framework. In some ways, MCOs may see self-direction as a more efficient means of delivering services rather than working through traditional providers. We have seen managed care policy in Pennsylvania, Virginia, and Florida that encourages competition among MCOs regarding how well they are supporting consumer direction. In states where participants have a choice of MCO providers, consumers have moved to the plans where they believe they can preserve their ability to self-direct.

However, to ensure that *all* participants are introduced to self-direction as an option, it will be necessary for state Medicaid agencies to spell out their expectations for self-direction in MCO contracts. Tennessee's MCO contract provides an example of how a state can influence the availability of self-direction. References to "consumer direction" are present throughout the Tennessee master contract with long-term managed care. The specific portion of the Tennessee CHOICES contract that addresses self-direction runs to 19 pages and includes detailed implementation guidelines regarding how self-direction will be offered and managed. The introductory subsection of the contract states:

> The CONTRACTOR shall offer consumer direction of eligible CHOICES HCBS and eligible ECF CHOICES HCBS to all CHOICES Group 2 and 3 and ECF CHOICES members

who are determined by a Care Coordinator or Support Coordinator, as applicable, through the comprehensive assessment/reassessment process, to need (for CHOICES) attendant care, personal care, in-home respite, companion care services and (for ECF CHOICES) personal assistance, including supportive home care, respite, and community transportation and/or any other service specified in TennCare rules and regulations as available for consumer direction. (Tennessee MCO Statewide Contract, 2020, p. 222)

Another emerging trend is an increased emphasis on "integrated care." The model was developed ostensibly to address the social determinants of health by combining social and health services under one umbrella and providing a holistic set of services and supports for individuals with a range of challenges. Integrated care combines the expertise of mental health and substance use care with primary care clinicians. Integrated care is also an approach adopted in many European countries merging social and health care, particularly for the elderly. Marrying social models with clinical models, though promising, has some built-in conflicts. According to a study by Simon-Rusinowitz, Bochniak, Mahoney, and Hecht (2000) that entailed interviewing policy experts, there was a consensus that tensions between consumerism and managerial and clinical control could pose major obstacles to embedding self-direction with integrated care models. However, some observers argue that the inclusion of self-direction in integrated care models will "humanize" integrated care "by encouraging more flexible service use and greater consumer satisfaction and quality—without harming inherent efficiency and effectiveness goals" (Kodner, 2003).

Changes in Labor Protections and Accountability. A major change by the US Department of Labor in 2015, called the Home Care Rule, makes major changes in the companionship exemption that removed certain direct care workers from the Fair Labor Standard Act's minimum wage and overtime requirements. The new rule narrows the companionship exemption in several ways. First, the rule narrows the services that a worker can perform and still be classified as a companion and be exempted from minimum wage and overtime. Companion responsibilities are limited to fellowship and protection. Further, only 20% of the companion's time can be providing care, such as help with dressing, bathing, light housework, meal preparation, and toileting. If more than 20% of the worker's hours are spent providing such care services in a work week, then the companionship exemption cannot be claimed for that week, increasing the ability of the worker to earn higher wages. Further, the companionship exemption can only be claimed by individuals and households, not by third-party payers including private agencies and the county and state.

The new rule affects live-in staff who were previously exempt from overtime compensation (though they still received minimum wage). Like the companionship exemption, the live-in exemption can only be claimed by the individual and the household—not third-party payers. The new rule also imposes new record keeping regarding hours of care provided, and since DOL rules (as opposed to IRS provisions) allow for multiple coemployers, all of whom have responsibilities for payment of services, including overtime, payments could go up wherever a worker serves more than one participant if the total weekly hours are more than 40, requiring overtime payments. This can even require co-employers to pay for travel time between participants during the day.

An additional new requirement calling for electronic visit verification (EVV) was passed as part of the 21st Century Cures Act in 2016. The purpose behind the EVV mandate is to track personal care aides and home health providers to ensure that the visits and hours reported to CMS are taking place, that participants are getting the care they require, and that Medicaid is being accurately billed. Most EVV systems rely on Global Positioning Systems to accurately pinpoint when a caregiver arrives at and leaves a specific location, such as a client's home. Other systems utilize telephone lines, requiring the caregiver to call the agency office via a landline. The new law for personal care aides goes into effect in 2019 and for home health aides in 2020. Although this requires implementation of new systems for timekeeping and payroll, many states see the advent of EVV as a way to streamline the operation of self-direction, creating an opportunity to develop on-line methods for submitting accurate time sheets and direct deposit of wages. However, EVV also places burdens on those in rural areas without the internet and on individuals with cognitive limitations who must use new technology to verify the services and supports they receive.

All of these changes, while improving protections for workers and increasing protections against fraud, also add more levels of complexity and administrative requirements for people who are self-directing and their families—especially when participants are managing multiple staff and schedules.

Sustainability of the Workforce. The success of self-direction now and in the future is dependent on the availability of personal care attendants, direct support professionals, and other workers who can assist people to manage their needs. In general, support workers are among the lowest paid in the nation. For workers in the I/DD field, the most recent turnover figure is 44% annually (National Core Indicators, 2019). The DOL payment rules were an acknowledgment of this problem. Given the importance of stable and dependable workers in the lives of people who are self-directing, pay and turnover issues pose real challenges to the well-being of participants. Typically, research on worker needs centers on wages, benefits, training, and working conditions. A major study that examined these issues was supported by the Robert Wood Johnson Foundation and the Atlantic Philanthropies. The initiative was named "Better Jobs, Better Care" (Leading Age, 2008).

The lack of adequate pay and benefits for direct support staff affects both agency and self-directed staff. However, self-direction does entail some different approaches. Traditional providers view workforce enhancement in terms of training, recruitment, and career ladders. In self-direction, training—in addition to basic health and safety—is more likely to be determined and delivered by the participant and based on his or her individual needs. To support recruitment, many states allow participants to hire family members or friends who know the person with disabilities. For those without a network of family and friends, finding staff can be a challenge, and registries have been developed in some states to match individuals with potential qualified support workers.

Regardless of the setting, support workers continue to be at the bottom of the pay scale, and many are forced to work more than one job. These problems have been somewhat ameliorated in those states where support workers are unionized. Unionization is discussed as it relates to California in chapter 4, but it is also relevant here as a factor that has and will affect self-direction. By 2009–2010, unionization of independent providers working for self-directing participants had become enough of a trend that some advocates of self-direction became concerned about the possibility that unionization of these workers could erode self-direction. At the same time, many disability rights advocates looked to unions as allies in advocating for both direct care workers and people with disabilities who rely on their services. Some said that they wanted to voice their support for unionization of direct care workers employed by self-directing beneficiaries since they believed these efforts would result in better pay and benefits for such workers but also wanted to make sure that unionization of participant-directed aides would be compatible with self-direction.

Tom Nerney, founding director of the Center for Self-Determination in Wayne, Michigan (and longtime advocate of self-determination for people with disabilities, especially intellectual developmental disabilities), approached Andrew Stern, then president (1996–2010) of SEIU, with a request to initiate dialogue and consensus building between disability rights advocates and SEIU representatives. Nerney facilitated face-to-face meetings: an informal meeting in May 2008 and a more formal meeting in December 2008. Participants included representatives of disability rights activists, including ADAPT and independent living organizations; and self-determination/self-direction advocates, including Nerney and staff from the Boston College National Resource Center for Participant-Directed Services. The key staff person from SEIU was Mark Polit, who worked for SEIU in California and who, as the parent of a child with intellectual and developmental disabilities receiving Medicaid-funded supports, considered himself an advocate for people with disabilities and their families.

Nearly four years of negotiations—primarily between ADAPT and SEIU, with the NRCPDS serving as facilitator—resulted in a consensus document in 2011 entitled *Guiding Principles for Partnerships with Unions and Emerging Worker Organizations When Individuals Direct Their Own Services and Supports*. This document tackled difficult issues, ranging from the rights of participants as employers, to required training, to collecting worker signatures to force a vote for unionization.[1] These guidelines establish practical approaches for states with public employee unions to support and expand self-direction.

Our Son—His Life: A Transition Story

Our son JS is an active 22-year-old young man who lives at home with us and his two younger siblings. JS was born with hydrocephalus, better known as "water on the brain." This resulted in other disabilities: cerebral palsy, intellectual disabilities, cortical visual impairment (legally blind), and epilepsy. He walks with a walker. He talks, though sometimes he needs interpretation. These challenges have never stopped him from engaging in a full life.

When JS was approaching his momentous 22nd birthday, we thought about the type of life that he would like to live. He will always require assistance for his personal skills, and our goal was to have reasonable accommodation for him by building a handicapped-accessible apartment onto our home. This would allow him privacy and independence while still being close to the family.

Through various funding, loans, and hard work, we were able to complete his "bachelor pad."

Then we began to think about what JS would like to do during the day. For our son, a traditional day program was not going to be a great choice. We visited some day habilitation programs and some supported employment programs, but none of them were a good fit. Staying at home all day or being stuck in a building all day was not an option. We knew he wanted to be physically, mentally, and socially active to have a meaningful and purposeful life. He loves people, and he enjoys being "where the action is."

We heard about self-directed services, which could enable a person to design their own supports in order to live a meaningful life of their own choosing. We asked JS what he wanted to do for a job, and he answered, "Sell hot dogs at the ballpark." Although a major league stadium did not seem feasible, selling hot dogs seemed like a great idea!

Self-directed services were the way to make it happen. We found a great deal on a hot dog cart, and through a combination of our savings and other funding, we bought the cart and got into the hot dog business. The Agency with Choice model of self-direction helped make the transition to adult services a smooth one. The ARC in our county made it easier for us to hire a great staff person, who is also a wonderful companion, working side by side with John at "DogHouseDog."

DogHouseDog is now a thriving business. JS is cooking and selling hot dogs at high school football games, public events, and parties. In December, JS was an important part of our town's Christmas celebration, selling warm hot dogs on a cold night!

When JS is not busy selling hot dogs, he is an active member of his community. He works part time at the local barber shop, volunteers for Meals on Wheels and his church, exercises at the YMCA, and takes the train to explore the nearby city. He is learning how to cook, how to paint, and how to do public speaking.

Our son has a great life, doing what he loves. JS is a wage earner, socializes with people of all ages, has responsibility to meet some of his own needs, works on staying physically fit, helps others through volunteerism, is involved with his family, and is maturing while experiencing life in his community.

JS says, "I like selling hot dogs and eating them too." And so do his customers!

Conclusion

This chapter provided an overview of the demographic, workforce, and management trends that will affect the uptake of self-direction. We have looked at policy reforms in states and at the federal level that have and will place a priority on self-direction, and the growing willingness of national membership and professional organizations to prioritize the importance of empowerment strategies such as self-direction. The discussion also described current and emerging factors in the human services system that may add complexity to the process and create constraints to self-direction. While on balance there appears to be substantial momentum for the expansion of self-direction, the impact of workforce issues and increased regulation will require careful scrutiny going forward. Our conclusions and recommendations building on and responding to these trends are addressed in chapter 11.

Chapter 9

The Expansion of Self-direction to Other Participants

Self-direction has become a support option for people who are aging, have physical disabilities, and have intellectual and developmental disabilities. The potential benefits of self-direction are not limited to these participants but can also enhance the empowerment of other individuals. The following discussion highlights the emerging application of self-direction for two groups: veterans and people with serious mental health conditions.

Self-direction for Veterans

In 2008, leaders in the Veterans Health Administration (VHA) were trying to deal with several challenges. Large numbers of service men and women were returning with major disabilities from wars in Iraq and Afghanistan. Many of these veterans were in their late teens, twenties, and thirties and didn't see themselves living in a nursing home for the rest of their lives. The amount of homemaker/home health services available to them was limited. VHA's existing long-term service and support (LTSS) options, especially in rural areas, were not set up to meet their needs. In addition, veterans of earlier wars were also aging and increasingly required LTSS. The VHA was challenged to meet the needs of these veterans, particularly in the community. Recognizing how important it was to rapidly put in place supports for people with disabilities, as well as the desire to rebalance the US Department of Veteran's Affairs (VA) commitments and devote more effort to home and community based services, the VHA embarked on a groundbreaking partnership with the US Department of Health and Human Services Administration on Aging (now part of the Administration for Community Living) utilizing the existing nationwide aging and disability network to meet veterans' needs.

On October 1, 2008, officials from the VHA and ACL met with staff from the National Resource Center for Participant-Directed Services (NRCPDS) to lay the groundwork for what would become the Veteran-Directed Home and Community Based Services (VD-HCBS) program. Both federal agencies were impressed with the results from the Cash and Counseling Demonstration and Evaluation (funded by HHS and the Robert Wood Johnson Foundation) and wanted to explore a similar participant-directed approach that would offer veterans with their families the opportunity to control and tailor their care to best meet their needs. This level of flexibility and individual control over a monthly budget seemed most appropriate for addressing the varied situations of each veteran. The *HANDBOOK on Developing and Implementing Self-direction Policies and Programs* had just been completed, and it became the blueprint for the new VD-HCBS program (RWJ and NRCPDS, 2010). The VHA, in close collaboration with ACL, acted quickly. The first VA Medical Centers to roll out the program were situated in locations that enabled them to take advantage of the Cash and Counseling infrastructure within the aging and disability network. By early 2009, Veterans in these early programs had begun managing their budgets to address their long-term care (LTC) needs. Over the next two years, the Robert Wood Johnson Foundation and Atlantic Philanthropies funded the NRCPDS to provide technical assistance to the VHA to conduct readiness reviews and assist in developing policies and procedures for VD-HCBS.

The VA chose to expand the program slowly to gain experience. Rather than serve large numbers of veterans at any one site, the VHA worked to have at least one VA Medical Center in each state as they incrementally aimed at nationwide coverage.

Current Scope of VD-HCBS. As of August 2018, 69 VA Medical Centers in 36 states and the District of Columbia and Puerto Rico had partnered with 219 Aging and Disability Network Agencies (ADNAs), including State Units on Aging (SUA), Aging and Disability Resource Centers (ADRCs), Area Agencies on Aging (AAAs) and Centers for Independent Living (CIL) to offer VD-HCBS. Across these sites, 2,152 Veterans were being served in the program; a total of 7,163 veterans have been served over the last 10 years.

Unique Aspects of VD-HCBS. There are many unique and innovative aspects of this self-direction program within the VHA. For example, VD-HCBS involved an historic partnership between the VHA and HHS that offers the VA the opportunity to leverage the existing aging and disability network infrastructure in the community rather than developing its own. This not only enabled efficiencies on the VA side, but it promoted community collaboration, and provided opportunities for veterans to access other home and community based programs through referral by the ADNA. The VHA pays the ADNA an administrative fee for conducting a veteran centered assessment, as well as a monthly fee for coordinating services, providing a Financial Management Service to handle the employer-related requirements, and administering the program.

The VD-HCBS has largely remained decentralized in the sense that it has been an option, among a suite of other VA services, for each VA Medical Center to adopt. For example, the VHA's other home care program, offering homemaker and home health aide services (H/HHA), continued to be available. It is up to each VA Medical Center to determine whether and how to invest in its Geriatrics and Extended Care LTC services. The VHA Office of Geriatrics and Extended Care initially provided start-up funds to VA Medical Centers, but after two years, each center had to decide whether to continue and expand its program. That start-up funding ended in 2015 when the funding processes for VA Purchased Care changed with the Veterans Choice Act.

Other unique attributes of VD-HCBS developed over time and include the following:

- A standardized VA Readiness Review for ADNA's interested in serving veterans in VD-HCBS to verify that all supportive services (e.g., Financial Management Service Agency) and policies are in place prior to enrolling veterans.

- The policy of offering the self-direction option to all Veterans in need of LTSS who access care at VA Medical Centers; no one is excluded based on the type of disability or availability of supports. Veterans have the right to have an unpaid representative if they cannot manage alone.

- The ability to hire family, friends, and neighbors, including legally liable relatives, as paid caregivers.

- The ability to combine VD-HCBS program resources with other VA benefits including the Comprehensive Assistance for Family Caregivers and the cash allowance from the Veterans Benefit Administration's Aid and Attendance and Housebound programs, which offers enhanced pension/special monthly compensation benefits.

- A standardized assessment instrument adapted from one used in the state of Minnesota, which helps create resource utilization groups tied to budget amounts. This standardized tool—the Purchased Care HCBS Case Mix and Budget Tool—takes into consideration activities of daily living, behavioral characteristics, and special nursing needs.

- A nationwide methodology to price an equitable home and community based service benefit for Veterans. The case-mix methodology enables a veteran living in one part of the country to receive an equitable benefit as a veteran with the same needs living in another part of the country.

Evaluations of VD-HCBS. To understand veterans' experiences in VD-HCBS, Mahoney and colleagues conducted interviews and focus groups with 21 veterans currently enrolled in VD-HCBS (Mahoney, Milliken, et al., 2018). Participants called the program "life changing," and all said they would recommend VD-HCBS to other veterans. For example, one veteran said, "It's changed everything." Interviews also revealed the ways in which VD-HCBS impacted the lives of veterans, illustrated by the following themes: "I'm a Person! It's a Home-Saver, Coming Back to Life, Keeping Me Healthy & Safe, and What a Difference Choice Makes." An exemplary quote about how the program promoted personhood was expressed by one veteran saying, "I know this probably don't sound right for somebody that's homebound in a wheelchair, but it makes me more . . . independent." In referencing the way this program was a "home saver," one veteran shared, "If it wasn't for this program, I would be in an assisted living situation, no doubt about it. You know, with all the disabilities I have, and this is a home saver for me." Another stated, "So, for me, it was the difference between going to the VA home and filing bankruptcy or being allowed some dignity and staying in my own home." As it relates to providing choice, one veteran stated, "It eliminates [worries like] are they going to show up? Who's going to show up? Are they going to know what to do when they get here?" Veterans also spoke about the numerous ways they let other veterans know about the program. During the focus groups, they shared practical ideas including ways to find workers who were themselves veterans utilizing the contacts at unemployment offices.

Milliken and colleagues (2016) also conducted the first study to understand the experiences of *caregivers* of Veterans enrolled in the VD-HCBS program. Interviews and focus groups conducted with 23 caregivers of VD-HCBS participants uncovered five major themes that the program afforded them: coming home and staying home; taking the pressure off; providing security; giving time as a couple; and the importance of choice. For example, one caregiver who was caring for her father described the way that the program was "life-saving" by saying, "I think, personally, I was almost at a breaking point, you know? Because I couldn't do any more . . . and it came just in the nick of time . . . it made the difference between . . . I think my own personal sanity and survival, you know?" The interviews and focus groups revealed sources of stress as well as the mechanisms behind stress relief and support through participation in VD-HCBS. For example, one caregiver said, "Now I don't have to work out of the home just to make a living. I can be at home, take care of him. And it helps make ends meet."

In addition to research documenting the impact of the program from the vantage point of the veterans and their caregivers, there have been several evaluations at the local VA Medical Center level as well as studies across VD-HCBS programs from the perspective of the VA VD-HCBS coordinator and the Aging and Disability Network Agency coordinator.

Recently, VHA conducted analysis to compare veterans' demographic characteristics and health care utilization after receiving VD-HCBS to veterans who receive H/HHA services across seven VA Medical Centers (Administration for Community Living, Centers for Medicare and Medicaid, 2018). In unadjusted difference in difference analyses, they found that veterans enrolled in H/HHA experienced a 55% increase in home utilization in the year after enrolling in the program compared to the year before enrollment; conversely, veterans in VD-HCBS experienced a 37% decrease in nursing home utilization in the year after receiving services compared to the year prior. While additional work is needed to confirm these findings, this does suggest that VD-HCBS is more effective in decreasing nursing home utilization than traditional, agency-based services.

In 2012, Diane Kayala and Ellen Mahoney published the first report on the program. These researchers surveyed VD-HCBS coordinators at 27 VA Medical Centers and asked them to submit case mix levels, current spending, service plans, and invoices for VD-HCBS participants. Coordinators indicated that VD-HCBS is filling a niche for veterans at risk of nursing home placement, and that it served veterans with higher needs than those using traditional, agency-based services despite having comparable costs. Coordinators perceived the program as meeting veterans' needs (92.3%), helping veterans remain at home (96.2%), improving satisfaction (96.2%), and improving access to care (96.2%). Results further suggested that, for many, collaboration between VA Medical Centers and Aging and Disability Network Agencies has been of mutual benefit; but in some cases, these partnerships were complicated. The evaluation report concluded that role clarification and coordination efforts were critical to maximize the roles of the VA and Aging and Disability Network Agencies. In complementary work, Thomas and Allen (2016) interviewed 26 VD-HCBS Aging and Disability Network Agency coordinators. Those interviewed suggested that the experience of collaborating with VA Medical Centers was positive, and interviews identified several key mechanisms for facilitating a successful partnership (e.g., frequent communication, training, designated VA Medical Center personnel, and the VA Medical Center's active involvement). In addition, coordinators unanimously noted many benefits of the VD-HCBS program to veterans, including allowing for autonomy in determining the services that will best meet veterans' identified needs and residence in the least restrictive setting.

In 2016, the VA solicited a call for applications to evaluate a randomized rollout of the VD-HCBS program to the 90 or so remaining VA Medical Centers. Working closely with the office of GEC, the Partnered Evidence-Based Policy Resource Center and investigators at the Providence and Durham VA Medical Centers are currently leading an outcomes and implementation evaluation of this rollout (Garrido et al., 2017). To collect information for the evaluation, researchers with VA Health Services Research and Development Service will be conducting administrative data analysis, as well as surveys and interviews with veterans, caregivers, and VD-HCBS program coordinators in an effort to capture (a) veterans' experiences, including improvements in health, healthcare utilization, and satisfaction;

(b) caregivers' experiences, including improvements in stress, burden, health, and satisfaction; and (c) implementation of the program within the VA.

Prospects for the Future. The speed with which the VD-HCBS option will become available at all VA Medical Centers is unclear as it depends on two major factors: funding availability/incentives and local VA Medical Center interest. The "early adopters" have been very pleased with the program and its ability to meet veterans' needs and reduce service utilization, as attested to by evaluations conducted at a number of VA Medical Centers (Bowen et al., 2017; Veterans-Directed Home and Community-Based Services Program, 2015; Snider-Meyer et al., 2013; VA Boston Healthcare System, 2013; Veterans-Directed Home and Community-Based Services Program, 2015), and Chilicothe, New Haven, and Milwaukee. The program has become ensconced in the VHA panoply of service options. It even has its own payment code. Despite the concerns about sustained funding leading to slower uptake in recent years (Administration for Community Living, 2018; Thomas & Allen, 2016), recent and proposed federal legislation shows some promise by enabling the VA to engage in agreements with Aging and Disability Network Agencies, including State Units on Aging, Area Agencies on Aging, Aging and Disability Resource Centers, and Centers for Independent Living. How VA Medical Centers without programs will react to the possible availability of funding and experiences of their peers remains unknown; however, the building evidence supports this unique program in its ability to reduce health care expenditures while providing veterans requiring LTSS the autonomy, flexibility, and choice needed to remain in their homes and the community.

Conclusion. The reasons that led the VHA to implement VD-HCBS (i.e., a growing population of aging veterans and younger veterans with disabilities, as well as veterans' clear desire to receive care at home) will remain.

Self-direction in Mental Health

In mental health self-direction—as with other self-direction approaches—participants manage an individualized budget with assistance from a support broker. While it is possible for self-directing participants to hire support staff, mental health self-direction is more commonly centered on nontraditional goods and services to meet recovery goals. Mental health self-direction participants work on goals related to employment, education, physical and emotional wellness, housing independence, and community engagement. Common purchases include transportation, computers, gym memberships, dental and eye care, medical copays, and complementary and alternative therapies (Croft, Isvan, et al., 2018; Snethen et al., 2016).

Recovery is central to mental health self-direction. Emerging from the mental health consumer/survivor/ex-patient movements in the late 20th century, recovery is a nonlinear, self-defined process of living a full life in the community characterized by hope, purpose, and connection (Anthony, 1993; Davidson & Roe, 2007). Self-direction is also strongly aligned with the concept of personal medicine, which acknowledges that individuals employ a range of strategies to embody recovery in their daily lives, beyond traditional clinical mental health treatment (Deegan, 2005).

Compared to self-direction approaches for individuals with physical, intellectual, and developmental disabilities and older adults with long-term care needs, self-direction for people with serious mental health conditions is relatively newer and less well developed. However, self-direction, despite the added problem of stigma, has gained increasing traction in mental health systems, and recent developments discussed in this chapter represent key steps toward increased adoption of the approach in mental health systems.

Many factors make the calculation of cost-effectiveness of self-direction in behavioral health an extremely complicated endeavor. When calculating program costs, it is critical to factor in costs associated with planning and securing service provision. Additionally, there may be "one-off" costs associated with initiating supports for self-direction that will have an impact on cost-effectiveness calculations during the start-up phases of demonstrations (Alakeson & Duffy, 2011; White, 2011). Determining participant budget amounts can have an impact on costs: if amounts are set too low, participants may appear to overspend their budgets and cost savings will be underestimated; if amounts are set too high, cost savings may be overestimated. These calculations are more difficult in behavioral health as expenditures are known to vary considerably from year to year. While calculating costs is difficult, so is calculating savings. Alakeson (2007) writes that calculating the full range of possible savings across multiple funding streams that support people with mental health needs is an extremely complex endeavor. Many savings could accrue to the behavioral health system; on the other hand, cost savings (or increases) could result from a shift in funding streams from other service areas, including employment, general healthcare, criminal justice, and housing subsidies.

Current Mental Health Self-direction Efforts. The person-centered orientation of self-direction and its ethos of self-determination and empowerment align with the vision of many federal and state behavioral health agencies of a good and modern behavioral health system (Croft, Simon-Rusinowitz, et al., 2018; Institute of Medicine, 2006; New Freedom Commission on Mental Health, 2003; SAMHSA, 2011b). Despite this alignment, however, current self-direction efforts are modest in size and scope and differ from one another in many respects. Mental health self-direction is best characterized as being in the early stages of development. One reason for the more limited adoption in a mental health context is that until recently, Medicaid HCBS waiver authorities did not cover services that are considered alternatives to institutional treatment for adults age 22 to 64 with serious mental health conditions. The reason for the lack of reimbursement was the "Institution for Mental Disease" (IMD) exclusion (Smith et al., 2005), which barred Medicaid reimbursement for in-patient hospitals. Since waivers were originally considered as community offsets to Medicaid spending in institutions, no such offset was available in mental health.

In 2010, the Affordable Care Act contained changes to the 1915(i)-state plan option that allowed states to use needs-based rather than institutional eligibility criteria for services, which created a pathway for states to fund self-direction for individuals with serious mental health conditions outside of the IMD exclusion. Despite its promise as a financing strategy for mental health self-direction, no state has yet elected to use the 1915(i) to offer mental health self-direction through the state plan. Notably, New York's self-direction pilot is part of the state's 1115 Research and Demonstration waiver and has been developed as a "1915(i)-like" service to allow for future inclusion in a 1915(i)-state plan amendment.

Absent a clear funding stream, most self-direction efforts are funded through a range of mechanisms that are often "braided" or combined with other funding sources. Funding sources include state and local general revenues, managed care funds, and other private and public funds. Mental health self-direction is administered through a variety of entities, including local and state mental health authorities, advocacy organizations, peer-run agencies, and other nonprofit social service providers.

Most self-direction efforts in the United States are pilots, including some newly launched efforts in Medicaid managed care contexts. Two exceptions are Florida and Michigan. The Florida Self-directed Care (FloridaSDC) is one of the first mental health self-direction efforts in the country. The product of concerted efforts from a group of advocates and mental health administrators in the state, FloridaSDC was established by state legislation and enrolled the first participants in 2002. Currently, 330 individuals in two parts of the state participate in the program. To be eligible, individuals must have a "serious and persistent mental illness" designation by the state and rely on public funds for mental health services. The FloridaSDC budget is a fixed yearly amount based on insurance status and income. For individuals with insurance, the budget is administered separately from traditional mental health treatment services (individuals do not control the funds for traditional services). Those without insurance work with a larger self-directed budget, with half reserved for direct purchase of traditional mental health treatment services.

In Michigan, self-direction is available to adults enrolled in Medicaid with mental health conditions through the state's Medicaid Managed Care and Specialty Services 1915 (b)(c) Waiver Authority. Unlike other mental health self-direction efforts, participants in Michigan primarily use an employer authority, hiring support staff—often peer specialists—to work on recovery goals. A 2003 *Self-Determination Policy and Practice Guideline* stipulated that self-direction arrangements must be made available to individuals with mental health conditions who receive services through the state's Community Mental Health Services Programs (Michigan Department of Health and Human Services, 2003). However, take-up of the self-direction option has been limited to date. With support from SAMHSA, a team has worked to increase engagement in self-direction in targeted areas of the state in recent years.

Pennsylvania's Consumer Recovery Investment Fund-Self-directed Care (CRIF-SDC) was established as a pilot program in 2009 and currently enrolls approximately 50 individuals in the Delaware County area who are enrolled in Medicaid managed care. CRIF-SDC participants manage a budget that includes outpatient mental health services, psychiatric rehabilitation, and approved alternative goods and services. Budgets are based on an individual's previous 24 months of spending, and funds for alternative goods and services are "banked" by reducing utilization of other services within the budget (Snethen et al., 2016; Croft et al., 2019).

Utah's self-direction effort, which took place between 2014 and 2016 in Salt Lake County, was based on the state's Access to Recovery (ATR) program. ATR is a SAMHSA discretionary grant program that provides funds to states to redesign their substance use treatment systems to promote more choice of treatment and recovery supports and expand existing provider networks to include nontraditional and faith-based organizations (SAMHSA, 2011a). Although the federal grant program ended in 2014, many states have continued to implement ATR programs using other federal and local financing mechanisms. ATR participants are given vouchers to purchase substance use treatment services as well as supports including childcare, transportation, housing, and goods to help secure employment, such as tools and clothing. In Utah's Mental Health ATR, participants used a fixed budget of $2,000 to purchase nontraditional goods and services.

In 2018, New York and Texas each launched pilots of mental health self-direction. New York's effort is part of the state's 1115 Research and Demonstration Waiver and is being piloted in two parts of the state. Eligible individuals are age 18 or older who are enrolled in a Medicaid Health and Recovery Plan (HARP) and eligible for Behavioral Health Home and Community-Based Services. Participants have either employer or budget authority to self-direct their HCBS service budget, which is either $8,000 or $16,000 per year based on an HCBS assessment. In Texas, self-direction is piloted in the Travis County Service Delivery Area (SDA) with two Medicaid MCOs as a Performance Improvement Project (PIP). Participants in the Texas pilot must be between 21 and 55 years old, have a serious mental health condition diagnosis, and have been engaged in outpatient mental health services in the past year. Texas participants self-direct a budget of approximately $1,400 per year that can be used to purchase nontraditional goods and services.

The Role of the Robert Wood Johnson Foundation. Since 2009, the Robert Wood Johnson Foundation (RWJF) has played an important role in furthering experimentation and evaluation of this approach. The RWJF efforts began with an environmental scan conducted by the National Resource Center for Participant-Directed Services at Boston College which included a mixed methods study of state and county behavioral health department leadership as well as interviews with participants, traditional providers, and innovative providers. This study documented strong interest in the model (Croft, Simon-Rusinowitz, et al., 2018) and presented implementation facilitators and barriers identified by study participants. In general, mental health leaders had a high level of interest in self-direction, and they expected self-direction to have a significant impact on mental health systems in the coming years. They expressed the need for clear implementation guidance for self-direction, stressing that this information would be an important tool for champions within mental health systems to promote greater adoption in coming years (Croft, Simon-Rusinowiitz et al., 2018), and they expressed a need for a large-scale demonstration that would allow one to examine system-level effects. All respondents discussed the importance of cost to any discussion on self-direction, particularly the importance of demonstrating cost-effectiveness. Respondents spoke of the salience of a "win-win" proposition—that self-direction leads to greater recovery and lowers costs.

Though cost effectiveness is important, a few respondents also added that an overemphasis on cost could be problematic: "It is always a problem when a program gets sold on cost benefits as primary" Many respondents noted that self-direction had the potential for lower costs by enhancing recovery and increasing the efficiency of service dollars by enabling participants to determine which mix of services and supports will work best to help them achieve recovery. Some respondents expected that by enhancing recovery, self-directing participants might rely less on high-cost services like inpatient and emergency care, which could lead to cost savings in the long term. Similarly, self-direction might lead to a reduction of inappropriate service use and an increase in appropriate service use, resulting in lower costs in both the short and long term.

In 2012, a study supported by the Assistant Secretary for Planning and Evaluation, the "Feasibility of Expanding Self-directed Services to People with Serious Mental Illness," conducted by Eric Slade from the University of Maryland, also called for additional research on this promising topic. In 2014, RWJF, in partnership with the federal Substance Abuse and Mental Health Services Administration (SAMHSA) and the New York State Health Foundation (NYSHF) began funding a Multi-State Demonstration and Evaluation of Self Direction for People with Serious Mental Illness. SAMHSA awarded transformation grants to the six states listed above (FL, MI, PA, NY, TX, and UT) and continued to use its traditional funding mechanism with the National Association of State Mental Health Program Directors to pay for the technical assistance these states needed. RWJF paid for some additional technical assistance, the establishment of a Learning Collaborative, so these states could share ideas and discuss common problems. RWJF also paid for an overall systems-level evaluation, and the NYSHF contributed significantly toward the cost of New York State's individual level evaluation. Results from this multistate effort are expected in 2020.

Research Findings to Date. Mental health self-direction first appeared in the peer-reviewed research literature in the late 2000s, beginning with two studies involving data from the Cash and Counseling Demonstration and Evaluation (Shen et al., 2008a; Shen et al., 2008b). These studies compared outcomes for Cash and Counseling participants with and without mental health diagnoses. In both studies, the authors found associations between self-direction and improvements in participant-reported satisfaction and reductions in unmet need. Then, in a study in England in the National Health Service, Forder, Jones, Glendinning, Caiels, Welch, Baxter, and Dolan, P. (2012) found that self-direction was especially successful in mental health services, and people who had more choice and control over a personal budget had better outcomes and lower inpatient and outpatient service costs.

Additional early studies of self-direction in the United States and abroad provided data points suggesting self-direction's cost-effectiveness, although these pre-post and observational studies carried methodological limitations (Spaulding-Givens & Lacasse, 2015). In 2014, Webber and colleagues conducted a systematic review that examined 15 studies of mental health self-direction across the world, including four studies conducted in the United States. The authors concluded that mental health self-direction was associated with increased quality of life and cost-effectiveness, although more rigorous research is needed to confirm preliminary findings and develop a stronger evidence base.

Some tools and resources have been developed (Cook et al., 2017; Bazelon Center for Mental Health Law & UPENN Collaborative on Community Integration, 2008), but fidelity or best practice standards have yet to be established. The implementation research currently taking place will help to further establish these standards for mental health self-direction. In addition, recently published studies point to key implementation factors, including the central role of the support broker in educating participants about program mechanics and supporting them in the person-centered planning process (Croft & Parish, 2016).

Many articles have been published since the 2014 review that add to the evidence base for self-direction. In a descriptive study of the Florida Self-directed Care program, Spaulding-Givens and Lacasse (2015) documented that participants had improved mental-health-related functioning and spent many days in the community as opposed to inpatient settings. Croft and Parish (2016) conducted a qualitative study of the experiences of 30 Florida Self-directed Care participants. In that study, self-directing participants described meaningful recovery gains in employment, housing stability, community integration, social connections, and access to appropriate mental health supports. Participants also described how they used self-direction to meet basic material needs that were impeding their recovery. Finally, participants in that study described how self-directing enhanced their independence, self-esteem, and self-confidence, which facilitated further progress on recovery goals. Also, in 2016, Snethen and colleagues explored purchasing behaviors of participants in Pennsylvania's Consumer Recovery Investment Fund Self-directed Care program. The authors concluded that self-directing participants were better able to address their recovery-related needs through "personal medicine" or individualized strategies that support wellness and increase engagement in meaningful activities. A recent quasi-experimental study compared housing and employment outcomes for 364 self-directing participants and a matched comparison group of 2,659 non-self-directing individuals over a four-year period (Croft, Isvan, et al., 2018). In that study, self-directing participants were significantly more likely than nonparticipants to have positive housing and employment outcomes, controlling for individual effects and program dosage.

These positive finding were reinforced in 2019 in a study by Croft, Battis, Ostrow, and Salzer that looked at costs for 45 Pennsylvania Medicaid participants before they started in the self-direction program and then again three years later; the study concluded that median monthly mental health clinical outpatient costs were significantly lower after self-direction, and overall self-direction was cost neutral; it did not significantly alter costs. Results from a randomized, controlled experiment conducted in the Dallas, Texas area from 2010–2013 in a system where behavioral health was carved out from other medical care were also very promising. In this experiment, with 114 people with serious mental illness in the treatment group and 102 in the control group receiving traditional care, Cook and colleagues (2019) found that self-directing participants had significantly greater improvements over time in recovery, self-esteem, coping mastery, autonomy support, somatic symptoms, employment, and education. "The budget neutral self-directed care model achieved superior client outcomes and greater satisfaction with mental health care."

Future Directions. A 2015 gathering of self-direction experts from around the world resulted in the identification of key priorities for self-direction (Croft et al., 2017). Among those priorities was ensuring that people with lived experience—often called peers—are engaged and supported in multiple ways in self-direction efforts. The participants were staff, advisory-group members, managers, administrators, and researchers. Similarly, program directors identified grassroots advocacy and peer-run organizations as facilitators of self-direction adoption. They also noted that enhancing the visibility and role of people with lived experience in mental health systems enhances the system's recovery orientation, which increases the likelihood that self-direction will be implemented successfully (Croft et al., 2017).

Peer specialists—individuals with lived experience who receive training in the practice of peer support—have key roles in most self-direction efforts in the United States. Peer support has been increasingly adopted in mental health systems and is a natural fit with self-direction because of its emphasis on recovery, individualization, and self-determination (Davidson et al., 2006). In Pennsylvania and Michigan, Certified Peer Specialists perform the role of support broker. Lived experience is preferred for support brokers and program managers in New York as well, and both agencies administering self-direction in New York have extensive experience with peer-delivered services. In Florida, individuals with lived experience—including program participants—comprise at least 51% of the advisory councils, and people with lived experience are also represented on Texas's advisory council.

Consistent with populations receiving publicly funded mental health services nationwide, between one-third and one-half of self-directing participants have a co-occurring substance use issue (Croft & Parish, 2016; Norris et al., 2010). In recent years, England has piloted self-direction efforts for individuals with a primary substance use disorder, with promising preliminary results suggesting that self-direction can support linkages between inpatient detoxification and follow-up services and improve relationships between participants and providers (Welch et al., 2013; Welch et al., 2016). There is also some interest in applying self-direction for individuals with a primary substance use disorder in the United States (Humphreys & McLellan, 2011). As Utah's self-direction effort suggests, there are key similarities between self-direction and Access to Recovery, which has been associated with increased treatment engagement and reductions in Medicaid costs, including hospital emergency room spending (Krupski et al., 2009; Wickizer et al., 2009).

As mental health self-direction's evidence base continues to grow, we will learn more about whether and how the approach supports recovery and enhances quality of life and what aspects of implementation constitute best practice. Current mental health self-direction research will also help to generate a needed understanding of the cost implications of self-direction. This information will inform efforts to scale up existing efforts and to scale out the approach to other states and other populations such as individuals with substance use disorders.

MM: Self-direction and Recovery

From the start, participating in Self-directed Care put me on a path of self-awareness and self-reflection. I was given choices from the beginning, starting with my support broker (a coach). After reviewing information about each coach, I picked mine for her passion for creative arts and her kindhearted spirit.

My coach encouraged me to create a vision. Since I was brought up in a home where my father had a mental illness, and since I had been diagnosed over twenty years ago, I knew that I wanted to use the creative arts to help tell the story, our story, of what mental illness looks like, how people experience it, how they suffer, and how they overcome. The vision that I penned is, "Being a powerful and passionate creative arts professional who moves people by speaking to their hearts and souls." It has been so important for me to have that statement at hand, written down and close by because when I wrote it, I had been in remission from my illness and things were looking very hopeful. Until they weren't.

I had taken an intensive acting course with a well-regarded studio in a city out of state, which turned out to be too stressful for me and caused me to have a serious mental health crisis. I was in a near fatal automobile accident and arrested for reckless driving and destruction of property. It was the most horrifying time of my life. After I was released, I had to go through mental health court, a program that involves engaging in court-supervised treatment rather than serving time in prison.

I was stable over 14 years on medication before the crisis, car accident, and arrest. I was shocked at what happened to me, at the criminalization of my mental illness. I was broken in a way that I had never experienced. I was afraid of my illness and afraid to live outside the walls of my apartment. My coach's love and support helped me walk through the darkest time of my life. She wrote to me while I was in jail and tried to connect me with supports. She continued to meet with me as I tried to make my way through the mental health court process. The support and encouragement I received from her brought a flicker of hope to me like a candle in the darkness. She helped keep me hopeful during the darkest time of my life. This part of Self-directed Care has been life-saving.

My coach and I came up with a plan of supports that needed to be in place if I were to experience another crisis. When I'm in crisis, I struggle with self-awareness, so it was important to create a plan when I was feeling well. My coach helped me write a plan, put down people who would have authority to make decisions for me if they felt I couldn't make decisions for myself, and write down red flags of things that might come about before a crisis. We gave copies to those who were part of the plan. This is an important safeguard for me.

Self-directed Care has helped me explore alternatives to mainstream psychiatric care. I have been able to try different kinds of therapies that have been very helpful in my staying well. One has been massage therapy. This has helped me take a break from my fast-paced life and result-orientated mindset and stop to take time to take care of myself. Self-directed Care has helped me learn and implement self-care that has been just as important to my body as my mind.

Self-directed Care has given me a vision. It has also given me help in funding things to complete my goal. It has given me ample time to invest in myself in building a strong foundation to success. Working with my coach has reminded me that the world's success does not have to drive my vision of success. Today, my success means staying healthy, well, and stable. For someone who is results-orientated, it has taken a major crisis to understand my own limitations. I have had to say no to many offers in the past two years because I truly wasn't certain if I could complete them and stay heathy.

Slowly but surely, I am taking the steps necessary that will help lead me to fulfill my vision. I started speaking at Crisis Intervention Team (CIT) trainings, which are designed to teach law enforcement professionals how to respond to people experiencing a mental health crisis. Self-directed Care funds have helped me purchase office equipment and business clothes for when I present at CIT trainings. The funds have helped me find a therapist out of my plan, who is not part of my support team. Self-directed Care helped me to transition to a better living situation by covering moving expenses, which alleviated some of the burdens of living on a limited income. It has been an amazing part of my recovery. I am living proof that it helps save lives, it lowers costs by helping people stay healthy, and it gives people like me someone to walk with as they continue to walk towards the person they were created to be.

Chapter 10

International Examples of Self-direction in Human Services

Even though well over a million people in the United States are self-directing, and the number continues to grow every year, self-direction has been slow to develop and has yet to be broadly understood as a program approach that creates positive outcomes and is cost beneficial. Additionally, there is no uniform national policy on self-direction; instead, states bear the responsibility of designing and implementing their own programs. Most states use Medicaid Home and Community-Based Services waivers as the mechanism to offer self-direction, and some do so through two, three, or four waivers written for different populations. There is language in the Patient Protection and Affordable Care Act, Section 2402(a) that "requires the Secretary [of HHS] to ensure [that] all states receiving federal funds develop service systems that are responsive to the needs and choices of beneficiaries receiving home and community based long-term services (HCBS), maximize independence and self-direction," but this is more of an exhortation than a mandate. In other countries, however, self-direction has been embedded in national health and long-term-care (LTC) policy for many years.

Representatives from 17 countries with self-direction programs attended an international conference held at the University of British Columbia in Vancouver in 2015. The conference, titled Claiming Full Citizenship: Self Determination, Personalization, Individualized Funding, highlighted the international self-direction movement and examined the progress made in self-direction since the first international self-direction conference was held in Seattle in 2000. The conference brochure (Claiming Full Citizenship, 2015) laid out the importance of the self-direction movement:

With the passage of the UN Convention on the Rights of Persons with Disabilities, self-determination, personalization and individualized funding initiatives have new foundations upon which to build. In countries all over the world, these initiatives are transforming the lives of people with disabilities. Like the shift from institutions to community services, these initiatives are a momentous step forward in assisting people with disabilities and seniors to achieve meaningful and rewarding lives as full citizens.

The conference included several presentations from self-direction programs in Europe, Asia, Canada, and several states in the United States.

In this chapter, we will look at how self-direction developed and how it is used as part of a national LTC and human services policy in Germany, the Netherlands, England, and Australia—with a focus on how it has changed and the lessons to be learned. Each of these countries uses individual budgets as a form of self-direction policy. In Germany and the Netherlands, personal budgets are an option in a complex national policy developed more than twenty years ago. The German program has gone through several phases as it has evolved, but self-direction remains one of the most popular cornerstones of Germany's LTC system. The Dutch program has been revised several times as LTC has gone through substantial changes in philosophy and financing; individual budgets remain, but greater priority has been given to policies to contain total costs. In England, personal budgets were developed as part of a national reform movement for people with disabilities carried out at the local district level over the past decade. Although there have been mixed results across the local districts, self-direction continues as national policy. In contrast, Australia's program is in its infancy, but it was written as national reform legislation affecting almost half a million participants across the country. Australia has created a complex and unique insurance system that creates individual budgets for all persons in the country with disabilities up to the age of 65.

Germany

Germany has provided LTC through a compulsory social insurance program for people of all ages, regardless of the individual's financial status, since

1994. It is helpful to look at the program in three phases: its inception, its implementation and growth through 2008, and changes that led to major long-term reforms beginning in 2015.

The Long-Term Care Insurance (LTCI) program (*Pflege-Versicherungs-gesetz*) was enacted under Chancellor Helmut Kohl in 1996. It was designed to be entirely self-financing through insurance premiums. Premiums were pooled and redistributed depending on user needs. The contribution rate was initially set at 1.7% of gross income, and this rate remained unchanged until 2008. Half of the premium was paid by the participant's employer. Since the program was designed to be financed as a pay-as-you-go system, focused initially on older individuals, workers were paying for the costs of current users as well as for themselves in the future. People without children paid a slightly higher premium because their benefits would be paid by other people's children. One other unique financing attribute is that about 10% of all workers purchase basic LTCI coverage through private insurance companies. These are civil servants, working for governmental agencies, who must purchase their health insurance from private companies. It does not affect their coverage for public LTCI benefits.

LTCI was designed as a universal program for all ages to provide basic LTC services for those having a physical, psychological, or mental disability who were expected to need a substantial amount of help to carry out the routine activities of daily life for six months or longer. One of the initial goals of the program was to address the growing burden of care on the means-tested social assistance programs in the German states that coincided with the reunification of the country. The program was also a response to the growth of the aging population and the reduced availability of family caregivers due to a demographic trend toward smaller family sizes and the changing role of women in the workforce. When the program was launched in 1996, 16% of the population was 65 or older; this figure rose to 21% in 2014 and is projected to increase to 32% by 2050.

The LTCI was national in scope and relatively straightforward. Public supports were designed to be basic, not comprehensive, leaving room for private contributions as well as private insurance. They were not intended to meet all needs. Eligibility for the national program was determined based on assessments conducted in the individual's home by nurses and doctors working for independent medical review boards who were trained to care for geriatric patients. Initially, three levels of benefits were established based on the extent of support needed for activities of daily living (ADLs). Hospice care was partly covered if the medical review board determined there was a need. There was a focus on rehabilitative services, including the need for medical equipment and technical aides to support independence. Support for families to avoid "care burnout" was also taken into consideration. The service system was designed to encourage home care and family care and to avoid nursing home and institutional care.

Germany's LTCI initially provided people with either residential care (primarily nursing home care) or home-based care depending on an individual's functional status. The size of the benefit was determined by the level of need established by the Medical Review Board assessment. When eligible individuals chose home-based care, they had the option of receiving either a cash benefit or a service benefit provided by agencies, or a combination of both. The cash benefit was structured as a self-direction program.

At the start of the program, about two-thirds of the individuals in need of home-based care chose cash budgets despite a 50% discount compared to the service benefit. The amount of care provided varied widely. Among those choosing cash budgets, 36% received care from one primary caregiver, 29% from two caregivers, and 27% from three or more caregivers. The overwhelming number of eligible individuals chose to pay their own workers, usually family members and friends. In fact, a national survey in 2010 that investigated the uses of the cash benefit documented a strong preference for care from family members and an aversion to care from "strangers." No doubt the decision to pay family members directly was improved by exempting caregiver wages from income taxes and providing payments into their pension, health insurance, and unemployment funds when family caregivers provided more than 14 hours of paid assistance in a week—partially offsetting the 50% budget reduction. Since there was no required documentation for the cash benefit, actual use was determined by what participants claimed and what the government learned from survey research.

The program included centers that provided information and coordination services for consumers who wanted to stay at home. The centers served as the intersection between family caregiving and professional service providers. They provided counseling and support to the individuals as well as their families and reduced the isolation that many families felt when providing care for a loved one at home.

Of the three levels of care available, more than half of German consumers choose to manage their own budgets and pay for their own staff despite losing half the value of their formal service budget (See table 10.1).

Table 10.1. Comparable Utilization From 1994 to 2013

Year	Homecare Cash Utilization	Homecare Service Utilization	Homecare Total Utilization	Institutional Care Utilization
1994	66%	7%	73%	27%
1998	55%	19%	74%	26%
2005	48%	19%	67%	33%
2013	56%	14%	70%	30%

Adapted from "The German health care system" by M. Blümel and R. Busse, 2015, Department of Health Care Management, Berlin Centre for Health Economics Research, Technische Universität Berlin.

Most recent data suggest an increase in self-direction to the point where four times as many participants (56% to 14%) use cash budgets rather than professional services to remain at home. On the other hand, there was a modest rise in utilization of nursing homes, from 27% in 1994 to 33% in 2005 to 30% in 2013. This led to the development of new housing models as alternatives to nursing home care; these alternatives included sheltered housing, self-organized collective living, villages for older people, and house communities. These intermediate housing options remained small in scale and grew slowly (Blümel & Busse, 2015).

It should be noted that when consumers chose professional services, they could also receive some cash for their purchases. It appears that since the program started, more than half of all participants chose to receive cash, and almost three-quarters chose to receive both cash and professional services.

A national survey in 2010 revealed a strong preference by participants for care from family members, friends, and neighbors. Participants also appreciated the ability to use the benefit to supplement basic living expenses. The survey reported that 64% said they were "very contented or contented"; 26% said they were "less contented"; and only 8% said they were "not contented" with the cash approach (Nadash et al., 2017).

As the program grew, the German LTC system compared very favorably in cost to other European Union countries (European Commission Directorate-General for Economic and Financial Affairs, Economic Policy Committee [Aging Working Group], 2016). In fact, public spending on LTC was only 1.4% of the German gross domestic product in 2013, below the average EU level of 1.6% of GDP and substantially below the most expensive, 4.3% in the Netherlands. Of the total cost of care, 69% was spent on all formal services, while 31% was dispersed in cash benefits. In comparison, the EU average was 80% for formal services and 20% in cash benefits.

In 2013, the program expanded to include people needing "general supervision and care" in the home: typically, people with dementia, developmental disabilities, and mental illness. This increased the demand for LTCI services and, coupled with the growing population of aging adults, put more pressure on program costs and premiums.

At the end of 2015, the German parliament passed additional changes to the LTCI that expanded support for individuals in need of LTC and for their families. The changes included redefined levels of care that broadened eligibility for services that were previously only available to people with considerably restricted daily functions. This expanded eligibility to people with a wider range of physical, mental, and psychological impairments. There are now five levels of care. Eligibility and level of care continue to be assessed in the individual's home by medical staff using national standards from an independent medical review board.

Additionally, the new legislation established a career education process to make the job of caregivers more attractive, provide a career ladder, and improve the quality of care. Last, it created opportunities for improved local coordination of services to better align incentives for care. An analysis from the European Commission reviewing all national health plans noted: "Germany has taken significant steps to establish a coherent financing mix, ensure the fiscal sustainability of LTC expenditures and provide adequate coverage to the population" (Nadash et al., 2017).

Recipients of LTC services can continue to choose among cash benefits for in-home care, home care professional services, and formal residential care, including institutional care, depending on their needs. Cash benefits continue to allow recipients to live at home and be taken care of typically by relatives and friends; the benefits also cover formal home care provided by professional caregivers, paid directly by the recipient from his or her budget to the provider. Institutional care refers primarily to a short-term or long-term stay in a nursing home. The value of monthly budgets ranges from $1,800 to $6,700, depending on the level of disability, with higher amounts for individuals with a higher level of need.

The social insurance program does not have an official "care manager," so participants are on their own when choosing and arranging the care. Coordination centers have developed in the private marketplace, but they are not used by many participants. All participants receive an in-home visit every 6 months to assess the quality of care, but there is little published data on the impact of these visits and the corrective actions, if any, that have been taken. For the elderly with dementia, however, there is a legal program, Adult Guardianship for the Cognitively Impaired, that plays a role in coordinating care. The guardianship program includes coordination of the necessary support, such as administration of property, housing, and general supervision in daily life for cognitively impaired adults. The most vulnerable population receives coordinated care from the system, while all others are responsible for assessing the options, making their own decisions and managing their care.

LTCI was designed to be sustainable through premiums, but changes in eligibility and demographic shifts made this challenging. Therefore, in 2017, the five eligibility categories were simplified to combine the needs of people with cognitive disabilities and physical disabilities. The lowest level of benefits includes monthly stipends but allows the participant to receive a range of ancillary benefits to increase independence—including home modifications, respite care, and counseling. The new focus places a priority on functional abilities rather than diagnosis.

Benefits continue to support basic services rather than comprehensive care. Participants continue to have broad discretion insofar as how budgets are spent. Caregivers who work at least 14 hours per week continue to receive a range of benefits, including tax-free income, coverage of unemployment insurance and health insurance, up to 6 months full-time leave and 24 months part-time leave, and interest-free loans.

Notably, room and board costs are not covered for participants. This affects the cost of nursing home care for people substantially, increasing the amount of out-of-pocket costs or reliance on means-tested social assistance programs for those eligible. The small but continued rise in nursing home utilization was expected to halt after these changes.

The LTCI system sets ceilings on provider rates, but providers can set their own rates within the ceilings, creating a range of rates across the country. The number of service providers—primarily non-profits—in both home care and residential care has tripled since the start of LTCI, creating more competition and better quality. A medical advisory service monitors all long-term services and supports providers and reviews them annually without advanced notice. Nursing homes are also subject to comparable national standards and unannounced reviews.

The reforms instituted in 2015 also focused on economic viability and long-term financing of the program for all participants. LTCI was designed to be universal, covering all citizens, primarily through public insurance premiums with small numbers covered through private insurance premiums. In the early years, when the number of participants was low, the premiums exceeded the program's costs. As the program became better understood, and as eligibility criteria expanded to include more people with mental and physical disabilities, costs rose, requiring a decline in the level of benefits and a need to increase premiums.

In 2015, the premium increased from 1.7% of gross income to 2.35%. In 2017, it increased again, to 2.55%. Employers continue to pay half the premium for their employees; meanwhile, retirees pay the full premium. Childless persons 23 and older pay a supplementary premium of 0.25% of income to help offset the policy that Germans with children would not have to pay LTSS during their old age. A small, automated adjustment for inflation was added in 2015. These changes are expected to keep the LTCI program solvent through at least 2022 without further financing. Last, the policy of prefunding the program in the future was established by creating a national demographic reserve fund that enabled 0.1% of the income premium to go into a national reserve that will become available in 2035.

After more than twenty years, the LTCI has become an integral component of the country's social security program. It has both a high level of acceptance and a financial framework for continued funding for all users. About 3% of the total population is receiving benefits, and about 250,000 jobs in LTC have been added to the economy. More than two-thirds of those receiving care receive it at home, and more than half of those receiving care at home use cash budgets (Nadash et al., 2017). LTCI has been able to meet the country's cultural values for care, emphasizing the importance of personal responsibility for care and payment while providing universal benefits to meet basic needs but not provide for the total cost of care.

The Netherlands

In the Netherlands, a national LTC policy was established in 1968 under the Exceptional Medical Expenses Act (AWBZ). The act covered people over age 65 as well as those with physical and mental disabilities and those requiring chronic care at all ages. Coverage was broad and included home care, home help, nursing, treatment, and residential care in institutions. The policy included cost sharing based on a sliding scale for practically all LTC services and required people to contribute to the costs of their room and board in institutions. All participants were assessed by an independent care assessment center. The center decided if participants were eligible for care in an institution or at home and, using ten different levels of care for the development of individual budgets, determined the amount of care they were entitled to. Other persons in the same household were expected to supply the "usual care" that family members give one another. The assessments were need based but did not create funding for comprehensive services.

For institutional and home care, 32 regional care agencies were mandated to purchase care with public funds. The agencies were generally subsidiaries of the dominant health insurer in each region. These agencies had no budget of their own (except for administrative costs) since care providers were paid directly from a public fund. Hence, purchasing agencies had no financial risk in purchasing care. (Later, municipalities became responsible for purchasing homecare services and took on the risk for the cost of care.)

Once assessed, participants chose to either receive care from a service provider (including institutional care) or to receive a cash benefit (personal budget) that allowed them to hire people and contract with agencies on their own. If they chose a cash benefit, they received 75% of the equivalent cost of agency care. Up to 10% of the benefit could be spent on "individual wishes"; the remainder was spent on service workers, including family members, and provider organizations. All workers were paid in accordance with applicable labor law and tax requirements.

Initially, personal budgets were a solution to overspending, given the 25% discounted rate relative to agency-based service benefits. Over time, however, concern grew that the cash benefit was attracting an unanticipated group of individuals in need of services—persons with IDD and mental illness—as the result of local government's success in shifting the costs of local disabilities services to the new national LTC program. Personal budgets became a way to avoid waiting lists for formal services, enabling participants to purchase supports and services with cash. Also, there was growing evidence that personal budgets were used to purchase services that had little to do with documented service needs and sometimes to hire home care providers who had lost their jobs with service organizations.

At the beginning of the program, there was a strong preference for using formal service providers. But as LTC expenses more than doubled from 2002 to 2012, the personal budget became a "growth industry." From 2005 to 2008, the number of budget holders grew by an average of 28% a year; overall, the number quintupled between 2002 and 2012. The number of program participants with physical disabilities or mental health problems substantially increased, constituting about two thirds of the budget holders.

This was a significant change from the start of LTC when it focused on aging participants. In 2010, the Netherlands spent 4.3% of its gross domestic product on LTC, the highest in the European Union, with projections of 7% to 9% of GDP spending by 2040 (Wammes et al., 2017).

The root of the problem, according to Dutch economists, was not the cash benefits themselves but rather insufficient screening and monitoring of the process that enabled movement from one service system to another to avoid waiting lists and service criteria (Nelsen, 2016). This was worsened by the fact that there was no financial payment agency or benefit administrator in the Dutch system to manage the payment system or monitor expenditures in real time. Instead, expenditure monitoring, when it was done, occurred after the fact, resulting in continuous surprises.

The first step in the reform of LTC took place in 2007 with the introduction of the Social Support Act (WMO), which placed more financial responsibility on municipalities for nonresidential care and more family responsibility for providing LTC. The most conspicuous change was that the coverage of all domestic home care services was shifted from the AWBZ to the new WMO with a substantial budget cut for these services. The municipalities took on the risk of managing service budget reductions. In the government's view, the broad coverage of LTC and its high level of public funding had created a supply-driven and "over-medicalized" policy that fostered dependence. Instead, the government wanted to foster more individual and social responsibility for managing care. The underlying policy assumption was that care should be the joint responsibility of families and local community networks as well as the government.

Second, the reform included a substantial shift of clients from residential to non-residential settings. While residential care remained available to clients for whom non-residential care was not a realistic option, clients with only "mild" problems were no longer eligible for residential care. The assumption was that persons with mild problems could be better cared for in their home setting, at a lower cost, which would also coincide with people's personal preferences.

Third, informal care continued to play a considerable role in LTC. Part of the informal care is the usual care that members of a household should give each other without payment. Consumer assessments took into account "usual care," potentially reducing the magnitude of publicly financed care. Cash benefits from individual budgets could still be used to pay informal caregivers, and consumers were free to choose who should deliver their care; however, the payments had to come out of their individual budget, creating more accountability and incentive on unpaid, informal caregiving. This created more responsibility for participants to show how they spent their funds.

Last, participants who preferred formal services could specify their choice but not determine which care organization delivered their care; instead, the responsibility for organizing and buying this type of care rested with the regional care offices. This led to institutional care playing a relatively substantial role in LTC in the Netherlands compared to many other countries, despite the policy to use formal care at home instead of institutional care.

After major reform, LTC in the Netherlands continued to include a broad range of health and social-care services for various categories of clients including persons with cognitive, physical or sensory handicaps, persons with long-term mental health problems, and older persons with chronic care problems. The number of people being served continued to increase (Wammes et al., 2017). By January 2014, nearly 5% of the population received LTC, with 45% receiving some form of residential care. About one-sixth of all persons 65 years and older received either residential or non-residential publicly funded LTC.

In 2011, new waiting lists were imposed on LTC to slow the growth. In 2012, cash benefits (individual budgets) accounted for 11% of the total program expenditure (Wammes et al., 2017). This led the government to restrict new access to cash beneficiaries in 2012 to only those people eligible for institutional care: about 10% of the current 130,000 cash benefit recipients. The growth of personal budgets slowed down in 2014 to 9% of all LTC costs, averaging $27,500 per person per year.

During 2012 and 2013, the Netherlands underwent a severe economic recession. The country's economic growth rate fell to –1%, and its debt-to-GDP ratio rose to its highest level in twenty years. This led to a reconsideration of the Dutch welfare state and the responsibilities of people who needed services and supports. There was a national philosophical move from a "welfare state" to a "participation state."

The rising cost of LTC, particularly for the elderly but also for those with disabilities, was a contributing factor and became part of the solution. Major changes in the philosophy, management, and funding of LTC became a national issue. The initial changes were announced by the new king, Willem-Alexander, when he took office at the end of 2013. Viewing dependency on the state for the provision of services as a last resort, he remarked in a speech written for him by Prime Minister Mark Rutte's government that people must take responsibility for their own future and create their own social and financial safety nets (Wammes et al., 2017):

It is an undeniable reality in today's network and information society people are more assertive and more independent than in the past. This combined with the need to reduce the budget deficit, means that the classical welfare state is slowly, but surely, evolving into a participation society. Everyone who is able will be asked to take responsibility for their own lives and immediate surroundings. (p. 11)

The reforms enacted in 2015 were the largest overhaul of LTC since the AWBZ became law in 1968. LTC costs (including social support costs) had been steadily rising—from 2.9% of GDP in 2000 to 3.6% of GDP in 2006 to 4.3% of GDP in 2012—with no end in sight. This was more than twice the 1.6% GDP paid for by other EU countries (European Commission, 2016). It is important to note, however, that the overhaul of LTC was also the result of larger financial trends that had slowed down the national economy, increased the costs of the health care system in general, and created a change in the country's philosophy of caregiving.

As of January 2015, the AWBZ ended and was replaced by the Long-Term Care Act (*Wet Langdurige Zorg*), also known as WMO 2015, which contained several major changes in policies and regulations. Just like the former AWBZ, it is set up as a statutory health insurance scheme where applicants undergo a national eligibility and needs assessment procedure. The changing premise was that citizens would be active consumers of public services rather than passive recipients of benefits from the welfare state. The new legislation expected everyone with disabilities to work from their strengths, to participate in society as fully as possible, and to use public services as a last resort. The responsibility for most public services was moved from a national organization to local governments.

Care and support were to begin in the home with paid and informal caregivers, moving up to local support from professional local services and ending with a public safety net for those who need intensive supports. Residential care was redefined as a place for clients who needed permanent supervision or for those who could potentially be a danger to themselves or others and for those who needed 24-hour care because of physical problems or self-control problems. The emphasis on individual responsibility, the restructuring of financing, the importance of nonresidential care, and the greater involvement and risk of municipalities in nonresidential care are the most conspicuous structural elements of change. Under WMO 2015, municipalities were obligated to give support to clients, but they have significant policy discretion in carrying out their obligation.

In another major policy change, eligibility for the personal budget was substantially reduced after large increases in participation led to annual spending increases of up to 20% annually. The budgets were initially seen as a way of empowering participants, enabling continuous care by family members, and stimulating a market for care that would better meet consumers' needs. As of 2015, however, only citizens who would otherwise have to move to a nursing or residential home would be eligible for personal budgets, allowing those on personal budgets not meeting the criteria to be "grandfathered" into the new program. And because of reports of budget fraud and poor financial reporting, budgets would be managed by a government agency.

All other non-residential care—including services for older people, people with disabilities, people with substance abuse disorders, and people with psychiatric problems—became decentralized to municipalities under the WMO 2015. Municipalities received a state budget to carry out their tasks under the new law. The reform has substantially upgraded the role of local government in LTC. This change is based on the policy assumption that municipalities are not only best informed about local needs but also best able to deliver an efficient, tailor-made, and integrated package of LTC services given their responsibility for various adjacent policy areas including housing, welfare programs, transport, and local planning.

WMO 2015 gives applicants a right to publicly funded support if they could not run a household on their own and/or participate in social life. However, municipalities possess much policy discretion for the type and extent of assistance to be delivered. For example, each municipality is free to organize non-residential care and its own local needs assessment procedure. The procedure may include an assessment of the capability of the applicant's social network to provide informal care. Municipalities may also introduce their own copayment schedule; means-testing, however, remains forbidden.

Initially, the government intended to implement large spending cuts in LTC, but during the follow-up negotiations with provider organizations, unions, and municipalities, the size of these cuts was gradually scaled back as the program was so popular. What remained were characterized as "efficiency cuts." The government assumes that municipalities and insurers can organize LTC more efficiently than the regional care offices under the former AWBZ. Further savings are expected to come from a substantial drop-in residential care and nursing home care. It was projected that these changes were expected to save the equivalent of €3.5 billion, about $4.3 billion USD (Maarse & Jeurissen, 2016) annually.

The implementation of the 2015 reform created many issues that were covered in the press. An independent commission underscored the need for coordination between health and other professionals in the so-called neighborhood teams to make LTC more client centered. The Court of Audit criticized the government for underestimating the feasibility of its reform plans, including the reform of LTC. The media regularly reported on municipalities failing to provide tailor-made services and on large provider staff layoffs and poorer conditions of employment. The number of legal appeals by participants against a reduction of the care increased significantly. There were also reports of increasing administrative costs. So far, the delayed payment of many personal budgets under the new municipal management caused the most political trouble for the state. Other concerns included the capacity of the smaller municipalities to carry out their new tasks properly and stay ahead of implementation. And of course, the wide range of municipal management ability has created concerns about very different levels and quality of services available across the country.

Despite the magnitude of the reform, LTC, including personal budgets, remains a popular, largely publicly funded provision and a statutory health insurance scheme that is responsible for a growing number of persons eligible for care. Furthermore, the benefit package of LTC continues to be generous compared to most other European countries.

England

In England, self-directed support, also known as "personalization," has been piloted, researched, and analyzed for persons with disabilities and mental illness since the early 2000s. Although it was implemented nationally, utilization has varied across the country. However, it has continued to grow despite harsh economic conditions in the public health sector. Most recently, it has been adapted for use in personal health budgets. It is useful to view the development of self-direction in the country in three stages: conceptual development and pilots, national implementation with continued research on use and outcomes, and response to the national austerity policy.

The initial work on self-direction and personal budgets was undertaken in a public-private partnership between England's Department of Health and Social Care and the learning disability charity Mencap. This work led to the creation of In Control, an organization dedicated to developing and testing new person-centered services and controls for persons with disabilities. In Control developed and promoted a seven-step model for self-directed services and tested its use in six small-scale demonstration sites (Hatton et al., 2006). This model was intended to replace the previous traditional care management model by shifting power in the process to those requiring support, assigning them control over decisions on how resources are spent and managed. The seven steps are shown in Figure 10.1.

In Control built on the pioneering work of the British Independent Living and Inclusion movements led by disabled activists and family advocates, with support from some professional, policy, and managerial leaders and groups. In preceding decades, these activists had achieved success in creating legislation on direct payments and the policy and practice of deinstitutionalization. These goals were characterized as a shift from the "Professional Gift" to the "Citizenship" model of public services (Hatton et al., 2006).

Figure 10.1. Seven-step model. Adapted from "A report on In Control's first phase 2003–2005" by C. Hatton, C. Poll, S. Duffy, H. Sanderon, and M. Routledge, 2006, In Control Publications. Copyright 2006 by In Control Productions.

Following the promotion of the seven-step model and the results from six small-scale demonstration sites, interest from the prime minister's advisors led to the development of a major national pilot program. This was described in the 2005 white paper *Our Health Our Care Our Say* (London Department of Health, 2006). The national pilot program extended self-direction to all groups eligible for adult social care in England; it was tested in 13 pilot sites across a range of English localities. The Individual Budget Pilot Programme also extended beyond adult social-care income funding to incorporate other funding streams relevant to a wider range of outcomes, including employment. It also expanded the responsibility of three government departments.

A group of social scientists and economists from prominent universities undertook an evaluation from 2005 to 2008. The findings were broadly positive (with some caveats for outcomes for older people), essentially suggesting cost neutrality with positive outcomes and satisfaction improvements for most groups. The attempt to merge a range of income streams, however, was largely judged to have been unsuccessful as those with policy and administrative responsibility for the various income streams effectively withheld their support (Glendinning et al., 2008; London Department of Health, 2008.)

After several years of pilots and the evaluation, several ministers decided to press forward with policy implementation, albeit in the more limited sphere of adult social care. Local district authorities became responsible for implementation. There was a change in terminology from "individual" budgets to "personal" budgets. The early years were characterized by continuing broad cross-party support but uneven implementation across the country of personal budgets in social care. Great variation in numbers and outcomes across local authorities reflected challenges with the national implementation approach as well as disparities in preparedness and the differing approaches of the local districts charged with delivery (London Department of Health, 2006).

By the end of 2007, self-directed support was implemented nationally as a personal budget concept. The rollout was announced in a cross-departmental paper, *Putting People First in December 2007*, which was issued jointly with the key social care sector bodies and across many government departments (HM Government, 2007). Personal budgets, termed "personalization," were the centerpiece of the initiative, which also included prevention and early intervention, generic services, and developing "social capital" for participants. A local authority paper outlined the policy direction and set out the availability of £520 million for implementation, mostly to be allocated to local authorities over a three-year period (London Department of Health, 2008). The policies, regulations, monitoring, and other factors driving implementation were not well developed in the central-local government approach to policy delivery, leaving many issues to be resolved by local authorities, who often took different approaches. Target levels for personal budgets were set and then increased, and a formal definition of self-directed support was established by the Department of Health to structure data collection. Modest national and regional resources were made available to provide local administrative support (London Department of Health, 2011).

Personal budgets were initially implemented for 166,000 participants with disabilities in the social care sector. Goals included achieving increases in self-determination and a shift from institutional and segregated forms of services for people with physical disabilities, people with intellectual and developmental disabilities, and people experiencing mental illness. The use of personal budgets grew substantially under the 2014 Care Act which established personal budgets as the primary means through which people with disabilities eligible for state funded adult social care would receive their resources (The Care Act 2014, 2014). Resources available to participants were wide ranging and included care at home, services in the community, improvements in the home, and other community services and supports. Budgets could be managed by direct care payments to participants, or by third parties, or by local district offices. The total number of personal budget holders grew by 300% in nine years, rising to 648,000 by the end of 2014; almost 3 in 4 people using social care services were formally defined as having a personal budget, although most did not manage their budget directly, using third parties or the local district offices. Only direct care payments provided participants with budgets that they managed directly and made their own choices. Unlike the Netherlands and Germany, there was no discount for using personal budgets.

A significant financial challenge emerged as the national policy of "austerity," introduced in 2010, had a dramatic impact on local government resources. Since the Putting People First policy did not establish self-directed support or personal budgets in law, it was vulnerable as national health budgets contracted and as the austerity policy led to a decrease in spending on adult social care between 2010 and 2017.

The success of the policy of personalization has been strongly debated. Differences of opinion reflect different definitions of success and, to some extent, different views about the approaches to implementation. There is a narrative held by some of the early advocates that government has corrupted essential principles of self-direction; others view this as naïve and take the view that policy implementation is complex and adaptions and partial delivery success are the prices to be paid for policy success.

In 2016, a National Audit Office report entitled *Personalised Commissioning in Adult Social Care* pointed out a lack of systematic collection and use of robust evidence following the evaluation report of the original pilot and proposed an improvement of the evidence base. The authors recommended making better use of existing survey data to understand the relationship of different ways of using personal budgets and improvement in outcomes. To date, the response to this call at the national and local government level has been very limited. The report did conclude that personal budgets are popular and effective in regions where they are properly implemented and supported by well-equipped local managers and effective commissioning and that there is widespread support for "personalization" in those areas (Think Local Act Personal, 2017).

Relevant evidence is collected via the national Adult Social Care Outcomes Framework based on questions set by the Department of Health and Social Care and data collected from all local district authority councils. Online summary reports have been made available; these are aimed at helping councils compare and benchmark their performance. The Think Local Act Personal report noted that the study found significant variations between local authorities in the numbers of people choosing personal budgets and the kind of personal budget used: direct cash payments, budgets managed by the local authority, and budgets managed by a third-party entity. There was also a wide range of definitions and understanding as to what a personal budget was and how it could be used.

In answering the question "Does personalized commissioning result in better outcomes for people?," they concluded that while the existing evidence does suggest that personal budgets benefit most people, they could not find any direct link between the proportion of people with personal budgets and overall levels of satisfaction at a local authority level. They also concluded that the available data do not make it possible to analyze the best way to implement personal budgets to maximize improvements in individual outcomes.

There is, however, further evidence relating to personal budgets in health based on a three-year pilot study with a control group and an evaluation undertaken by a consortium of UK academic institutions (Forder, Glendinning, et al., 2012). Core findings included cost-effectiveness for the study group and positive impacts on quality of life as well as high levels of user satisfaction. The evaluation established higher levels of confidence of outcomes and effectiveness for certain groups, including people with higher support needs and people with mental health problems. The evaluation also suggested a range of "process conditions" during implementation that were associated with better results. In social care, the program of practice-based evidence collection and analysis by In Control with volunteer localities also suggests a correlation between a range of positive outcomes and the practices and processes in place to deliver personal budgets (Think Local Act Personal, 2017).

Political consensus in support of personalization and personal budgets generally remains strong despite the austerity policy and mixed evaluation results. Notably, personalization has been maintained by both conservative and labor governments, and it is expected to remain well established in national policy going forward. The Care Act stipulates that personal budgets should serve as the core mechanism for those in receipt of publicly funded social care support and that support should be allocated and managed through two different options: cash payments to providers directed by participants and local council managed personal budgets done on behalf of the participant.

In the National Health Service, the number of people accessing personal health budgets has started to rise significantly with an increasingly feasible target of 100,000. This is aided by policies giving certain groups a "right to have," setting challenging targets for Clinical Commissioning Groups and establishing a significant "Personalized Commissioning Group" within NHSE, the national body charged with driving the delivery of health policy (Think Local Act Personal, 2017). National partnerships of organizations continue to champion personalization in health and social care led by Think Local Act Personal and the Coalition for Collaborative Care with continued attention from researchers and advocates.

Australia

In Australia, a broad reform that encompasses the principles of self-direction for people with disabilities in LTC is just getting off the ground. Although still in its infancy—and therefore with little available data on outcomes—it is included here because of the radical nature of the changes envisioned. The authors of the reform used some of the elements in the social insurance programs in Germany, the Netherlands, and England but have greatly enlarged those elements to develop a national policy that is designed to transform the system of services and supports, using self-determination and individual budgets as the cornerstones of the new system for all participants. Budgets are meant to be comprehensive and detailed, changing annually as participants' needs change. If successful, it could become the global model to address the growing LTC needs of people with a growing range of physical and mental disabilities.

In 2011, the Australian government determined that its current disability system, funded and administered at the state and territory level, was failing to meet the needs of Australians (Australia Productivity Commission, 2011):

> The current disability support system is underfunded, unfair, fragmented and inefficient. It gives people with a disability little choice, no certainty of access to appropriate supports and little scope to participate in the community. People with disabilities, their careers, service providers, workers in the industry and governments all want change. (p. 3)

The government determined that most families and individuals could not adequately prepare for the risk and financial impact of significant disability; consequently, it tasked the Productivity Commission—an independent research and advisory body—with looking at the costs, cost-effectiveness, benefits, and feasibility of replacing the current arrangements with a properly funded and managed long-term disability plan for the entire country. Created in 1998 as an independent authority within the treasury portfolio, the Productivity Commission has the role of helping governments make better policies in the long-term interest of the Australian community; it provides research and advising on a range of economic, social, and environmental issues.

The commission conducted detailed investigations across all six Australian states and two territories, and the work included extensive actuarial analysis to determine the costs of different approaches and to make projections for the total costs and financing of the policy recommendations. It also included weeks of public hearings around the country. The result, published at the end of 2011 and revised in 2013, proposed major changes in the philosophy of providing services, the structure of the system and the financing of long-term services and supports. It was the single largest reform ever proposed for public services since the introduction of the Australian Medicare program for national health care (Australia Productivity Commission, 2013).

First, the Productivity Commission recommended there should be a single national scheme (plan) to replace the different schemes run by the six states and two territories. The National Disability Insurance Scheme (NDIS) would be run by the National Disability Insurance Agency (NDIA), a new agency with agreements with all states and territories. It would have strong governance arrangements, an independent commercial board, an advisory council of key stakeholders, clear guidelines to ensure a sustainable and efficient scheme, and legislation to protect the scheme from political influences of changing governments. The main function of the NDIS would be to fund and administer high quality comprehensive care and support through individual budgets—but not income replacement—for people with significant disabilities up to the age of 65. Those over 65 would be supported in a similar program that would be phased in several years later. Those in the NDIS turning 65 would continue with individual budgets. Individual assessments for eligibility would be completed by the NDIA, following national standards and leading to detailed individual plans and budgets for all participants. Everybody eligible would be covered, and the program was expected to support about 410,000 people.

Second, people would be able to choose their own provider or providers in a market-based system. Control of services and supports would shift from local disability service providers to participants. Also, participants could decide how to manage their own service packages: use the NDIA, use a support organization (plan-management) to help them manage it on their direction, or do it themselves (self-management) within certain rules. Participants would be supported to work in the community and become more involved in community activities. Traditional services such as those for health, public housing, public transport, mainstream education, and employment would remain outside the NDIS, with the NDIS providing referrals to the responsible agencies. Service packages were designed as individual plans that would change over time to provide the required services and supports needed to meet each person's goals within the plan's funding level. Services and supports would include care in the home, one-time expenditures to support independence, and a wide range of services in the community. Australia provided an individualized service package and cash budget for all participants, not just for those who chose self-direction. No country in the world had taken this step of individualizing services and budgets for all eligible participants.

Third, the financing of the program was proposed to function as an insurance program where the cost of the services was to be fully offset by premiums paid. Premiums would come from all Australians since all were eligible for coverage under the NDIS. It was estimated that the current system, funded by taxes levied by the states and territories and awarded in block grants to service providers, totaled $7.1 billion AUD and was seriously ineffective. The total cost of the system in 2011 was projected to be $13.6 billion AUD, an increase of more than 90% in funding for direct care, not including the cost of the new NDIA and other startup costs. The Productivity Commission proposed that funding be nationalized through the creation of a new national revenue source, a national disability insurance premium, and that current state and territory taxes for disability services be eliminated. The cost of the new premium eventually totaled a one-half percent increase of national income tax (NDIA Annual Report, 2017). By the time the final program was designed and implementation began, the population to be served had increased to 460,000, and the annual cost of full implementation by 2020 was projected to be $22 billion AUD, including the costs of new agency administration, inflation, startup, and population growth since the original 2011 projections.

The increased costs were expected to be partly offset by many economic gains. These included the implicit income transferred by the NDIS to people with disabilities into the consumer economy, the use of a single national agency to administer the program replacing six states and two territories, the use of the private marketplace by participants to get better prices and services, increased employment outcomes for participants who would pay taxes and require fewer supports while making payments into their pension, health insurance and unemployment funds, and the reduced use of institutional services. The Productivity Commission estimated that by 2050 there would be a one percent increase in the country's GDP because of the NDIS.

Following the commission's report, there was an active national discussion, additional consulting engagements to refine the implementation and design of the NDIS, and national legislation in 2013 that was supported across party lines. Small pilot programs were begun across the country in 2015. They enrolled approximately 30,000 participants before the official program rollout began in June 2016. After one year, approximately 90,000 participants were enrolled.

The NDIS annual report of 2016–2017, after the first full year of implementation, documented many outcomes and challenges. First, the number of participants enrolled was below first year projections by 17%, or about 25,000 below the plan. Since larger numbers of children were entering the plan, and smaller numbers were leaving the plan as had been projected, discussion began about the three years allowed for implementation and whether that would be enough. Data collection efforts resulted in completed surveys of 98% of all participants, creating a very strong database for continued research and projections. Participant satisfaction with the plan was 84%, a slight decline from the pilot year but still very strong. As expected, the number of registered providers grew substantially, more than doubling in a year from 3,519 to 8,698, including 3,291 new providers who entered the marketplace specifically to respond to participant decision-making. Overall plan costs were estimated to be "broadly on track with NDIA's long term modeling" and 26% of all participants over the age of 25 had been paid for work in 2016–2017 (National Disability Insurance Scheme, 2017).

Although the first year of implementation proceeded well, many implementation issues were documented, including the need to improve the national database system for enrollment and budget planning, the need to expand the disability services market to meet the needs of a population estimated to be five times the size of the first year of enrollment, and the need to prepare for the scaled growth of the NDIA and its capability to manage the plan as it expands. The first year reports from the chairman of the NDIA board and the new NDIA CEO, as well as the NDIS report on market development, were promising and upbeat on the new plan reaching and exceeding its implementation goals (National Disability Insurance Scheme, 2017).

The final quarter report of the second year, published at the end of the 2017–2018 implementation year, continued to show promising results. Annual enrollment was about 87,000 participants. The levels of high satisfaction with the planning process increased to 88% (rating it "good" or "very good") and spending levels per person remained lower than projected (Council of Australian Governments, Disability Council, 2018).

The number of registered providers increased to 16,755, almost a doubling of providers registered at the start of the year. This included individual caregivers providing at-home care, service provider agencies, and providers of generic community services. Outcome data continues to tell a good story. Among adults 25 and over, 71% said that the NDIS helped them in activities of daily living, 67% said they had improved choice and control in their lives, and 59% said they had increased participation in their community. About one-quarter of all participants over the age of 25 continue to report having a paid job (Council of Australian Governments, Disability Council, 2018). Although the annual enrollment continued to increase, it remained behind projections and would have to grow another 60% annually to meet the 460,000 goal by June 2020. Additionally, a review was launched into how plans are managed—by individuals, plan managers and the NDIA—and how these approaches can be improved to meet NDIS goals while enabling choice and control and reducing the likelihood of fraudulent activities.

Publicly, the rollout of the scheme continued to be covered and discussed in newspapers, on television, and in radio shows throughout 2017 and 2018. Stories focused on individual successes, the slowness of the planning process, difficulties getting in touch with the NDIA, and the slowness of approval of individual plans. Some people drawn to the program through aggressive marketing on the part of the government have been frustrated by the slow plan approval and implementation process. On the other hand, there are many memorable stories on how the plan has created unheard of opportunities for individuals to grow.

For all the issues raised by the implementation of the NDIS, however, Australia's experiment in nationwide self-direction is indeed a bold and ambitious reform—more far-reaching than the programs in the other three countries reviewed in this chapter. It will be important to continue to study this reform and its implications for the United States.

Case Study: Australian Family Interview

IS is a mother in Sydney, Australia, trained as a nurse, who has two adopted children with severe special needs. Her daughter, T, is 12 years old and has cerebral palsy and quadriplegia with very limited use of her hands. Her son, R, is 38 years old, also with cerebral palsy, and has complex medical conditions including epilepsy. She enrolled them both in the NDIS program about seven months ago after many years of receiving services from agencies that were funded by grants. She is very pleased with the changes and with the ability to use their individual budgets to meet their own goals and aspirations. Also, she has noticed that the NDIS pays more attention to individual needs, and she receives budgets that respond to their desires to learn and build their own individual capabilities.

She uses their individual plan and budget to develop and support new hobbies and activities both at home and in the community. For her daughter, this includes gardening and taking care of the lawn, learning photography with an iPad, and making beaded jewelry. Another of her daughter's new hobbies is the care and breeding of tropical fish in a small pond. She learns these hobbies and develops new skills at home with specialists who visit weekly; she also participates in church activities where there are group learning opportunities. Her son is learning from an in-home worker to prepare food and cook meals using a thermomixer and a cooking appliance that can make full meals. He is also getting more caregiver hours at home to enable him to learn how to take care of his personal needs, dress himself, and live more independently.

One of the big changes in their lives is not having to go to disability agencies to receive services. IS observed that her daughter and son would often imitate and learn inappropriate behavior from other participants using the agency. She noticed they are now learning age-appropriate behavior and striving to meet standards of community activities, including church groups and educational programs. They are learning to make individual decisions and choices that support their goals rather than imitate others in their environment.

She observes that the NDIA expects T and R to have more choice and control and to learn how to do both well. This is not something that agencies had previously supported. She has found that using a plan manager gives her family more information to manage their budgets and make good choices. Now she is very conscious of the costs of services and supports, whereas in the past she was dependent on getting whatever the agency wanted to deliver. This has given her the confidence to object to certain NDIA decisions and file appeals when she sees budget decisions unsupportive of her son's and daughter's goals. After about seven months in the program, she says: "The changes in my kids' behavior are absolutely remarkable. They are more independent and happier."

She has noticed that some agencies she uses have not developed a consistent billing practice for services provided, sometimes with several months passing before she receives a bill. She has let the agencies know that submitting a bill more than a month after services are delivered puts their resources at risk. And she has also observed that some families have difficulty managing their budgets because of the long delay in agency invoicing. She assumes this will improve over time and families will learn to take control.

IS observes that some agencies are improving and are providing more individualized services because they are learning the new

> model and don't want to lose business. But she also has noticed that some parents are very conservative in developing new goals for their sons and daughters because they don't want them to fail. She is working with a group of families receiving NDIA services, so they can support each other and learn from each other. And she sees plan management agencies helping families exercise more choice and control while helping families manage their budget.

Conclusions and Lessons Learned

First, the national programs reviewed in this chapter suggest that personal budgets should be an intrinsic part of an LTC system, focused on the needs of the individual. This requires significant investment in program design, technology, and management. In Germany, the Netherlands, and England, the personal budget is an alternative to traditional services, requiring that the costs and trade-offs be well understood. In Australia, every person eligible has a personal budget, requiring more time and support for participants to learn how to use the new system. It is also important that the individual budget can be spent on a wide range of options that support individual needs and desires. German and Dutch participants who have chosen personal budgets have done so even though the amounts are substantially less than what would be available for formal agency services. The flexibility to employ family members and friends as caregivers, as well as to choose to purchase from both formal and informal service providers, is appealing to the participant population. Participants should have the information and time they need to make well-informed decisions about their new purchasing choices.

Second, it is important for the long-term financing of self-direction programs to be in place by national law from the start, while changes in eligibility, services, and demographics should be reviewed and accounted for on a regular basis. The differences in the financial viability of the Netherlands and Germany are striking outcomes of systems that took very different approaches to long-term financial viability and had to go through major reforms to achieve stability. The English system was seriously affected by the national move to austerity since personalization was not legally mandated. Australia appears to have been focused on long-term viability from the start, and its program is well supported by national legislation that has been successfully transferred across changes of government.

Third, it is helpful for the eligibility criteria and determination process to be centrally managed and consistent for all users. The decentralization of decision making and management in the Netherlands and the United Kingdom resulted in a lack of uniformity and equity across both countries and highly variable results. Standardization supports a system that is both more efficient and fairer. It allows decisions to be made based on need and program goals rather than managing against funding sources or enabling costs to be passed onto different systems. Also, it enables evaluation studies to be conducted nationally from the start of the program using a consistent database.

Fourth, introducing self-direction, or reforms in self-direction, should be part of a process that takes the time to develop and test all processes and technology at all levels before implementation. A fundamental reform of this size with new regulations and a new financing regime requires a new administrative and technology infrastructure. Technical implementation problems turn into policy and political problems that could undermine self-direction if they are not properly addressed. Variation at the local implementation level of the program in England has created differential results and limited its growth. Australia is learning this as it goes through implementation.

Last, managing the use of personal budgets should be done as part of the current financial system, not afterwards as part of a monitoring and accounting process. Managing budgets after the transactions have occurred fails to prevent spending problems or identify fraudulent activities in a timely manner. Also, it takes more time and is more expensive. The existence of multiple budget management options creates the possibility of differential results and inconsistent documentation, as well as less effective cost projections. In the United States, this is the role usually played by each state's Medicaid agency, which contracts with one or more private financial management service agencies to achieve consistent and timely financial results. The process is often aided by support brokers or specially trained case managers, who help participants manage their budgets, hire staff, and make expenditures in real time, enabling them to make choices that are effective, efficient, and allowed by their budgets.

Chapter 11

Reflections and Recommendations

What We Know

Self-direction continues to be a state-by-state initiative and not a standardized national program. Although there are many national policies that support self-direction, including federal options in HCBS waivers, language in the Affordable Care Act, aspirations in the HCBS Settings Rule promulgated by the Centers for Medicare and Medicaid, and IRS provisions that clarify the tax treatment of individual budgets, it is left to the discretion of the states to design and implement self-direction. Without an overarching long-term care program in the United States that embraces self-direction, there are no standardized rules or expectations for the states. While self-direction remains a cost-effective option that empowers individual participants to shape their own supports, the growth and extent of the program depends substantially on individual state decisions.

Evaluations of self-direction have been uniformly positive. The Cash and Counseling model in Arkansas, Florida and New Jersey, funded by the assistant secretary for planning and evaluation and the Robert Wood Johnson Foundation, highlighted positive outcomes and cost effectiveness. The Cash and Counseling approach has become a best practice that has influenced the design of self-direction in many states. Evaluations of the Robert Wood Johnson funded Self-Determination Pilots for Persons with Developmental Disabilities also showed positive outcomes for participants lending further momentum to the expansion of the adoption of the program in many states.

Though self-direction began in California almost 40 years ago with the IHSS program, it did not become an explicit option in HCBS waivers until 2003. Since then, programs have slowly expanded and now exist in all fifty states serving about 1.2 million people. Self-direction, depending on the state, now encompasses programs for persons with physical disabilities, intellectual and developmental disabilities, children with autism, and older adults. Some states have as many as four separate waivers, each serving a different group of participants. Recently, self-direction has gained the support of other groups, including people with serious mental illness and veterans with needs for continuing support. Research on the impact on both groups has been very positive.

We believe that self-direction will continue to grow across the country given the strong support for the option among participants. As self-direction expands nationally, it reinforces the principle of person-centeredness by enabling individuals to determine where and how services are delivered. Agencies no longer make decisions about who provides what service—those choices are now made by participants and their families. As a family member told us: "Choice makes it personal, focuses on meeting needs and creates accountability."[1] This level of personalization also creates opportunities for members of different racial and ethnic groups to get services from providers who share similar cultural and linguistic traditions.

Recently, legislation in two states—Hawaii and Washington—provides a path for the inclusion of self-direction in long-term care. Both states established programs that enable the participant to train and hire family members and friends to provide in-home care, in turn reducing reliance on agency care and potentially lowering Medicaid costs. The Washington long-term care program is funded by payroll deductions, substantially expanding the number of participants who could choose to direct their own care.

Interviews with state directors of long-term care and disability programs across the country suggest that self-direction will continue to grow. Patti Killingsworth, Director of TennCare in Tennessee noted: "Self-direction perfectly aligns with personalization and the individualization of services. I can't see a long-term care program without this as an option."[2] Bill Moss, the Assistant Secretary for Aging and Long-Term Support in Washington stated that "[self-direction is] definitely growing—many are moving to individual providers—and it will continue to grow because personal care is very intimate, and participants want to have a relationship with their provider. It's what people want."[3]

Even in the California IHHS program, the largest in the country, self-direction is expected to continue to grow at about 5% annually according to interviews with Peter Cervinka and Debbi Thompson, administrators overseeing the program. Ms. Thompson explained the popularity of the program by stating: "It is an incredible benefit to remain safely at home, in your own community, and prevent the need for out of home care (Cervinka, P., personal communication, September 2018; Thompson, D., personal communication, September 2018). There is no sign that these priorities will change. As noted in chapter 8, if anything, more people requiring long-care services will want to age in their home and communities and will see the use of self-direction as a way to reach their goals. Given the projections of demographic growth among those who will require long-term services and supports, there should be a strong incentive for all states to expand self-direction.

Self-direction can create many efficiencies that are helpful to individuals as they use their budgets to meet their needs. When budgets are based on individual levels determined by functional needs (as opposed to the costs of traditional services), as described in chapter 5, it is possible to budget in a more accurate, equitable, and efficient fashion. Further, by enabling participants to design their own services and make their own provider choices, they often spend less money because they get what they want and need, not what the agencies are funded to deliver. As a national health care policy maker and parent of a daughter with a disability told us, "A cash benefit avoids a cookie cutter approach where people use more services than they need and don't necessarily get what they want. It can build self-esteem and cost less" (Garner, C., personal communication, August 2018).

The research has shown that individual budgets are rarely overspent, and in fact are often underspent during the first two or three years. Further, few participants leave the program, creating a stable platform for providing long-term care at a reasonable and predictable cost.

The use of individual budgets to help people remain at home rather than in nursing homes and other congregate settings has resulted in a reduction of long-term-care costs. In a California survey completed by 4,846 participants, one of the largest surveys of its kind, 96% of consumers say that the IHSS program services are either "very important" or "important" in allowing them to live independently and remain at home. Significantly, almost half of the people responding did not use English as their home language, however, 97% were "very satisfied" or "satisfied" with the language used in the program indicating that they were able to hire staff from their own culture. And we have seen how Tennessee has used self-directed care to help decrease its reliance on nursing home care from one of the highest in the country to a median level.

Given all the positive aspects of self-direction, the question remains: Why do some states lag far behind others in the numbers of people self-directing, and why hasn't self-direction become an official national policy for long-term care? Furthermore, why have most states used it primarily as a niche option for a limited number of participants? In part, the answer may be that self-direction is still viewed in some states as an approach for a narrow group of more competent constituents rather than as a way of delivering a range of services and supports for all. It is also an approach that requires a different infrastructure—including financial management services and support brokers—from the one that supports traditional services. Creating a new state infrastructure for self-direction can be costly and has necessitated substantial changes in IT systems, billing protocols, and planning templates. In many states, self-direction is seen as competition to well-established provider agencies who may see the initiative as cutting into their funding. Because self-direction is still viewed as a "boutique" service in many states, there is a concern that the emergence of managed care may halt any forward progress given what some perceive to be the mismatch between the flexibility of self-direction and the data-driven and more rigid managed care approach.

What steps can be taken to foster the growth of self-direction? Just as reforms that led to the deinstitutionalization of people from large institutions, the inclusion of children with disabilities in regular classrooms and removal of physical barriers to accessibility of public places for people with mobility impairments challenged the status quo and took many years, even decades, to fully implement, self-direction also presents a dramatic change that disrupts the traditional service system. Disruption causes tensions, and as self-directed options have begun to grow, public managers have been faced with pressure to monitor and regulate self-direction while attempting to maintain the flexibility that is the hallmark of the program. Self-direction also poses challenges to established provider organizations and to case managers used to facilitating placement in group settings. As noted above, the existing human-services and long-term-services infrastructure in most states is not compatible with self-direction. The future of self-direction will be determined by whether public managers at the state level can retool some or all of the infrastructure to accommodate this new "disruptive" option.

Reflections from Practitioners, Administrators, and Advocates

To provide a solid basis for final recommendations, the authors consulted federal and state government leaders, advocates, and researchers for their suggestions about the future of self-direction. We are deeply grateful for the ideas these leaders shared and the time they gave us. Rather than report on each interview, we will cluster their comments around specific topics. Whereas those interviewed did not always agree on specific next steps, they all saw significant advantages to self-direction and shared a consensus that the option should be expanded to all those who are interested.

Overall, our key informants anticipate that self-direction will continue modest growth over the short run. A case in point is California, which still has almost half of those self-directing in the United States. As one of our informants said (Doty, P., personal communication, September 2018), if you follow self-direction in California's IHHS program over the last 25 years or more, you see that the model has withstood a range of setbacks, including competition from proprietary home care agencies, charges of fraud and abuse, state economic downturns, and new, complex federal mandates regarding auditing and staff time tracking. Despite these challenges, IHSS has survived and continued to grow over 40 years. How? In California's case, the program has prospered because of community support and advocacy, especially through the county-based public authorities. IHSS has also received significant support from organized labor and has continued to balance the interests of the unions with the interests of the participants.

The reasons why IHHS is successful and growing are similar to those that have bolstered self-direction in other states. These factors include strong citizen participation and advocacy, support of state legislatures and public agencies, and documentation of positive outcomes. In Wisconsin, for instance, advocates in Dane County created individual budgets for almost every participant with developmental disabilities. This approach grew into a statewide HCBS Waiver program—IRIS—that garnered enough support to defeat attempts by the governor to abolish the IRIS option. The growth of self-direction in Virginia and West Virginia was also sustained by strong consumer advocacy over many years, and the support of Medicaid managers aligned with the values and goals of self-direction.

So, is strong constituent involvement the solution to the growth of self-direction? National leaders say that the answer is not simple. Having a consistent advocacy voice at the policy-making table is not always easy to accomplish. The feedback from leaders of the National Participant Network—an organization of people who use self-directed services—indicates how difficult it is to sustain a participant advocacy group when the members are mostly poor and have significant disabilities—disabilities that periodically make it difficult or impossible for them to be activists. Advocacy comes at an extraordinary cost. In addition, there is a growing concern that some programs, as they mature, are creating obstacles to the growth and quality of participant direction. "Participants were offered more freedom in return for more responsibility, but over the years the freedoms have been eroded and the responsibilities increased."[4]

For the foreseeable future, the expansion of self-direction will be up to state public agency managers, participants, families, and advocates. Unlike some of the international models highlighted in this book, the United States has not undertaken the type of national transformation that could result in a robust self-direction option such as that described in Australia. It is hoped that in the future, policy makers in the United States will look to international experiences to shape a national long-term care policy. We think many helpful lessons can be learned from Germany, the Netherlands, England, Australia, and other countries where self-direction and individual budgets have become key components of their national long-term care policy.

The following recommendations are based on a synthesis of the findings and lessons described in the previous chapters and interviews with experienced informants from many states. Suggestions fall into two categories: program changes to promote and improve self-direction itself, and systems changes that elevate self-direction to an integral part of new long-term support systems. There are eleven program recommendations and three system recommendations that we believe will improve the quality of self-direction, expand the number of participants self-directing, and elevate self-direction to a national priority.

Recommendations for the Future of Self-direction

Program Recommendation 1—Continue to develop and implement the HHS guidance on person-centered planning and self-direction as required by Section 2402a of the Affordable Care Act. The Affordable Care Act included a specific requirement that the Secretary of HHS establish guidelines for each agency to integrate the principles of self-direction into its program policies. That provision, 2402(a), was further explicated in policy guidance and, recently, was translated into a curriculum for person-centered planning by the US Administration for Community Living (ACL). Person-centered Planning is now required by CMS in all HCBS services. Similar attention (including curriculum guidance) needs to be devoted to the process of self-direction. Because self-direction is one important way to support person centeredness, it should be used as a national standard for implementing person-centered planning. HHS should take the leadership role in expanding self-direction policies and practices seeking legislative authority as necessary.

Program Recommendation 2—Develop comprehensive training in self-direction for case managers and support brokers to ensure that they provide a robust introduction and necessary support to participants and family members. Case managers and support brokers are the gate keepers for self-direction. If they do not fully understand the potential benefits of self-direction for their clients, or do not agree with the principles of self-direction, utilization of the option will be constrained. As the "ambassadors" of self-direction, case managers should receive adequate training in the values of self-direction as well as the mechanics of the process. If these staff are well-armed with information, they will be able to answer questions from participants and family members regarding whether self-direction is a good match for their needs. States should also explore developing a network of support brokers who can work directly with participants to help with recruiting staff, understanding their budget, making choices about services and supports, and working with the fiscal intermediary. Like case managers, support brokers will need training in the values and mechanics of self-direction.

There are training modules available for case managers and support brokers thanks to the pioneering work of the Council on Social Work Education in collaboration with the National Resource Center for Participant-Directed Services and nine leading social work schools from around the country (Sciegaj, Hooyman, et al., 2018). The training videos and modules were developed through a grant from the New York Community Trust. But this work is just the beginning. We are past the time of foundation funding for training and recommend that the Administration for Community Living support the development of a training curriculum as part of the self-direction mandate outlined in Section 2402(a) of the Affordable Care Act. It is also recommended that social work programs include self-direction as part of under-graduate and graduate curricula and be part of the profession's accreditation process. Finally, there should be skill standards for support brokers that can lead to certification requirements.

Program Recommendation 3—Ensure that new federal labor laws and regulations minimize obstacles for self-direction growth and development. Recent federal legislation and regulations regarding the treatment of staff providing personal care and other services have the potential to further complicate self-direction for the state, participants, and caregivers. In chapter

8, we discussed the impact of changes to companionship rules under the Fair Labor Standards Act as well as the requirements for electronic verification of staff hours as part of the CURES Act by 2020. These changes were originally aimed at home care agencies and other support organizations, not necessarily for staff hired by participants and families who are self-directing. We recommend that federal and state funds be made available to explore more flexible and adaptable systems to document hours worked by staff hired by participants, including systems that enable consumers to easily change their schedule and sign off on all hours worked by their staff. In addition, the regulations recently proposed by CMS that prohibit payroll deductions for union dues, benefits, and training for home care workers create additional burdens on staff as well as participants. We recommend that CMS, in collaboration with the Administration for Community Living, revisit this rule to reduce the impact that it will have on staff recruitment and quality.

Program Recommendation 4—Increase awareness of the self-direction option for users. We discovered in talking to consumers and workers that they often found it was difficult to get clear, understandable information about self-direction. As one of the participant advocates noted, "No one even knows about this option." Certainly, this is true in Veteran-Directed HCBS where the understanding of the self-direction option varies widely across the country. For example, legislation in the state of New York first required the counties to offer the Consumer-Directed Personal Assistance option. A few years later, the New York legislature had to return to require the counties to tell participants about this option! States like Massachusetts and California recently have passed legislation for IDD populations stipulating the self-direction option be offered at every assessment and annual reassessment. New and better tools, processes, social media, and written materials need to be developed and tested to inform potential participants of the opportunity to self-direct.

The tools used must speak to the participants and families about the opportunities and challenges of self-direction. The handbook written by Virginia consumers discussed in chapter 4 is one example of an orientation tool that had good results. Information should not come solely from professionals but should also be provided by individuals and family members and those with lived experience who have experienced self-direction and who can answer questions and respond to concerns.

Program Recommendation 5—Work to keep the self-direction option before policy makers and Medicaid public managers as a management option that leads to higher consumer satisfaction, improved

outcomes, and managed costs. Self-direction has the potential to bring about a comprehensive reform in the way social and long-term care services are provided. The positive aspects of such system change were highlighted when the Gerontological Society of America devoted an entire issue of *Public Policy and Aging Report* to self-direction. Further, the special issue on self-direction in *the Journal of Gerontological Social Work*, published in March 2019, featured a number of articles showing what the self-direction option has meant to veterans, caregivers, and people with dementia. To further bolster the delivery of self-direction, the Office of the Assistant Secretary for Planning and Evaluation has commissioned a revision of the *Handbook on Self-direction Policies and Procedures,* which is a powerful tool for public managers who want to expand self-direction. National organizations such as the National Association of Medicaid Directors could play an important role by reviewing the status of self-direction and providing examples of outstanding programs and outcomes for their members.

Program Recommendation 6—Provide information and guidance to policy makers and public managers regarding the administrative and infrastructure requirements for self-direction. Self-direction that entails participant authority over services and goods in addition to employer authority requires new management systems and technology to administer the program and assure its quality. Self-direction is not easily grafted onto legacy systems. California has developed and operated most of its system changes in-house for its IHSS program, but other states have relied on contractors for design and operations. Both approaches have been successful. Policy makers and administrators will need to understand and implement these new requirements including a onetime development cost to design and build new systems, as well as an ongoing administrative cost.

The larger and more complex the program, the higher the development cost, although per member administrative costs decline substantially as the program grows into the thousands. New costs cover financial management services to manage individual budgets, ensure that correct wages, including overtime, are paid on time, that proper taxes are deducted and deposited, that workers receive the benefits required under federal and state law, and that all goods and services are paid for properly and on time. In some programs, this includes the cost of federal and state criminal background checks and multilingual customer services systems—telephonic and online—that support participants, workers, and service providers. Both the total cost of self-direction initiatives and the one-time development costs need to be continually monitored and audited as enrollment grows. Additional resources may be required to manage the growth, meet new federal requirements, and take advantage of new technology to improve quality. Once fully implemented, we have seen that self-direction administrative costs are less than legacy systems costs per member.

Program Recommendation 7—Support continued research to monitor the progress and outcomes of self-direction. To track the growth of self-direction, it will be important to continue to collect data on the numbers and characteristics of people who are self-directing Medicaid HCBS services and supports. Without data, it will be difficult to gauge the success of initiatives to increase utilization. With the advent of managed care, there is a concern that such utilization data may not be publicly available unless Medicaid agencies include a requirement to track self-direction in the contracts with MCOs. Further, we strongly recommend that CMS require the submission of such data annually as stipulated in the new T-MSIS.

The growth of managed care and the renewed interest in the integration of acute, long-term care and behavioral health create the opportunity to examine how self-direction works in these settings. Research should be funded to explore how self-direction is introduced and implemented in order to identify best practices and to highlight constraints. Without such an effort, integration may merely mean a return to medicalization of support services. Research reviewed in previous chapters has shown that self-direction can reduce institutionalization and hospitalization. Research should also focus on the costs and benefits of self-direction within managed and integrated care, including relying on family and trained support staff to administer medications and monitor health indicators rather than employing more expensive medical staff.

There should also be continued research on fraud and abuse in self-direction programs. The Department of Health and Human Services, Office of the Inspector General (2012), did conduct a recent review that identified a number of weaknesses, including lack of documentation, lack of appropriate worker qualifications, and lack of adequate cost controls. Though the study identified a few specific incidents of fraud, it failed to document the amount of fraud or the potential cost to the program. It did assert that FMSAs can identify and prevent fraud when they use standard operating procedures employing current technology. Research is needed to document the most effective types of timekeeping systems and technology required to identify and mitigate potential fraud and abuse.

Given the low wages and relatively small individual budgets for most participants, it is not surprising that the potential magnitude of fraud incurred in self-direction programs is relatively small when compared to Medicaid programs, which pay for medical services, pharmacy services, hospitalization, and other health care services. Still, because fraud is a topic often brought up when self-direction is proposed, expanding available data on the financial exploitation of both the participant and the public purse will be necessary. Research should also consider whether the amount spent on monitoring is commensurate with the savings accrued or fraud prevented.

Self-direction relies on the availability of workers, which may be limited in some regions of the country. To augment staff, technology offers support that can supplement personal care and other support workers. Research will be important to document how such technology can be deployed and how it impacts the costs and the outcomes for participants and families. When participants have control of the budget for purchasing goods and services, they have a practical way to get labor-saving devices into the home. Research should document whether technology can generate sufficient cost savings, including monitoring health status, identifying health issues before they require intervention, and enabling in-home workers to provide quasi-nursing services under proper supervision. As one of the consumers we interviewed pointed out, self-direction makes it possible for participants to use their budgets in creative ways. Self-directed budgets may be a key to speeding the spread of technological innovations, but processes for purchasing such devices need to be streamlined.

Finally, what is needed now is more research on the details of implementation of self-direction with special emphasis on approaches that prove to be cost effective. As we have noted throughout this book, the penetration rate among specific groups of participants (e.g., people with intellectual disabilities versus older adults) varies widely. Why? To answer that question, more research is needed to understand how different implementation approaches work with different groups of participants and how states can adapt their processes to expand enrollments across diverse groups of participants.

Program Recommendation 8—Document how self-direction can impact the impending worker shortage in the home care industry. We have written about the aging of the population and the potential increase in demand for in-home services (see chapter 8). We need to document and quantify how employing families and friends as support staff can expand the available pool of workers. We have seen how the use of family members has helped fuel the growth of the California IHSS program, where 70% of all workers are family members and 50% of all workers are family members who reside in the participant's home. This has brought almost 350,000 staff into the state's home care work force. We have seen similar results in the programs in Germany and the Netherlands. Even though individual budgets in both countries were substantially discounted from agency-based services, as many as half of all recipients chose to receive care from family members. This needs to be clearly understood as projections are made for the growth of the in-home worker industry in America. In any case, the needs of family caregivers deserve additional attention.

Self-direction will require the continued use of well-trained "authorized representatives" in all programs whose purpose is to ensure the participants make informed decisions and are treated with respect. Fortunately, the role of representative is not a paid service, rather one performed without fee by a family member or friend who is not on the payroll. The needs of such representatives are documented in the recent special issue of the *Journal of Gerontological Social Work* (Mahoney, Simon-Rusinowitz, et al., 2019).

Last, the issue of training in-home workers under self-direction should be addressed. There is an active debate about training that ranges from those who argue that training should be modularized and under the guidance of participants, to states that require over 70 hours of classroom training. Concern has been expressed that extensive classroom training may needlessly eliminate well-qualified workers from the labor force. Research needs to be done to determine the impact of the formal training with an eye to the needs of particular groups of participants. People with physical disabilities may have different needs and preferences than people with I/DD or older adults. Again, research can identify best practices in training requirements that recognize the diversity of needs among those who are self-directing.

Program Recommendation 9—Use individual budget methodologies that are based on user needs, transparent and replicable, and that are aligned with available resources. We have seen in chapter 5 that states use many kinds of methodologies to develop individual budgets. Some are based on historical expenditures, some on user requests, and some on a documented evaluation of user needs. It will be important to better understand these methodologies and the impact they have on meeting the needs of participants and their ability to help participants reach their goals and desires within available funds.

In the United States, each state will continue to develop its own methodology to support participant needs within certain CMS guidelines. It is important that these methodologies are clear and transparent so that all users and their families understand what is possible and how the process works. Although it may be desirable to start with historical spending, that should only be the beginning. Individuals should be able to use their budgets and allocations to secure supports that meet their evolving needs. Since self-directed budgets are rarely overspent, and in fact are often underspent as participants learn how to use them, meeting this criterion requires constant monitoring and documentation but should be easily met.

Program Recommendation 10—Develop and implement national models and plans for the widespread use of self-determination for veterans and for people with serious mental illness. We have seen early success with new self-direction service models for both veterans and persons with serious mental illness in chapter 9. But it is clear that self-direction has just touched the surface of the needs of these large and growing groups.

Self-direction for Veterans. Satisfaction with Veterans-Directed Care by every stakeholder group from veterans to their caregivers, and from the aging and disability coordinators to the coordinators at the VAMCs has been overwhelmingly positive. Four VAMCs in Boston, Ohio, San Diego, and Wisconsin have done evaluations of their own, which have shown how important this option is in helping veterans remain in the community and avoid institutional care (Veteran's Health Administration, 2017). In addition, the program offers the ability to employ large numbers of veterans as in-home care givers. More than 7,000 veterans have been participants over the past seven years, and about 2100 are currently in programs. Still, nine years after this program was initiated, only one-third of the Veterans Medical Centers offer self-direction, averaging about thirty veterans per program. Veterans and their caregivers complain that they had to fight to have the chance to manage their own supports and services (Milliken et al., 2016).

Compared to the few thousand self-directing, in 2017, there were almost 114,000 veterans in nursing homes across the country, costing more than $5.7 billion annually. This number is expected to grow as veterans age. Given the experience in rebalancing efforts in civilian long-term care programs, there are potentially tens of thousands of veterans currently in nursing homes who could be supported in their homes at less cost through self-directed programs.

The VHA should undertake a three-point strategy to change this. First, every veteran qualifying for nursing home services should first be offered the self-direction option. We know that if presented properly many eligible veterans would opt for self-direction. Second, every VAMC should be required and funded to offer the self-directed program model. This should be a requirement, not a choice. Last, the program model needs to be scalable if it is to be sustained. Each program should be designed to serve hundreds, if not thousands. Expansion should be accompanied by the creation of an advisory board of veterans who are both consumers and direct care workers in VD-HCBS.

Self-direction for People with Mental Illness. A growing body of evidence shows that self-direction can improve the quality of life of people with mental illness across a number of domains, including the following:

- Employment and education
- Meaningful relationships
- Community participation
- Independent, stable housing
- Self-sufficiency and self-esteem
- Culturally competent support
- Access to health services

These positive self-direction outcomes in behavioral health have the potential to fuel the expansion of the option across the country.

However, evidence on the cost benefits associated with mental health self-direction, while encouraging, is not yet conclusive. Research has indicated that participants use fewer traditional mental health services, particularly in-patient services, and suggests potential cost savings in housing, employment, and health care services. Additional research will help to more fully understand the magnitude of these savings.

Because change in behavioral health systems is complex, and because current efforts are based on very different approaches, it is likely that additional, sustained efforts will be needed to establish self-direction as common practice in behavioral health systems. Regarding the evidence base, more research will be needed in the areas of fidelity standards and the cost implications of self-direction. This research will be essential to support large-scale adoption, inform best practice, and ensure sustainability over the long term. In keeping with the ethos of self-direction, it is essential that people with lived experience are involved in the planning, implementation, and evaluation of future self-direction efforts.

Given the significant co-occurrence of mental illness and substance use among participants in public systems, and given the early promise of self-directed models for people with substance use disorders, states should consider expanding the option to individuals with primary substance use disorders. This work will need to be accomplished by policy makers, administrators, advocates, and other behavioral health stakeholders. Recent programs have been most successful when state and local behavioral health administrators partner with advocates and providers to set self-direction as a priority and identify strategies for making it a reality within their unique state and local contexts.

Most importantly, the experiences of people self-directing show that they value the freedom and choice that it represents. They have used self-direction to change their lives. We encourage policy makers, program administrators, advocates, family members, and mental health service users to learn more about mental health self-direction and how it can work in their state.

Program Recommendation 11—Support a national focal point for self-direction. From 2009 to 2015, the Robert Wood Johnson Foundation with Atlantic Philanthropies, funded a National Resource Center for Participant-Directed Services at Boston College. The mission and vision of this center were as follows:

- Mission: to infuse consumer-directed options into all home- and community based services by providing national leadership, technical assistance, education, and research, leading to improvement in HCBS quality and performance and improvement in the lives of individuals of all ages with disabilities.

- NRCPDS envisions a world where people, of all ages, with disabilities will explore and be able to easily access participant-directed support and service options with the hallmarks of Cash and Counseling as the default, and traditional agency-managed approaches as an option.

The experience during those six years showed the value of having one place to go to learn about the latest developments in self-direction; one organization whose sole reason for being was to advance this concept. With the retirement of the NRCPDS's director, the center left Boston College and is housed at Applied Self-direction, LLC, but its mission has, of necessity, been limited, and there is no secure long-term funding. We believe private and government funds are needed to ensure that there is a permanent home and national leadership for self-direction for all participants.

System Recommendations

The second group of recommendations made by our national informants were focused on changes that can foster system change and that will sustain the progress that has been made in self-direction. It will also be important to revisit unsuccessful system change efforts, such as the CLASS Act, under which a self-directed budget was a core element of a much larger reform.

System Recommendation 1—States moving to managed long-term care should specify their expectations for the inclusion of self-direction requirements in their contracts with MCOs. Contracts should set annual goals and require the MCOs to develop a data base of utilization, cost, and outcomes. Some of the people we interviewed felt managed care could be a great boon to self-direction, especially after industry leaders discover the efficiencies, lower costs, and increased consumer satisfaction that self-direction could bring. Some told us of ways to use MCOs to implement the state's self-direction goals. Others felt strongly that managed care was unfortunately a way to distance decision makers from day to day operations and policy responsibility. As one consumer leader said, "I used to be able to call my state representative or bring people to protest at the capitol, now I am dealing with company executives who are five levels down in the bureaucracy and have little ability or incentive to be responsive." Some informants pointed to a particular state where the move to managed care was a time to get rid of budget authority and stop collecting publicly available data on usage of self-direction.

Currently, there is very little data collected from MCOs that shed light on the scope of self-direction, cost, and satisfaction issues. Though information is limited, it does appear that managed care has led to a growth in self-direction in states such as Tennessee, where there were strong contractual requirements regarding the option of self-direction. However, even with strong commitment to self-direction, the implementation is not uniform across the states we talked to.

A few MCOs have evinced an interest in self-direction, even if they have not invested heavily in either its operation or research to demonstrate whether it is cost effective in their environment. On the other hand, many MCOs have little experience with long-term care services and supports or with self-direction. Leadership will have to come from state Medicaid directors and other public-agency managers to educate MCOs and hold them accountable.

System Recommendation 2—Advocates for self-direction should support efforts to improve the circumstances of direct care support staff. This means supporting initiatives that improve worker wages and acknowledging the positive role that unions can and do play in self-direction. Disability advocates should remain in regular communication with worker representatives and insist that the principles of self-direction be respected. Public employee unions have played a significant role in self-direction in several states, most notably California, Oregon, and Washington. This was not always the case. In the early days of the Cash and Counseling program, union officials in Washington State wrote to the Robert Wood Johnson Foundation asking that the foundation not fund replication of the budget authority of Cash and Counseling. Some union officials felt that participants should not be the employers. In Washington State, union leaders even objected to using HCBS funds to purchase assistive devices and other labor-saving goods and services, saying this option would take money away from workers. These same union officials wanted seniority rules to apply to participant hiring, and they objected to participants being able to pay workers more than the union-negotiated wage. These objections did not stop the foundation from selecting Washington as a replication site, and over time, many of these areas of contention were resolved as unions accepted the premises of self-direction and the role of the participant as employer and decision maker.

The unions learned several valuable lessons from their early state experience with self-direction. First, with favorable leadership in governors' offices or in the legislature, they could, via executive order or legislation, gain the opportunity to represent many thousands of workers for collective bargaining purposes subject to an affirmative vote of home care workers. Tensions between unions and advocates for people with disability did arise over such issues as whether workers were in fact state employees. A high-level mediation took place between ADAPT and the SEIU, with the NRCPDS serving as facilitator, resulting in a consensus document entitled "Guiding Principles for Partnerships with Unions and Emerging Worker Organizations When Individuals Direct their Own Services and Supports." In November 2011, SEIU hosted a signing ceremony at the union's national headquarters in Washington, DC, and SEIU president Mary Kay Henry signed on behalf of the union, as did Tom Nerney on behalf of the Center for Self-Determination, Bob Kafka and Mike Oxford on behalf of ADAPT, and Kevin Mahoney on behalf of the Boston College NRCPDS.

This agreement was sorely tested when many in the disability community felt that union efforts to secure minimum wage and overtime pay for workers did not consider the immediate impact on state budgets and the ability of participants to find workers. There continue to be disagreements between participants and some unions over union efforts to mandate uniform training, often of up to 70 hours, for participant-hired workers. Participants point out that such efforts tend to weed out valuable workers who are not comfortable in classroom settings, many of whom may not speak English, and lead to potential workers not taking or completing the training.

However, since unions have acknowledged that the consumer in self-direction has the hiring, supervising, and firing authority over the union workers they have continued to play a key role in supporting self-direction. The most important role of the union is to negotiate wages and benefits on behalf of the care worker, not to negotiate or bargain with the consumer. In California, the two public employee unions have participated with consumers, advocates, and county authorities to continually expand the program and protect it from legislative or gubernatorial cuts.

However, the power of unions may be diminished as Right to Work laws have passed in many states, and recent federal court rulings limit the ability of unions to organize and expand membership. Recent CMS policy has drafted regulatory efforts to prevent states from collecting union dues, training fees, or even benefit copayments on behalf of participants. Some states, where the legislature was not involved in union agreements such as Wisconsin and Michigan, have decertified unions with a change in governors.

System Recommendation 3—Include a self-directed budget as a benefit in any long-term care policy, whether state or national in scope. As we have seen throughout this book, the country has not developed an appetite for a national long-term policy. Long-term care has been largely shaped by the states and more recently through the initiation of private MCOs. There have been some attempts to launch a national long-term care policy, but those attempts have been unsuccessful to date. Reform legislation, such as the CLASS Act passed as part of the Affordable Care Act but subsequently repealed, included a cash payment to people who joined a voluntary national social insurance program. The CLASS Act would have mainstreamed self-direction to all beneficiaries. The demise of CLASS was related to actuarial problems given that it would have provided coverage for all individuals with disabilities—not just those who became disabled once they enrolled. This meant that the requirement that the program would be financially sound in 75 years could not be met. But CLASS is not the only national long-term care initiative to rely on a self-directed budget.

Recent discussions have focused on a new catastrophic Medicare benefit that would include self-direction. The proposal, the Medicare Long Term Services and Support Act, was recently submitted as a discussion draft by New Jersey congressman Frank Pallone. In announcing the draft, Representative Pallone said, "It's time to expand Medicare to include a long-term care benefit so that millions of seniors and individuals with disabilities no longer have to face individual ruin before they get assistance" (press release, May 2, 2018). The proposal includes a monthly self-direction budget for services to be purchased by beneficiaries who meet certain disability criteria. As part of the rationale for the proposal, he estimated that 70% of seniors over the age of 65 will need long-term care services and supports and that 90 million Americans are expected to be over the age of 65 by 2055. He projected that the cost of long-term care will double over the next thirty years.

Regardless of the future success of this or other long-term care policy payment initiatives, it appears clear that self-direction will be a key component of proposals going forward. Research done at Brown University supported by the Commonwealth Foundation (Miller et al., 2010) found that 61% of policy leaders from all walks of life and all political persuasions agreed that self-direction will be a key part to any future national approach to paying for long-term services and supports.

Conclusion

We need to think about whether self-direction is a program option or a comprehensive system change, a change in how we think about service delivery, a change in where the power lies, and a response to the demographic pressures facing the long-term care system. Self-direction can be the key to empowering program participants, leading to real person-centered support. Or it could remain a boutique option in many states, without the resources and infrastructure necessary to realize the potential of self-direction to reform the traditional long-term care system. We believe it has the potential to transform the way human services are purchased and delivered, substantially expand the availability of direct care workers, and improve outcomes and consumer satisfaction without raising costs. The work has only begun.

Postscript

This overview of self-direction was completed early in 2020, before the onset of the COVID-19 pandemic. Since that time, self-direction has become an even more important option. When policy makers and program administrators faced an urgent need to increase access to home and community based services and supports, they turned to self-direction and augmented the types of caregivers who could be paid. When policy makers and program administrators faced an urgent need to increase the flexibility of LTSS so that participants could get the personal protective equipment and access to telehealth, they turned to self-direction and personalized budgets and expanded the list of purchasable items. But as the nation worked to increase access and promote the flexibility to tailor individual plans, policy makers realized the need to streamline eligibility and operational policies and improve benefits for personal care workers, raising wages and providing family and sick leave. The next step is to study the effects of these changes and keep those that served the nation well. Documenting and improving self-direction should become the "new normal."

Notes

Chapter 1

1. Sections 1915 (c) Home and Community-Based Waiver Services; 1915 (i) State Plan Home and Community-Based Services; 1915 (j) Self-directed Person Assistance Services Under State Plan; and 1915 (k) Community First Choice; Social Security Act.

Chapter 2

1. See (Sebelius, 2014).

Chapter 3

1. Interview with Pam Doty, PhD, Senior Policy Analyst, Office of Disability, Evaluation, Office of the Asst. Secretary for Planning and Evaluation, U.S. DHHS, October 2018.

Chapter 4

1. Interview with Peter Cervinka, Chief Deputy Commissioner, California Dept. of Social Services, September 2018; interview with Deborah Thompson, Director of Senior Services, California Dept. of Social Services, September 2018.

2. Interview with Karen Kimsey, Director of Complex Populations VA DMAS, March 2017; interview with Terry Smith, Director of Long Term Care, VA DMAS, April 2017.

3. Interview with Patti Killingsworth, Director of Long Term Care, Bureau of TennCare, June 2017.

Chapter 5

1. The idea of considering "what is important to and for a person" is attributed to Michael Smull and the Essential Lifestyle Planning process.
2. See American Association on Intellectual and Developmental Disabilities, n.d.
3. More information at: https://rtcom.umn.edu/database/instruments/icap.
4. More information at InterRAI website: http://www.interrai.org.
5. See State of Florida, Agency for Persons with Disabilities, 2010.
6. See Wisconsin Department of Health Services, n.d.b.
7. See Minnesota Department of Human Services, n.d.
8. See Hawaii Department of Health, Developmental Disabilities Division, 2018 for more information.
9. See North Carolina Department of Health and Human Services (n.d.) for more information.

Chapter 6

1. The Cash and Counseling budget was based on what that individual would have received in the traditional system. The amount in AR was based on a brief study of what proportion of a care plan was typically delivered. That amount was discounted at a rate of .86, based on the percentage of a care plan that was typically delivered, in order to stay budget neutral. The MEDIAN monthly allowance in AR was $313 and it was determined by taking $8 an hour and multiplying that by the number of hours in the care plan times the agency-specific discount rate.

Chapter 7

1. The discussion of Arkansas's ongoing cost experience and cost containment strategies is based primarily on numerous (2008–2009) personal communications (including data shared by email) with former Arkansas state officials. This material was previously published in Doty, P., Mahoney, K. J., and Sciegaj, J., 2010.
2. Chapter 1 of the revised *Handbook on Self-direction* published by the Office of the Assistant Secretary for Planning and Evaluation includes results from a number of other credible state evaluations, including Florida.

Chapter 8

1. The full text is available on the website of Applied Self-direction, an independent organization that now provides some of the same technical assistance in self-direction previously provided by NRCPDS. See (Guiding Principles for Partnerships with Unions and Emerging Worker Organizations When Individuals Direct their Own Services and Supports, 2011).

Chapter 11

1. Interview with Connie Garner, Vice President for Disability Policy and Education Policy, ML Strategies and mother of participant, August 2018.
2. Interview with Patti Killingsworth, Tennessee Director of Long Term Care, TennCare, July 2018.
3. Interview with William Moss, Washington Assistant Secretary, Aging and Long Term Support Administration, August 2018.
4. Interview with Althea McLuckie, Executive Director, National Participant Network, National Resource Center for Participant Directed Services, September 2018.

References

AARP (2017). *Long-Term services & supports state scorecard. Retrieved from* http://www.longtermscorecard.org/methodology.

An Act related to long term services and supports. State of Washington House Bill #1087. (2019).

Administration for Community Living (2014). *Section 2402(a) Affordable Care Act—Guidance for implementing standards for person-centered planning and self-direction in home and community-based services programs.* Retrieved from https://acl.gov/sites/default/files/programs/2017-03/2402-a-Guidance.pdf.

Administration for Community Living (2018). Veteran-Directed care program. Retrieved from https://www.acl.gov/programs/veteran-directed-home-and-community-based-services/veteran-directed-home-community-based.

Administration for Community Living, Centers for Medicare and Medicaid (2018). *VD-HCBS educational webinar.* Retrieved from https://nwd.acl.gov/pdf/VDHCBS_Educational_Webinar%20-%20January%2018th%202018.pdf.

Agosta, J., Fortune, J., Kimmich, M., Melda, K., & Smith, D. (2010). *Using individual budget allocations to support people with intellectual and developmental disabilities.* Tualatin, OR: Human Services Research Institute.

Agosta, J., Kidney, C., & Vazquez, A. (2018). *Moving from seven to five support levels for determining personal supports budgets.* Tualatin, OR: Human Services Research Institute (prepared for the Idaho Department of Health and Welfare).

Alakeson, V. (2007). *The Contribution of Self-direction to Improving the Quality of Mental Health Services.* U.S. Department of Health and Human Services Assistant Secretary for Planning and Evaluation Office of Disability, Aging, and Long-Term Care Policy. Retrieved from https://aspe.hhs.gov/basic-report/contribution-self-direction-improving-quality-mental-health-services.

Alakeson, V., & Duffy, S. (2011). *Health efficiencies: The possible impact of personalisation in healthcare.* Centre for Welfare Reform. Retrieved from https://lx.iriss.org.uk/content/health-efficiencies-possible-impact-personalisation-healthcare.

American Association on Intellectual and Developmental Disabilities & The Arc (2016). Autonomy, decision-making supports and guardianship position statement. Retrieved from http://aaidd.org/news-policy/policy/position-statements/autonomy-decision-making-supports-and-guardianship.

American Association on Intellectual and Developmental Disabilities (n.d.). Supports Intensity Scale. Retrieved from https://aaidd.org/sis.

American Bar Association (2016). *PRACTICAL tool for lawyers: Steps in supported decision making*. Retrieved from http://www.ambar.org/practicaltool.

The Americans with Disabilities Act of 1990, 42 U.S.C. § 12101 (2008). Retrieved from https://www.law.cornell.edu/uscode/text/42/12101.

Anderson, A. (2013). Ed Roberts: The father of independent living. Retrieved from http://www.foundsf.org/index.php?title=Ed_Roberts:_The_Father_of_Independent_Living.

Anthony, W. A. (1993). Recovery from mental illness: The guiding vision of the mental health service system in the 1990s. *Psychosocial Rehabilitation Journal 16*(4), 11.

The Arc (n.d.). *Autonomy, decision-making supports, and guardianship*. Retrieved from the Arc website https://www.thearc.org/who-we-are/position-statements/rights/Autonomy-Decision-Making-Supports-and-Guardianship.

The Arc (n.d.). *Our history*. Retrieved from the Arc website: http://www.thearc.org/about-us/history/.

Arkansas Department of Human Services (2008). *Independent Choices*. Final Report.

Australia Productivity Commission (2011). *Disability care and support: Executive summary, No. 54*. Retrieved from https://www.pc.gov.au/inquiries/completed/disability-support/report/disability-support-executive-summary.pdf.

Australia Productivity Commission (2013). *NDIS assessment summary*.

Bazelon Center for Mental Health Law & UPENN Collaborative on Community Integration (2008). *In the driver's seat: A guide to self-directed mental health care*. Retrieved from http://www.bazelon.org/wp-content/uploads/2017/01/Drivers-seat.pdf.

Bill of Rights for Persons Under Guardianship, Texas Estates Code Section 1151.351 (2018). Retrieved from http://www.txcourts.gov/media/1441683/bill-of-rights-guardianship-texas-code-english.pdf.

Bowen, C. N., Fox-Grage, W., Thomas, K., & Rudolph, J. (2017). *No wrong door: Supporting community living for veterans*. Retrieved from http://www.longtermscorecard.org/~/media/Microsite/Files/2017/2017%20Scorecard/Veterans/AARP1195_PP_NWDandVeterans_WEB.PDF.

Bradley, V. J. (1978). *Deinstitutionalization of developmentally disabled persons: A conceptual analysis and guide*. Baltimore, MD: University Park Press.

Bradley, V. J., Agosta, J. M., Smith, G., Taub, S., Ashbaugh, J., Silver, J., & Heaviland, M. (2001). *The Robert Wood Johnson Foundation Self-Determination*

Initiative: Final impact assessment report. Cambridge, MA: Human Services Research Institute.

Bradley, V. J., Knoll, J., & Agosta, J. M. (1992). *Emerging issues in family support*. Washington, D.C.: American Association of Mental Retardation.

Benjamin, A. E., & Mathias, R. E. (2000). Comparing consumer-and agency-directed models: California's in-home supportive services program. *Generations 24*(3), 83–87.

Benjamin, A. E., Matthias, R., & Franke, T. M. (2000). Comparing consumer-directed and agency models for providing supportive services at home. *Health Services Research 35*(1), 351–66.

Benjamin, A. E. Mathias, R. E., Kietzman, K., & Furman, W. (2008). Retention of paid related caregivers: Who stays and who leaves home care careers? *The Gerontologist, 48*(1), 104–113. DOI: https://doi.org/10.1093/geront/48.Supplement_1.104.

Bernanke, B. S. (2011). Promoting research and development: The government's role. *Issues in Science and Technology 27*(4), 37–41.

Blümel, M., & Busse, R. (2015). *The German health care system*. Department of Health Care Management, Berlin Centre for Health Economics Research, Technische Universität Berlin. Retrieved from https://www.mig.tu-berlin.de/fileadmin/a38331600/2015.lectures/Berlin_2015.09.03_mb_GermanHealthCareSystem.pdf.

Brown, R., Lepidus, B., Dale, S., Foster, L., & Phillips, B. (2007). *Cash & Counseling: Improving the lives of Medicaid beneficiaries who need personal care or home and community-based services, final report.* College Park, MD

California Welfare and Institutions Code—WIC DIVISION 4.5. Services for the developmentally disabled, Section 4685.8. (2013). Retrieved from https://leginfo.legislature.ca.gov/faces/codes_displayText.xhtml?division=4.5.&chapter=1.&lawCode=WIC.

Cameron, K., & Firman, J. (1995). *International and domestic programs using "cash and counseling" strategies to pay for long-term care*. Washington, DC: National Council on Aging.

The Care Act 2014, Chapter 23 (2014). Retrieved from www.legislation.gov.uk/ukpga/2014/23/pdfs/ukpga_20140023_en.pdf.

Carlson, B. L., Foster, L., Dale, S., & Brown, R. (2007). Effects of Cash and Counseling on personal care and well-being. *Health Services Research 42*(1pt2), 467–487. DOI: 10.1111/j.1475-6773.2006.00673.x.

Centers for Medicare and Medicaid Services (2014). Home and community-based settings requirements. Retrieved from Centers for Medicare and Medicaid Services website https://www.cms.gov/newsroom/fact-sheets/home-and-community-based-services.

Cervinka, Peter interview, California Department of Social Services, Chief Deputy Commissioner, September 2018.

Chamberlin, J. (1990). The ex-patient's movement: Where we've been and where we're going. *The Journal of Mind and Behavior 11*(3), 323–336.

Claiming full citizenship 2015: Self-Determination, personalization, individualized funding conference (October 15–17, 2015). University of British Columbia.

Colorado Department of Health Care Policy and Financing (2016). *Cost analysis of consumer directed attendant support services.*

Conroy, J. (1995). *Reliability of the personal life quality protocol.* Coffelt Quality Tracking Project–Report No. 7. Ardmore, PA: Center for Outcome Analysis.

Conroy, J., Fullerton, A. Y., Brown, M., & Garrow, J. (2002). *Outcomes of the Robert Wood Johnson Foundation's National Initiative on Self-Determination for Persons with Developmental Disabilities.* Narberth, PA: Center for Outcome Analysis.

Conroy, J., & Yuskauskas, A. (1996). *Independent evaluation of the Monadnock self-determination project.* Narberth, PA: Center for Outcome Analysis.

Cook, J. A., Curtis, L., Jonikas, J., Russell, C., Sweatland, N. (2017). *Self-directed care implementation manual: A comprehensive mental health program guide.* Solutions Suite. Retrieved from http://www.cmhsrp.uic.edu/download/SDC-manual-FINAL.pdf.

Cook, J. A., Shore, S., Burke-Miller, J., Jonikas, J., Hamilton, J., Ruckdeschel, B., Norris, W., Markowitz, A., Ferrara, M., & Bhaumik, D. (2019). Mental health self-directed care financing: efficacy in improving outcomes and controlling costs for adults with serious mental illness. *Psychiatric Services 70*(3), 191–201. Retrieved from https://ps.psychiatryonline.org/doi/pdf/10.1176/appi.ps.201800337.

Council of Australian Governments, Disability Council (2018). *COAG Disability Council quarterly report.*

Croft, B., Battis, K., Ostrow, L., & Salzer, M. (2019). Service costs and mental health self-direction: Findings from consumer recovery investment fund self-directed care. *Psychiatric Rehabilitation Journal 42*(4), 401–406. DOI: 10.1037/prj 0000374

Croft, B., Isvan, N., Mahoney, K., & Parish, S. (2018). Housing and employment outcomes for mental health self-direction participants. *Psychiatric Services.* DOI: https://doi.org/10.1176/appi.ps.201700057.

Croft, B., & Parish, S. (2016). Participants' assessment of the impact of behavioral health self-direction on recovery. *Community Mental Health J 52*(7), 781–792. DOI:10.1007/s10597-016-9999-0.

Croft, B., Simon-Rusinowitz, L., Loughlin, D. M., & Mahoney, K. J. (2018). Mental health leadership perspectives on self-direction. *Social Work in Mental Health 16*(4), 381–399. DOI: 10.1080/15332985.2017.1395783.

Croft, B., Wang, K., Cichocki, B., Weaver, A., & Mahoney, K. (2017). The emergence of mental health self-direction: An international learning exchange. *Psychiatric Services 68*(1), 88–91. DOI: 10.1176/appi.ps.201600014.

Crisp, S., Doty, P., Flanagan, S., & Smith, G. (2010). *Developing and implementing self-direction programs and policies: A handbook*. National Resource Center for Self-directed Supports, Robert Wood Johnson Foundation.

Crisp, S., Sciegaj, M., DeLuca, S., & Mahoney, K. (2013). *Participant direction in home and community-based services: Summary of selected provisions from integrated care RFPs and contracts*. Integrated Care Resource Center.

Dale, S. B., & Brown, R. S. (2006). Reducing nursing home use through consumer-directed personal care services. *Medical Care 44*(8), 760–767. DOI: 10.1097/01.mlr.0000218849.32512.3f.

Dale, S., & Brown, R. (2007). How does Cash and Counseling affect costs? *Health Services Research 42*(1p2), 488–509.

Dane County Developmental Disabilities Coalition (2017). *Building on the Dane County difference*. Wisconsin Supported Provider Coalition.

Davidson, L., & Roe, D. (2007). Recovery from versus recovery in serious mental illness: One strategy for lessening confusion plaguing recovery. *Journal of Mental Health 16*(4), 459–470. DOI: 10.1080/09638230701482394.

Davidson, L., Chinman, M., Sells, D., & Rowe, M. (2006). Peer support among adults with serious mental illness: A report from the field. *Schizophrenia Bulletin, 32*(3), 443–450. DOI: 10.1093/schbul/sbj043.

DeCarlo, M. P., Bogenschutz, M. D., Hall-Lande, J. A., & Hewitt, A. S. (2018). Implementation of self-directed supports for people with intellectual and developmental disabilities in the United States. *Journal of Disability Policy Studies*. DOI: 10.1177/1044207318790061.

Deegan, P. E. (2005). The importance of personal medicine: A qualitative study of resilience in people with psychiatric disabilities. *Scandinavian Journal of Public Health 66,* 29–35. DOI: 10.1080/14034950510033345.

DeMilto, L. (2004). *Independent choices: Enhancing consumer direction for people with disabilities*. Retrieved from Robert Wood Johnson Foundation website: https://www.rwjf.org/en/library/research/2004/06/independent-choices.html.

DeMilto, L. (2015). Cash and Counseling. Robert Wood Johnson Foundation. Retrieved from: https://www.rwjf.org/en/library/research/2013/06/cash---counseling.html.

Department of Health and Human Services, Office of the Inspector General (2012). *Personal care services: Trends, vulnerabilities, and recommendations for Improvement*. Retrieved from https://oig.hhs.gov/reports-and-publications/portfolio/portfolio-12-12-01.pdf.

Department of Health and Social Care (2014). *Statutory guidance issued under the Care Act 2014*. Retrieved from https://www.gov.uk/government/publications/care-act-statutory-guidance.

Developmental Disabilities and Bill of Rights Act, 42 U.S. Code, Chapter 144, Subchapter I.s (1975).

Doty, P., & Flanagan, S. (2002). *Highlights: Inventory of consumer-directed support programs.* U.S. Department of Health and Human Services, Office of the Assistant Secretary for Planning and Evaluation Retrieved from http://aspe.hhs.gov/daltcp/reports/2002/highlght.htm.

Doty, P., Kasper, J., & Litvak, S. (1996). Consumer-directed models of personal care: Lessons from Medicaid. *Milbank Quarterly 74*(3), 377–409.

Doty, P., Mahoney, K. J., & Sciegaj, M. (2010). New state strategies to meet long-term care needs. *Health Affairs 29*(1), 49–56.

Edwards-Orr, M., & Ujvari, K. (2018). *Taking it to the next level: Using innovative strategies to expand options for self-direction.* AARP Public Policy Institute. Retrieved from AARP website at https://www.aarp.org/ppi/info-2018/taking-it-to-the-next-level-using-innovative-strategies-to-expand-options-for-self-direction.html.

European Commission Directorate-General for Economic and Financial Affairs, Economic Policy Committee (Ageing Working Group) (2016). German health care and long-term care systems, joint report on health care and long-term care systems and fiscal sustainability. *European Economy Institutional Papers 37*(2), 349–354. DOI: http://dx.doi.org/10.2765/776073.

Fenton, M. (2008). *When individuals can choose, what do they choose?* Presentation at the 2008 Home and Community-Based Waiver Conference, Minneapolis, Minnesota.

Fenton, M. (2015). *Measuring the impact of self-direction at the state and national level.* Presentation at the Claiming Full Citizenship 2015 International Conference, Vancouver, British Columbia.

Forder, J., Jones, K., Glendinning, C., Caiels, J., Welch, E., Baxter, K., Davidson, J., Windle, K., Irvine, A., King, D., & Dolan, P. (2012). *Evaluation of the personal health budget pilot programme.* Department of Health. Retrieved from https://www.york.ac.uk/inst/spru/research/pdf/phbe.pdf.

Forder, J., Jones, K., Glendinning, C., Caiels, J., Welch, E., Baxter, K., Dolan, P. (2012). *Evaluation of the personal health budget pilot programme.* Department of Health.

Foster, L., Dale, S. B., & Brown, R. (2007). How caregivers and workers fared in Cash and Counseling. *Health Services Research 42*(1 Pt 2), 510–532. https://doi.org/10.1111/j.1475-6773.2006.00672.x.

Fraser, M. W., Richman, J. M., Galinsky, M. J., & Day, S. H. (2009). *Intervention research: Developing social programs.* New York: Oxford University Press.

Frick, W. (2015). Here's why people trust human judgement over algorithms. *Harvard Business Review.* Retrieved from https://hbr.org/2015/02/heres-why-people-trust-human-judgment-over-algorithms.

Friedman, C. (2018). Participant direction for people with intellectual and developmental disabilities in Medicaid Home and Community Based Services Waivers. *Intellectual Disabilities, 56*(1), 30–39.

Garner, Connie interview, Vice President for Disability Policy and Education Policy, ML Strategies and mother of participant, August 2018.

Garrido, M. M., Allman, R. M., Pizer, S. D., Rudolph, J. L., Thomas, K. S., Sperber, N. R., Van Houtven, C., & Frakt, A. B. (2017). Innovation in a learning health care system: Veteran-directed home- and community-based services. *Journal of the American Geriatrics Society 65*(11), 2446–2451. DOI: 10.1111/jgs.15053.

Gibson, M. J. (2003). *A report to the nation on independent living and disability.* Washington, DC: AARP Public Policy Institute.

Gibson, M. J., & Redford, D. (2007). *Comparing long term care, in Germany and the United States—What can we learn from each other?* AARP Policy Institute.

Glasgow, R. E., Vogt, T. M., & Boles, S. (1999). Evaluating the public health impact of health promotion interventions: The RE-AIM Framework. American Journal of Public Health. (89)2. Retrieved from: https://www.researchgate.net/publication/12824646_Evaluating_the_Public_Health_Impact_of_Health_Promotion_Interventions_The_RE-AIM_Framework.

Glendinning, C., Challis, D., Fernez, J., Jacobs, S., Jones, K., Knapp, M., Wilberforce, M. (2008). Evaluation of the individual budgets pilot programme: Final Report. University of York, York: Social Policy Research Unit.

Goldberg, L. (2012). *Vulnerabilities in personal care services.* Office of the Inspector General.

Governor of State of Hawaii (2017). Retrieved from website of the Office of Governor of Hawaii—David Y. Ige http://governor.hawaii.gov/.

Grayson, K., & Velkoff, V. (2010). *The next four decades: The older population in the United States: 2010 to 2050.* U.S. Census Bureau. Retrieved from: https://www.census.gov/library/publications/2010/demo/p25-1138.html.

Haass, R. (1999). *Bureaucratic entrepreneur: How to be effective in any unruly organization.* Washington, D.C.: Brookings Institution Press.

Hagopian, M. (2013). *Community-based long-term care programs in Wisconsin.* Disability Rights Wisconsin.

Halderman v. Pennhurst, 446 F. Supp. 1295 (E.D. Pa. 1977).

Harkins, D., Bear, M., & Rossiter, D. (2016). Dane County, Centers for Medicare and Medicaid Services (CMS) and Individualized Services. *TASH Connections 41*(4), 20–24.

Harry, M. L., Kong, J., MacDonald, L. M., McLuckie, A., Battista, C., Mahoney, E. K., Jeon, H., & Mahoney, K. J. (2016a). The long-term effects of participant direction of supports and services for people with disabilities. *Care Management Journals 17*(1), 2–12. DOI:10.1891/1521-0987.17.1.2.

Harry, M. L., MacDonald, L., McLuckie, A., Battista, C., Mahoney, E., & Mahoney, K. (2016b). Long-term experiences in Cash & Counseling for young adults with intellectual disabilities: Familial representative descriptions. *Journal of Applied Research in Intellectual Disabilities 30*(4), 573–786. DOI:10.1111/jar.12251.

Harry, M. L., Mahoney, K. J., Mahoney, E. K., & Shen, C. (2017). The Cash and Counseling model of self-directed long-term care: Effectiveness with young adults with disabilities. *Disability and Health Journal 10,* 492–501. DOI: 10.1016/j.dhjo.2017.03.001.

Hatton, C., Poll, C., Duffy, S., Sanderson, H., & Routledge, M. (2006). *A report on In Control's first phase 2003–2005.* In Control Publications.

Havercamp, S. (2009a). *Evaluating the reliability and validity of the questionnaire for situational information: Item analyses.* Tallahassee: Florida Agency for Persons with Disabilities.

Havercamp, S. (2009b). *Evaluating the reliability and validity of the questionnaire for situational information: Inter-interviewer reliability.* Tallahassee: Florida Agency for Persons with Disabilities.

Havercamp, S. (2009c). *Evaluating the reliability and validity of the questionnaire for situational information: Test-retest reliability.* Tallahassee: Florida Agency for Persons with Disabilities.

Havercamp, S. (2009d). *Evaluating the reliability and validity of the questionnaire for situational information: Concurrent validity.* Tallahassee: Florida Agency for Persons with Disabilities.

Hawaii Department of Health, Developmental Disabilities Division (2018). *Waiver Amendment #2 and Individual Supports Budgets.* Retrieved from http://health.hawaii.gov/ddd/files/2018/04/Supports-Budget-Info-Brief-1-18-18.pdf.

Hawaii Kapuano Care. Retrieved from: https://www.payingforseniorcare.com/hawaii/kapuna-care.

Head, M. J., & Conroy, J. M. (2005). Outcomes of self-direction in Michigan: Quality and costs. In. R. Stancliffe & C. Lakin (Eds.), *Costs and outcomes of community services for people with intellectual disabilities* (pp. 219–240). Baltimore, MD: Paul Brookes Publishing.

Health Resources and Services Administration, Bureau of Health Professions, National Center for Health Workforce Analysis (2004). *Nursing aides, home health aides, and related health care occupations: National and local workforce shortages and associated data needs.* Retrieved from https://bhw.hrsa.gov/sites/default/files/bhw/RNandHomeAides.pdf.

Health Services Research (2007). Volume 42, Issue 1p2. Pages: 353–586.

HM Government (2007). *Putting People First, A shared vision and commitment to the transformation of adult social care.* Retrieved from http://www.cpa.org.uk/cpa/putting_people_first.pdf.

House of Commons Committee of Public Accounts (HC74) (2017). *Personal budgets in social care.* Second Report of Session 2016–17.

Humphreys, K., & McLellan, A. T. (2011). A policy-oriented review of strategies for improving the outcomes of services for substance use disorder patients. *Addiction 106*(12), 2058–2066. DOI: 10.1111/j.1360-0443.2011.03464.x.

Individuals with Disabilities Education Act, 20 U.S. Code, Title 20, 3, Subchapter 1400 (1990).

Institute of Medicine (2006). *Improving the quality of health care for mental and substance-use conditions.* Washington, D.C.: National Academy Press.

Iowa Legislative Statute 225C.36. (1988).

Kietzman, K. G., Wallace, S. P., Durazo, E. M., Torres, J. M., Choi, A. S., Benjamin, A. E., & Mendez-Luck, C. A. (2011). *Holding on: Older Californians with disabilities rely on public services to remain independent.* Los Angeles: UCLA Center for Health Policy Research.

Killingsworth, Patti interview, Tennessee Director of Long-Term Care, TennCare, July 2018.

Kimmich, M., Agosta, J., Fortune, J., Smith, D., Melda, K., Auerbach, K., & Taub, S. (2009). *Developing individual budgets and reimbursement levels using the Supports Intensity Scale.* Houston, TX: Independent Living Research Utilization (ILRU), Community Living Partnership.

Kimmich, M., & Becker-Green, J. (2000). *Evaluation of the Maryland self-determination initiative: Brief findings.* Cambridge, MA: Human Services Research Institute.

Kimsey, Karen interview, Virginia Department of Medical Assistance, Director of Special Populations, April 2018.

Knickman, J. R., & Stone, R. (2007). The public/private partnership behind the Cash and Counseling Demonstration and Evaluation: Its origins, challenges, and unresolved issues. *Health Services Research, 42*(1), 362–377.

Kodner, D. L. (2003). Consumer-directed services: lessons and implications for integrated systems of care. *International Journal of Integrated Care 3*(2). DOI: http://doi.org/10.5334/ijic.80.

Krupski, A., Campbell, K., Joesch, J. M., Lucenko, B. A., & Roy-Byrne, P. (2009). Impact of access to recovery services on alcohol/drug treatment outcomes. *Journal of Substance Abuse Treatment 37*(4), 435–442. DOI: 10.1016/j.jsat.2009.05.007.

Leading Age (2008). Better Jobs Better Care. Retrieved from: https://www.leadingage.org/research-projects/better-jobs-better-care.

Lessard v. Schmidt, 349 F. Supp. 1078 (E.D. Wis. 1972).

London Department of Health (2006). *Our health, our care, our say: A new direction for community services.* National Health Service. Retrieved from https://assets.publishing.service.gov.uk/government/uploads/system/uploads/attachment_data/file/272238/6737.pdf.

London Department of Health (2008). *Transforming social care.* Department of Health, Local Authority Circular. Retrieved from http://www.cpa.org.uk/cpa/Transforming%20social%20care%20DH.pdf.

London Department of Health (2011). *The adult social care outcomes framework handbook of definitions–Version 2.* Retrieved from https://www.gov.uk/government/publications/the-adult-social-care-outcomes-framework-handbook-of-definitions.

Maarse J. A. M., Jeurissen, P. P. (2016). The policy and politics of the 2015 long-term care reform in the Netherlands. *Health Policy 120*(3), 241–245.

Mahoney, E., & Kayala, D. (2012). *Veteran-directed home and community-based services: A program evaluation.* National Resource Center for Participant-Directed

Services. Retrieved from http://www.appliedselfdirection.com/sites/default/files/VD-HCBS%20Program%20Evaluation.pdf.

Mahoney, K. J., Mahoney, E. K., Morano, C., & DeVellis, A. (2019). Unmet needs in self-directed HCBS programs, *Journal of Gerontological Social Work* 62(2), 195–215 DOI: 10.1080/01634372.2018.1451421.

Mahoney, E. K., Milliken, A., Mahoney, K. J., Edwards-Orr, M., & Willis, D. G. (2018). "It's changed everything": Voices of Veterans in the Veteran-Directed home and community-based services program. *Journal of Gerontological Social Work* 129–148. DOI: 10.1080/01634372.2018.1458054.

Mahoney, E. K., Simon-Rusinowitz, L., Loughlin, D. M., Ruben, K., & Mahoney, K. J. (2019). Preparedness of representatives for people with dementia in a self-directed program. *Journal of Gerontological Social Work* 62(2), 172–194 DOI: 10.1080/01634372.2018.1500965.

Massachusetts Real Lives Bill–H4237 (2014).

Massachusetts Department of Developmental Services (n.d.). DDS Autism Waiver Services. Retrieved from Massachusetts DDS website https://www.mass.gov/dds-autism-waiver-services.

Mattson, S., & Bergfeld, T. (2017). *Senior long-term care in Tennessee: Trends and options* Tennessee Comptroller of the Treasury, Office of Research and Education Accountability.

McLuckie, Althea interview, Executive Director, National Participant Network, National Resource Center for Participant Directed Services, September 2018

Medicaid.gov (2018). *Self-directed services*. Retrieved from www.medicaid.gov/medicaid/ltss/self-directed/index.html.

Meiners, M. R., Loughlin, D. M., Sadler, M. D., & Mahoney, K. (2003). *Findings on the purchase of goods and services under the cash and counseling demonstration and evaluation cash options in Arkansas and New Jersey*. Presented at the Annual Scientific Meetings of the Gerontological Association of America.

Meltsner, A. J. (1976). *Policy analysts in bureaucracy*. Berkeley: University of California Press.

Michigan Department of Health and Human Services (2003). Self-determination policy and practice guideline. Retrieved from http://www.michigan.gov/mdch/0,4612,7-132-2941_4868_4900-264686--,00.html.

Miller, A., Mor, V., & Clark, M. (2010). Reforming long-term care in the United States: Findings from a national survey of specialists. *The Gerontologist,50*(2), 238–252. DOI: 10.1093/geront/gnp111.

Milliken, A., Mahoney, E. K., & Mahoney, K. J. (2016). "It just took the pressure off": The voices of Veterans' family caregivers in a participant-directed program. *Home Health Care Services Quarterly* 35(3–4), 123–136. DOI: 10.1080/01621424.2016.1227010.

Minnesota Department of Health Services (n.d.). MnCHOICES. Retrieved from https://www.dhs.state.mn.us/main/idcplg?IdcService=GET_DYNAMIC_

CONVERSION&RevisionSelectionMethod=LatestReleased&dDocName=dhs16_180264.

Min, J. W., & Tomkiewicz, N. (2017). *Analysis of the 2015 in-home supportive services consumers satisfaction survey.* San Diego State University, School of Social Work Social Policy Institute, Center on Aging.

Moss, William interview, Washington Assistant Secretary, Aging and Long-Term Support Administration, August 2018.

Nadash, P., Doty, P., Mahoney, K. J., & von Schwanenflugel, M. (2012). European long term care programs: Lessons for community living assistance and supports?. *Health Services Research 47*(1), 309–328. DOI: 10.1111/j.1475-6773.2011.01334.x.

Nadash, P., Doty, P., & von Schwanenflügel, M. (2017). LLM Eur, The German long-term care insurance program: Evolution and recent developments, *The Gerontologist 58*(3), 588–597, DOI: https://doi.org/10.1093/geront/gnx018.

National Audit Office (2016). *Personalised commissioning in adult social care.* Retrieved from https://www.nao.org.uk/report/personalised-commissioning-in-adult-social-care/.

National Core Indicators (2016–2017). *Adult consumer survey: 2016–2017 Final Report.* Retrieved from https://www.nationalcoreindicators.org/upload/core-indicators/NCI_2016–17_ACS_NATIONAL_REPORT_PART_I_6_29.pdf.

National Core Indicators (2018). *Adult consumer survey 2016–17 Final Report.* Retrieved from https://www.nationalcoreindicators.org/upload/core-indicators/NCI_2016–17_ACS_NATIONAL_REPORT_PART_I_%286_29%29.pdf.

National Core Indicators (2019). *What can states learn from NCI results about the numbers of people who self-direct their services?* Retrieved from https://www.nationalcoreindicators.org/upload/aidd/Data_Highlight–self-direction_NCI.pdf.

National Core Indicators (2019). *2017 staff stability survey report.* Retrieved from https://www.nationalcoreindicators.org/upload/core-indicators/2017_NCI_StaffStabilitySurvey_Report.pdf.

National Council on Disability (2013). *Medicaid managed care for people with disabilities: Policy and implementation considerations for state and federal policymakers.* Retrieved from https://ncd.gov/rawmedia_repository/20ca8222_42d6_45a5_9e85_6bd57788d726.pdf.

National Disability Insurance Scheme (2016). *NDIS market approach: Statement of opportunity and intent.* Retrieved from https://www.ndis.gov.au/media/448/download.

National Disability Insurance Scheme (2017). *NDIA annual report 2016–2017.* Retrieved from https://www.ndis.gov.au/about-us/publications/annual-report/annual-report-2016-17.

National Employment Law Project (2017). *Surveying the home care workforce: Their challenges & the positive impact of unionization.* Retrieved from https://s27147.pcdn.co/wp-content/uploads/surveying-home-care-workforce.pdf.

National Guardianship Association (2013). *Standards of practice.* Retrieved from https://www.guardianship.org/wp-content/uploads/2017/07/NGA-Standards-with-Summit-Revisions-2017.pdf.

National Resource Center for Participant-Directed Services (2011). *Guiding principles for partnerships with unions and emerging worker organizations when individuals direct their own services and supports.* Retrieved from http://www.appliedselfdirection.com/sites/default/files/Guiding%20Principles%20with%20Signatures.pdf.

National Resource Center for Participant-Directed Services (2013). *An environmental scan of self-direction in behavioral health: Summary of major findings.* Boston, MA.

National Resource Center for Participant-Directed Services (2014). *Facts and figures: 2013 national inventory survey of participant direction.* Retrieved from Applied Self-direction website http://www.appliedselfdirection.com/resources/facts-and-figures-2013-national-inventory-survey-participant-direction.

Nelsen, L. (2016). *The realisation of the participation society. Welfare reform in the Netherlands: 2010–2015.* Radboud University, Institute for Management Research. DOI: 10.13140/RG.2.1.3405.9763.

Nerney, T. (2001). *Filthy lucre: Creating better value in long term supports.* Detroit, MI: Center for Self Determination.

Nerney, T., Crowley, R., & Kappel, B. (1995). *An affirmation of community: A revolution of vision and goals. Creating a community to support all people including those with disabilities.* Durham, NH: University of New Hampshire Institute on Disability.

New Freedom Commission on Mental Health (2003). *Achieving the promise: Transforming mental health care in America–Final report.* Retrieved from Suicide Prevention Resource Center website https://www.sprc.org/resources-programs/achieving-promise-transforming-mental-health-care-america.

Newcomer, R. J., Kang, T., & Doty, P. (2012). Allowing spouses to be paid personal care providers: Spouse availability and effects on Medicaid-funded service use and expenditures. *The Gerontologist 52*(4), 517–530. https://doi.org/10.1093/geront/gnr102.

Niu, X.-F., & Bell, L. (2010). *Statistical models for predicting resource needs and establishing individual budgets for individuals served by the Florida agency for persons with disabilities.* Tallahassee: Florida Agency for Persons with Disabilities.

Norris, W., Warnick, T., Moreno, L., Warren, J., & Razzano, L. (2010). *Self-directing your own recovery by controlling your own service dollars.* Presented at the Alternatives 2010, Anaheim, CA.

North Carolina Department of Health and Human Services (n.d.). *NC innovations waver.* Retrieved from https://medicaid.ncdhhs.gov/nc-innovations-waiver.

NRCPDS (2014). *Facts and Figures: 2013 National inventory survey of participant direction.* Retrieved from http://www.appliedselfdirection.com/resources/facts-and-figures-2013-national-inventory-survey-participant-direction.

O'Connor v. Donaldson, 422 U.S. 563 (1975).

O'Keeffe, J. (2009). *Implementing self-direction programs with flexible individual budgets: Lessons learned from the Cash and Counseling replication states.* Macon, NC: National Resource Center for Participant-Directed Services.

Olmstead v. L.C., 527 U.S. 581 (1999).

Oregon Department of Human Services, Office of Developmental Disabilities Services (2019). *Oregon needs assessment manual.* Retrieved from https://www.oregon.gov/DHS/SENIORS-DISABILITIES/DD/PROVIDERS-PARTNERS/ONA/ONA-Manual.pdf.

Oregon Department of Human Services (n.d.). Services for seniors & people with disabilities. Retrieved from http://www.oregon.gov/DHS/seniors-disabilities/Pages/index.aspx.

Ortman, J. M., Velkoff, V. A, & Hogan, H. (2014). *An aging nation: The older population in the united states population estimates and projections current population reports.* Washington, DC: AARP Public Policy Institute.

Patient Protection and Affordable Care Act 42 U.S.C. § 18001 (2010).

Pavelchek, D., Mann, C. (2007). *Evaluation of interventions to improve recruitment and retention: Summary of results.* Olympia, WA: Washington State University Social & Economic Science, Research Center–Puget Sound Division.

Petner-Arrey, J., Kardell, Y., & Kidney, C. (2019). *Making self-direction a reality: Using individual budgets to promote choice, control, and equity:* Tualatin, OR: Human Services Research Institute.

Petner-Arrey, J., Kidney, C., Kardell, Y., & Agosta, J. (2018). *Minnesota Waiver Reimagine Project: Analysis of budget methodologies and research into other state activities.* Human Services Research Institute. Retrieved from https://mn.gov/dhs/assets/Budget-Model-Other-States-accessible_tcm1053-390881.pdf.

Petroni, S. (2014, October 29). Real lives bill signed at Fenway Park: Victory for disability rights, *Boston Globe.*

Phillips, B. (2006), Presentation before the Pennsylvania Budget Agency. Harrisburg, PA.

Public Partnerships, LLC (2016). *Tennessee CHOICES satisfaction survey.*

Reinhard, S., Accius, J., Houser, A., Ujvari, K., Alexis, J., & Fox-Grage, W. (2017). *Picking up the pace of change: A state scorecard on long-term services and supports for older adults, people with physical disabilities, and family caregivers.* AARP Public Policy Institute. Retrieved from http://longtermscorecard.org/~/media/Microsite/Files/2017/Web%20Version%20LongTerm%20Services%20and%20Supports%20State%20Scorecard%202017.pdf.

Reinhard, S. C., Fox-Grage, W., & Friss Feinberg, L. (2016). *Family caregivers and managed long-term services and supports.* AARP Public Policy Institute. Retrieved from https://www.aarp.org/ppi/info-2016/family-caregivers-and-managed-ltss.html.

Reinhard, S. C., Fox-Grage, W., Friss Feinberg, L., Coulter Edwards, B., Downie, J., & Moscardino, D. (2017). *Emerging innovations in managed long-term services and supports for family caregivers.* AARP Public Policy Institute. Retrieved from http://www.longtermscorecard.org/-/media/Microsite/Files/2017/2017%20 Scorecard/AARP1202_EI_EmerInnovationLTSS_Oct31v2.pdf.

Rhee, N., & Zabin, C. (2009). Aggregating dispersed workers: Union organizing in the "care" industries. *Geoforum 40*(6), 969–979.

Robert Wood Johnson Foundation and The National Resource Center on Participant-Directed Services (2010). *HANDBOOK on developing and implementing self-direction policies and programs*. Retrieved from: http://www.appliedselfdirection.com/sites/default/files/Participant%20Direction%20Handbook.pdf.

SAMHSA (2011a). Access to Recovery Grants. Retrieved from https://www.samhsa.gov/grants/grant-announcements/ti-14-004.

SAMHSA (2011b). *Description of a good and modern addictions and mental health service system*. Retrieved from http://www.samhsa.gov/sites/default/files/good_and_modern_4_18_2011_508.pdf.

San Antonio, P. M., Simon-Rusinowitz, L., Loughlin, D., Eckert, J. K., & Mahoney, K. J. (2007). Case histories of six consumers and their families in Cash and Counseling. *Health Services Research 42*(1pt2), 533–549.

Sanjek, R. (2009). *Gray Panthers*. Philadelphia, PA: University of Pennsylvania Press.

Sciegaj, M., Crisp, S., DeLuca, C., & Mahoney, K. (2013). *Participant-directed services in managed long-term services and supports programs: A five state comparison*. U.S. Department of Health and Human Services, Assistant Secretary for Planning and Evaluation. Retrieved from http://aspe.hhs.gov/daltcp/reports/2013/5LTSS.shtml.

Sciegaj, M., Edwards-Orr, M., DeLuca, C. (In Preparation). The State of Self-directed Long-Term Services and Supports in 2016.

Sciegaj, M., Hooyman, N. R., Mahoney, K. J., & DeLuca, C. (2018). The times they are a-changing: Self-directed long-term services and supports and gerontological social work, *Journal of Gerontological Social Work 62*(2), 236–252, DOI: 10.1080/01634372.2018.1439852.

Sciegaj, M., Mahoney, K. J., Schwartz, A. J., Simon-Rusinowitz, L., Selkow, I., & Loughlin, D. M. (2016). An inventory of publicly funded participant-directed long-term services and supports programs in the United States. *Journal of Disability Policy Studies 26*(4), 245–251. http://doi.org/10.1177/1044207314555810.

Sciegaj, M., Mahoney, K., & Simone, K. (2008). State experiences with implementing the Cash and Counseling Demonstration and Evaluation project, *Journal of Aging & Social Policy 20*(1), 81–98, DOI: https://doi.org/10.1300/J031v20n0105.

Schoultz, B. (1993). *Like an angel that came to help*. Syracuse, NY: Center for Human Policy.

Sebelius, K. (2014). *Section 2402(a) of the Affordable Care Act—Guidance for implementing standards for person-centered planning and self-direction in home and community-based services programs*. Washington, D.C.: Department of Health and Human Services. Retrieved from www.acl.gov/sites/default/files/about-acl/2017-04/2402-a-Guidance.pdf.

Section 504 of Rehabilitation Act of 1973. 29 U.S.C. § 701. Pub. L. No. 93–112 (1973).

Section 1915(c) of Social Security Act 42 U.S.C. Ch. 7, § 1396n §§ 1915(c) (1983).

Shapiro, J. P. (1994). *No pity: People with disabilities forging a new civil rights movement.* Broadway Books.

Shen, C., Smyer, M. A., Mahoney, K. J., Loughlin, D. M., Simon-Rusinowitz, L., & Mahoney, E. K. (2008a). Does mental illness affect consumer direction of community-based care? Lessons from the Arkansas Cash and Counseling program. *The Gerontologist 48* (1), 93–104.

Shen, C., Smyer, M. A., Mahoney, K. J., Simon-Rusinowitz, L., Shinogle, J., Norstrand, J., Mahoney, E. K., Schauer, C., & del Vecchio, P. (2008b). Consumer-directed care for beneficiaries with mental illness: Lessons from New Jersey's Cash and Counseling program. *Psychiatric Services 59*(11), 1299–1306.

Smith, Terry interview, Virginia Department of Medical Assistance, Director of Long Term Care, April 2018

Shumway, D. (1999). Freedom, support, authority, and responsibility: The Robert Wood Johnson Foundation National Program on Self-Determination. *Focus on Autism and Other Disabilities 14*(1), 28–35. DOI: 10.1177/108835769901400104.

Shumway, Donald interview, Executive Director Crotched Mountain School and former New Hampshire Director of Health and Human Services, January 2018.

Simon-Rusinowitz, L., Bochniak, A., Mahoney, K., & Hecht, D. (2000). Implementation issues for consumer-directed programs: Views from policy experts. *Ethics, Law & Aging Review 6,* 107–130.

Slade, E. (2013). *The Feasibility of Expanding Self-directed Services to People with Mental Illness.* Washington, D.C.: U.S. Department of Health and Human Services, Assistant Secretary for Planning and Evaluation. Retrieved from https://aspe.hhs.gov/report/feasibility-expanding-self-directed-services-people-serious-mental-illness.

Smith, G., Kennedy, C., Knipper, S., & O'Brien, J. (2005). *Using Medicaid to support working age adults with serious mental illnesses in the community: A handbook.* Washington, D.C.: U.S. Department of Health and Human Services, Assistant Secretary for Planning and Evaluation. Retrieved from https://aspe.hhs.gov/report/using-medicaid-support-working-age-adults-serious-mental-illnesses-community-handbook.

Smith, T. (2016). *Consumer direction: A model making a difference.* Virginia Department of Medical Assistance Services, Director of Long-Term Care.

Snethen, G., Bilger, A., Maula, E. C., & Salzer, M. S. (2016). Exploring personal medicine as part of self-directed care: Expanding perspectives on medical necessity. *Psychiatric Services 67*(8), 883–889. DOI: 10.1176/appi.ps.201500311.

Snider-Meyer, M., Minkin, A., Olson, D., Gresser, S., Smith, H., & Kier, F. (2013). Comparison of a veterans-directed home care program vs. community nursing home placement. *Federal Practitioner 30*, 24–30.

Spaulding-Givens, J. C., & Lacasse, J. R. (2015). Self-directed care: Participants' service utilization and outcomes. *Psychiatric Rehabilitation Journal 38*(1), 74–80. DOI:10.1037/prj0000103.

State of Florida, Agency for Persons with Disabilities (2010). *The QSI and you: What you need to know about APD's questionnaire for situational information.* Retrieved from https://apd.myflorida.com/brochures/qsi-and-you-brochure.pdf.

Stein, J., & Boulton, G. (June 10, 2016). Scott Walker's administration drops plan to shift Family Care to for-profit insurers. *Milwaukee Journal-Sentinel.*

Supplemental security income for the aged, blind, and disabled, Social Security Act Title SVI, 42 U.S. Code, Chapter 7, Subchapter 16 (1974).

Swaine, J. G., Parish, S. L., Igdalsky, L., & Powell, R. M. (2016). Consumers and worker's perspectives about consumer-directed services in the United States. *Disability and Health Journal 9*(3), 464–471.

Taub, S., Chiri, G., Astor, L., & Grotpeter, M. (2004). *Benchmarks and trends in ISO performance: Third annual quality report.* Boston, MA: Public Partnerships.

Taylor, B., Aiken, F., & Agosta, J. (2015). *Analysis of instruments to assess support needs of people with intellectual and developmental disabilities.* Human Services Research Institute.

Tennessee Health Care Finance and Administration, Bureau of TennCare (2016). *2016 quality assessment and performance improvement strategy.*

Tennessee MCO Statewide Contract (2020). Section 2.2.9.7.1.1. Retrieved from https://www.tn.gov/content/dam/tn/tenncare/documents/MCOStatewide-Contract.pdf.

Title VII of the Rehabilitation Act, Sections 95–602, 95th Congress (1978).

Think Local Act Personal (2017). *Gathering the evidence. Making personal budgets work for all.* Retrieved from https://www.thinklocalactpersonal.org.uk/news/Gathering-the-Evidence-Making-Personal-Budgets-Work-for-All/.

Think Local Act Personal (2017). *Personal outcomes evaluation (POET) for adults in receipt of social care support—2017 report.* Retrieved from https://www.thinklocalactpersonal.org.uk/Latest/Personal-Outcomes-Evaluation-Tool-POET-for-adults-in-receipt-of-social-care-support-2017/.

Thomas, K. S., & Allen, S. M. (2016). Interagency partnership to deliver veteran-directed home and community-based services: Interviews with aging and disability network agency personnel regarding their experience with partner. Department of Veterans Affairs medical centers. *Journal of Rehabilitation Research and Development, 53*(5), 611–618. DOI: 10.1682/JRRD.2015.02.0019.

Thompson, Deborah interview, California Department of Social Services, Director of Senior Services, September 2018.

U.S. Census Bureau (2011). *2010 census shows 65 and older population growing faster than total U.S. Population.* Newsroom Archive. Retrieved from: https://www.census.gov/newsroom/releases/archives/2010_census/cb11-cn192.html#:~:text=According%20to%20the%202010%20Census,increased%20during%20the%20previous%20decade.

United Domestic Workers of America (2017). Celebrating 40 years of IHSS at Disability Capitol Action Day. Retrieved from http://www.udwa.org/2013/05/celebrating-40-years-of-ihss-at-disability-capitol-action-day/.

U.S. Department of Health and Human Services, Office of the Assistant Secretary for Planning and Evaluation (2013). *Participant-Directed services in managed long-term services and supports programs: A five state comparison.* Retrieved from https://aspe.hhs.gov/report/participant-directed-services-managed-long-term-services-and-supports-programs-five-state-comparison.

U.S Department of Health and Human Services, Office of the Assistant Secretary for Planning and Evaluation (2021). *Revised handbook on self-directed services.*

U.S. Department of Labor, Bureau of Labor Statistics (2005–2016). *Quality assessment and performance improvement strategy, Consumer Price Index.*

VA Boston Healthcare System (2013). *Veterans independence plus: Cost benefit analysis.* Retrieved from https://nwd.acl.gov/pdf/VDHCBS_Boston.pdf.

VA MISSION Act of 2018, 115–182 C.F.R. S.2372—(2018).

Vennochi, J. (2012, July 26). Real Lives bill would empower people with disabilities. *Boston Globe.* Retrieved from https://www.bostonglobe.com/opinion/2012/07/26/real-lives-bill-would-empower-people-with-disabilities/ay4mZWABxBirsOZxUXYTuI/story.html.

Veterans-Directed Home and Community-Based Services Program (2015). *San Diego Veteran's independence services at any age: SD-VISA.* Retrieved from https://nwd.acl.gov/pdf/SD%20Visa%20Flyer_100215_508.pdf.

Virginia Commonwealth University, Partnership for People with Disabilities (2007). *Virginia elderly or disabled with consumer-direction Medicaid waiver.*

Virginia Department of Medical Assistance Services (1996). *A study of consumer-directed services–Virginia House Document No. 18.* Retrieved from https://rga.lis.virginia.gov/Published/1996/HD18/PDF.

Virginia Department of Medical Assistance Services (1997). *Medicaid-Funded consumer-directed personal assistance services–Virginia House Document No. 22.*

Wammes, J., Jeurissen, P., Westert, G., & Tanke, M. (2017). The Dutch health care system, 2016. In E. Mossialos, A. Djordjevic, R. Osborn, & D. Sarmak (Eds.). *International Profiles of Health Care Systems.*

Webber, M., Treacy, S., Carr, S., Clark, M., & Parker, G. (2014). The effectiveness of personal budgets for people with mental health problems: A systematic review. *Journal of Mental Health, 23*(3), 146–155. DOI:10.3109/09638237.2014.910642.

Welch, E., Caiels, J., Bass, R., Jones, K., Forder, J., & Windle, K. (2013). *Implementing personal health budgets within substance misuse services: Final report*. Retrieved from https://kar.kent.ac.uk/37738/1/dp2858.pdf.

Welch, E., Jones, K., Caiels, J., Windle, K., & Bass, R. (2016). Implementing personal health budgets in England: A user-led approach to substance misuse. *Health and Social Care in the Community 25*(5). DOI: 10.1111/hsc.12396.

Weisman, R. (August 28, 2019). As costs mount, states scramble for new ways to pay for late-in-life care. *Boston Globe*.

White, C. (2011). *The personal touch—The Dutch experience of personal health budgets*. London, UK: The Health Foundation.

Wickizer, T. M., Mancuso, D., Campbell, K., & Lucenko, B. (2009). Evaluation of the Washington State Access to Recovery project: Effects on Medicaid costs for working age disabled clients. *Journal of Substance Abuse Treatment 37*(3), 240–246. DOI: 10.1016/j.jsat.2009.01.005.

Wikoff, R. (1989). *Inventory for client and agency planning*. From J. C. Conoley & J. J. Kramer (Eds.), *The tenth mental measurements yearbook* [Electronic version]. Retrieved May 15, 2006, from the Buros Institute's *Test Reviews Online* website: http://www.unl.edu/buros.

Wisconsin Department of Health Services (2016). Long term sustainability—IRIS and self-directed supports. Retrieved from https://www.dhs.wisconsin.gov/familycare/index.htm.

Wisconsin Department of Health Services (2018). Family care and IRIS programs to expand statewide. Wisconsin Department of Health Services website.

Wisconsin Department of Health Services (n.d.a). IRIS (Include. Respect. I Self-direct). Retrieved from https://www.dhs.wisconsin.gov/iris/index.htm.

Wisconsin Department of Health Services (n.d.b). Wisconsin's Functional Screen. Retrieved from https://www.dhs.wisconsin.gov/functionalscreen/index.htm.

Wolfensberger, W. P., Nirje, B., Olshansky, S., Perske, R., & Roos, P. (1972). *The principle of normalization in human services*. Toronto, Canada: National Institute on Mental Retardation. Retrieved from https://digitalcommons.unmc.edu/wolf_books/1.

Won Min, J., & Tomkiewicz, N. (2017). *Analysis of the 2015 In-Home Supportive Services (IHSS) consumer satisfaction survey*. California Department of Social Services, San Diego State University School of Social Work.

Wyatt v. Stickney, 325 F. Supp. 781 (M.D. Ala. 1971).

Your Guide to Directing Your Own Services (2011). CMS system transformation grant. Retrieved from https://partnership.vcu.edu/servicesfacilitators/Module%203-PartA/downloadables/SD_Guide_7_18_11.pdf.

Index

Note: Page numbers in *italics* indicate figures; those with a *t* indicate tables.

a priori logic model evaluation, 100–101
abuse, caregiver, 33
Access to Recovery program (ATR), 148–149, 153
activities of daily living (ADLs), 67, 120; assessment of, 69; TennCare CHOICES program and, 60, 62
acupuncture, 20–21
ADAPT, 135, 201–202
Administration for Community Living (ACL), 27, 30, 120, 190, 192; training programs of, 191; VD-HCBS and, 140
Administration on Aging (AoA), 25, 30
Adult Guardianship for Cognitively Impaired, 163
Adult Needs Assessment (ANA), 70–71
Adult Social Care Outcomes Framework (UK), 174
Advisory Board for Consumer Direction, 55
Affordable Care Act (2010), 18–19, 190–191; Community First Choice Option of, 26, 30, 37, 47, 59, 127; needs-based criteria of, 147; Section 2402(a) of, 26, 191. *See also* Patient Protection and Affordable Care Act

Aging and Disability Network Agencies (ADNAs), 140, 141, 143, 144
"aging at home" approach, 120, 187
Agosta, J., 11
Alakeson, V., 146
allocation algorithm amount, 72
American Association of Retired Persons (AARP), 41, 127–128
American Association on Intellectual and Developmental Disability (AAIDD), 128
Americans with Disabilities Act (1990), 11, 126
Applied Self-direction, LLC, 199
Area Agencies on Aging (AAA), 54–56, 140
Arkansas, 185; Agency Based care in, 106; cost studies in, 101–108, *103*, 104t, 107t; Independent Choices waiver in, 106; individual monthly budget in, 88; preference study in, 87–88
"Ask Me!" study (Md.), 94
aspirational goals, 67
assessment tools, 68–75, *74*
Assistant Secretary for Policy and Evaluation (ASPE) Office, xiv–xv,

229

Assistant Secretary for Policy and
Evaluation (ASPE) Office *(continued)*
14–15, 24, 28–29; on participant-
direction programs, 58; preference
studies by, 87; self-direction cost
studies of, 101
Association for Retarded Children
(ARC), 10
Atlantic Philanthropies, 16; "Better
Jobs, Better Care" initiative of,
134; National Resource Center for
Participant-Directed Services and,
90, 199; VD-HCBS and, 140
Attendant Care program (Calif.), 44
Australian long-term care programs,
158, 175–183
authorized representatives, 2, *3*, 5;
training of, 196; for veterans, 141
autistic individuals: Massachusetts
legislation for, 123–124; self-
direction programs for, 43–44,
115–117, 186

Behavioral Health Home and
Community-Based Services, 149
Bell, L., 72
Berkeley Center for Independent
Living, 10
Bernanke, Ben, 23
British Independent Living and
Inclusion movement, 171
"budget neutrality," 100, 152
Bush, George W., 30

California, 44–49, 197, 201; Attendant
Care program in, 44; consumer-
directed programs in, 44, 47;
cost studies in, 111–113, 112t;
Department of Developmental
Services in, 111–113, 112t;
Department of Disability Services
in, 125–126; In-Home Support
Services in, 24–25, 46–49, 185–189;
outcomes studies in, 93–94; polio
survivors in, 2, 99; self-direction
expansion in, 125–126
California Department of Social
Services (CDSS), 45–46
Carbonnell, Josefina, 30
case managers, 2, 129–130, 162, 191
Cash and Counseling Demonstration
Program, xiv–xv, 2–3, 14–16,
85–91, 201; "budget neutrality" test
for, 100; dissemination strategy of,
89; diversity needs in, 120–122;
Doty on, 34–35; effectiveness of,
89, 185; ethnic diversity of, *121*,
121–122; ethnographic study of,
88; federal roles in, 25–26; home
care worker impacts of, 96–97;
implementation research of, 89–90;
Mathematica Policy Research on,
101–102; Medicaid replication of,
89; mental health self-direction
programs and, 151; randomized
control experiment of, 23; self-
direction cost studies of, 99–108,
103, 104t, 107t
Center for Outcome Analysis, 91, 93,
112t
Center for Self-Determination (Mich.),
134, 201
Centers for Independent Living (CIL),
10, 54–56, 140
Centers for Medicare and Medicaid
Services (CMS), 18; cost evaluations
of, 105; COVID waivers of, xv–xvi;
on person-centered planning, 27;
Real Choice Systems Change grants
of, 25; self-direction expansion by,
126–127; on support brokers,
130; System Transformation Grants
of, 55–56. *See also* Medicaid/
Medicare

cerebral palsy, 115–117, 135–136, 180–182
Cervinka, Peter, 186–187
Chicago Center on Integrated Health Care and Self-directed Recovery, 32
Children's Needs Assessment (CNA), 70–71
chiropractic, 20–21
CHOICES waiver (Tenn.), 57–62; cost analyses of, 113; managed care organizations and, 56–59, 131–132
Claiming Full Citizenship Conference (2015), 157–158
Clinton Health Plan, 14–15, 24
cognition/memory support needs, 69
Colorado, 20–21, 101, 114
Commonwealth Foundation, 203
Commonwealth Fund Opinion Leader's Survey, 122
Community First Choice Option (CFCO), 26, 30, 37, 47, 127
Community Living Assistance Services and Supports (CLASS) Act (2010), 26–27, 200, 202–203
Community Mental Health Services Programs (CMHSP) (Mich.), 109, 148
community participation activities, 67
Community Services Boards (Va.), 54
complementing considerations, 75–81
Comprehensive Assistance for Family Caregivers, 142
Conroy, J., 93, 94, 96
consumer-directed programs, 192; in California, 44, 47; in Colorado, 20–21, 114
Consumer Recovery Investment Fund–Self-directed Care (CRIF-SDC) (Penna.), 148, 152
continuous quality-improvement process, 75–76
Cook, J. A., 152

cost-benefit analyses, 100
cost-effectiveness analyses, 100
cost studies, 99–118
Council on Quality and Leadership, 41–42
COVID-19 pandemic, xv–xvi, 205
Crisis Intervention Team (CIT), 155
Croft, B., 11, 154
Cures Act (2016), 27, 33, 192

Dane County Developmental Disabilities Coalition (Wisc.), 50
Davis, Judy, 32
day habilitation programs, 38
day-to-day support needs, 67
Decision Control Inventory, 93
Deficit Reduction Act (2005), 16, 25, 30, 37
del Vecchio, Paolo, 31
DeParle, Nancy-Ann Min, 35
Department of Developmental Services (Calif.), 111–113, 112t
Department of Labor Home Care Rule, 27, 32–33, 132–133
Department of Medical Assistance Services (DMAS) (Va.), 54–56
developmental disabilities. *See* intellectual and developmental disabilities (I/DD)
Developmental Disabilities Council: in Illinois, 84; in Maryland, 94
Developmentally Disabled Assistance and Bill of Rights Act (1975), 11
Disability Rights Wisconsin (organization), 51
diversity needs, 119–122, 187, 196
Doty, Pamela, 28–29, 34–35, 37, 39–40, 189

Education for All Handicapped Children Act (1975), 10
Edwards-Orr, M., 127–128

Electronic Visit Verification (EVV), 27, 33, 61, 133
Environmental Scan, 31
evidence-based policy making, 23
exceptional needs budget, 79–80

Fair Labor Standards Act, 132, 192
Family Care program (Wisc.), 50–53
family caregivers: individualized budgets planning for, 81, 181; respite care for, 54, 79; support of, 13, 83–84, 124, 196; training by, 115–117; of veterans, 142, 143
Fauci, Anthony, xvi
financial management services agency (FMSA), 5–6, 32, 58, 141; fraud and, 194; IRS and, 5–6, 32; VD-HCBS and, 141
financial manager, 2, *3*
Fiscal Employment Agent, 6, 55
Flanagan, S., 37, 39–40
Florida, 185; individualized budget approach in, 71–72; managed care organizations in, 131; peer specialists in, 153; self-direction cost studies in, 102–105, *103*, 104t
Florida Self-directed Care, 147–148, 151–152
Food Stamp waivers, 15, 28–29
Forder, J., 151
fraud, 27, 33, 46–47, 133, 183, 194–195
Friedman, Carli, 41–42

Garner, C., 187
Gerhard, Lori, 31
Germany: home care worker shortage in, 196; long-term care programs in, 14, 15, 158–164, 161t, 182
Gerontological Society of America, 193

Glasgow, R. E., 90
Gray Panthers, 10
guardianship, 128–129, 163

Haass, Richard, 35
Halderman v. Pennhurst State School and Hospital (1977), 13
Harrahan, Mary, 34
Hawaii, 74, 96, 124, 186, 201
Health and Human Services (HHS), 18–19
Health and Recovery Plan (HARP) (N.Y.), 149
Health Care Financing Administration, 24. *See also* Centers for Medicare and Medicaid Services
Henry, Mary Kay, 201
Heumann, Judy, 45
HIV/AIDS, 3
home and community based services (HCBS), 3, 149, 192; Medicaid expansion of, 126–127; Medicaid funding of, 18, 157; for people with I/DD, 41–42; Section 1915(c) waiver application for, 11, 25, 37–38; "Settings Rule" of, 126, 185; state-plan options with, 38. *See also* Veteran-Directed Home and Community Based Services
Home Care Commission (Ore.), 125
Home Care Rule, 132
home care workers: impact of self-direction on, 96–97; Labor Department rules for, 27, 32–33, 132–133; live-in, 133; payroll issues of, 61–62; recruitment of, 134; retention of, 134; shortages of, 122, 195–196; training of, 96, 196; turnover among, 20, 116, 122, 133–134. *See also* Service Employees International Union

homemaker and home health aide services (H/HHA), 141
Homemaker Chore Program (Calif.), 45
hospice care, 159–160
human rights, 128, 158
Human Services Research Institute (HSRI), xiii–xiv, 16–17, 91; family subsidy evaluation by, 84; NCI and, 42; self-direction program evaluations by, 91, 94

I/DD. *See* intellectual and developmental disabilities
Ige, David, 124
Illinois, 16, 32, 84
implementation analysis, 91–93
implementation research, 89–90
In-Home Support Services (IHSS) (Calif.), 24–25, 46–49, 185–189
Include, Respect, I Self-direct (IRIS) (Wisc.), 51–53, 189; individualized budgets for, 72–73; version 2.0 of, 53
Independence Plus Waiver (IPW) Program (Calif.), 47
Independent Choices program (National Council on Aging), 14, 106
individual education plans, 10
individualized budgets, 5, 65–82, 158, 185; assessment-based methods for, 68–75; categories of, 66–75, *74*; complementing considerations of, 75–81; conversational method for, 67–68; definition of, 66; flexibility of, 17, 117–118; Florida's approach to, 71–72; formula-based approach to, 71–73; Hawaii's approach to, 74; item-based approach to, 70–71; level-based approaches to, 73–75, *74*; for long-term care, 187;

North Carolina's approach to, 74; nursing home care versus, 187; recommendations for, 195–197; support broker for, 6; West Virginia's approach to, 73–74; Wisconsin's approach to, 72–73
Individuals with Disabilities Education Act (1990), 10
"Institution for Mental Disease" exclusion, 147
integrated care, 132. *See also* managed care organizations
Integrated Health Agency (IHA), 53
intellectual and developmental disabilities (I/DD), people with, 55, 59, 123, 125–126; guardianship for, 128–129; In-Home Support Services for, 49; National Core Indicators of, 41–44, *43*; RWJF programs for, 3, 16–18, 91–93, 109–111, 185; self-direction cost studies of, 108–112, 112t
intermediary service organization (ISO), 95
Internal Revenue Service (IRS), 5–6, 26, 32, 185
Inventory for Client Agency and Planning (ICAP), 74
Iowa, 84
IRIS. *See* Include, Respect, I Self-direct

Kafka, Bob, 201
Kayala, Diane, 144
Kessler, Keith, 55
Killingsworth, Patti, 57, 186
Knickman, J. R., 23
Kohl, Hermut, 159

Lacasse, J. R., 151–152
Learning Collaboratives, 150
learning objectives, 67

least restrictive setting, 12
Lessard v. Schmidt (1972), 13
long-term care, 120, 157–158; AARP Scorecard on, 41, 127–128; demographic trends in, 119–122; in Germany, 158–164, 161t; in Netherlands, 158, 164–170; self-direction in, 186–187, 202–203; in United Kingdom, 158, 170–175, *171*; veterans' programs for, 140
Long-Term Care Trust Act (2019) (Wash.), 124–125
long-term service and support (LTSS) of VHA, 139–141, 145, 164

Mahoney, Ellen, 144
managed care organizations (MCOs), 40–41, 130–132; recommendations for, 200; in Tennessee, 56–59, 131–132; in Wisconsin, 53
Maryland, 94, 96
Massachusetts, 84, 95, 110–111, 197; autism initiative of, 123–124; "Real Lives" legislation of, 123
massage therapy, 20–21, 155
Mathematica Policy Research (MPR), 101–105
McGill, Jason, 125
Medicaid/Medicare, 40–41; Cash and Counseling replication by, 89; catastrophic benefit proposal to, 203; Coordination Office of, 26; financial management services agencies and, 5–6; fraud in, 195; Health and Recovery Plan of, 149; Independent Choices waiver, 106; "Institution for Mental Disease" exclusion of, 147; mental health coverage of, 147; state plan options of, 30; Transformed Medicaid Statistical Information System of, 41, 194; waivers of, 28–29. *See also* Centers for Medicare and Medicaid Services
Medicaid Research and Demonstration Waivers, 15, 101
Medicare Long Term Services and Support Act, 203
Meltsner, Arnold, 35
memory support needs, 69
Mental Health Block Grants, 31
mental health care, 31–32, 145–155; criminal justice system and, 154; in Germany, 162; for serious illness, 31–32, 86, 146–152, 154, 186, 198–199; for substance use disorders, 146, 153–155
Mental Patients Liberation Front, 9
Michigan: Community Mental Health Services Programs in, 148; family subsidy program in, 83–84; peer specialists in, 153; self-determination evaluation in, 95–96; Self-direction Initiative of, 109–110
Milliken, A., 143
minimum wage, 29, 32, 46, 132–133, 202. *See also* labor laws
Minnesota, 70, 142
Monadnock Developmental Services pilot program (N.H.), 91, 108–109
Money Follows the Person grant, 25
Moss, Bill, 186
Multi-State Demonstration and Evaluation of Self-direction in Behavior Health, 26–27
muscular dystrophy, 60

National Advocacy to Reform Guardianship and Encourage Alternatives, 128–129
National Association of Medicaid Directors, 193

National Association of State Directors of Developmental Disabilities Services (NASDDDS), 42, 150
National Center for Health Workforce Analysis, 122
National Core Indicators (NCI), xiv; Adult Consumer Survey of, 95; of guardianship, 128; for long-term care, 127–129; for people with intellectual and developmental disabilities, 41–44, *43*; purpose of, 42; of worker turnover rate, 134
National Council on Aging, 14, 106
National Council on Disability, 11, 130–131
National Guardianship Association, 128
National Institute on Disability, Independent Living, and Rehabilitation Research, 31–32
National Participant Network, 29, 189
National Program for Self-Determination for Persons with Developmental Disabilities, 109
National Resource Center for Participant-Directed Services (NRCPDS), xv, 41, 90, 135, 199; behavioral health and, 149; formation of, 90; surveys by, 38; VD-HCBS and, 140
Nerney, Tom, 68, 134–135, 201
Netherlands, 14, 15; home care worker shortage in, 196; long-term care in, 158, 161, 164–170, 182–183
New Hampshire, 84–85, 91, 108–109
New Jersey, 84, 102–105, *103*, 104t, 185
New York, 147, 149–153, 192
New York State Health Foundation (NYSHF), 27, 150
Niu, X.-F., 72

North Carolina, 74
nursing aides, 122
nursing home care: "aging at home" approach versus, 120, 187; in Germany, 163; in Tennessee, 56–57, 113, 187; for veterans, 143–144, 197

O'Connor v. Donaldson (1975), 13
Office of the Inspector General, 28, 33, 194
Ohio, 96
O'Keeffe, Janet, 89
Older Americans Act (2006), 16, 25, 30
Olmstead v. L.C. (1999), 13–14, 25, 30; self-direction expansion under, 126; Tennessee lawsuits over, 56
Oregon, 42, 70–71, 84, 125, 201
overtime pay, 29, 32–33, 132–133, 193, 202
Oxford, Mike, 201

Pallone, Frank, 203
parents. *See* family caregivers
participant-direction program (Tenn.), 58
Partnered Evidence-Based Policy Resource Center, 144
Patient Protection and Affordable Care Act, 29, 157. *See also* Affordable Care Act
peer specialists, 153
Pennsylvania, 131, 148, 152, 153
person-centered care, 6, 119; CMS on, 27; HCBS Settings Rule on, 126, 185; individualized budget for, 67, 76; labor laws and, 33; of mental health programs, 147
"personalization," 170, 173–174
"Personalized Commissioning Group" (UK), 175

Petner-Arrey, J., 11, 70–73
polio survivors, xvi, 2, 44, 99
Polit, Mark, 135
preference studies, 86–88
Public Consulting Group (PCG), xiv
Public Partnerships, LLC, xiv, 55, 95, 111
Purchased Care HCBS Case Mix and Budget Tool, 142
Putting People First policy (UK), 172–173

quadriplegic individuals, 60, 180–182
quality control, 32–33, 46–47
Quality of Life Changes Scale, 85, 93–94
Questionnaire for Situational Information (QSI), 72

RE-AIM model, 90
readiness reviews, 31
Real Choice Systems Change program, 25, 30
"Real Lives" legislation (Mass.), 123
Rehabilitation Act (1973 & 1978), 10
Research & Demonstration activities, 23
respite care, 54, 79
Retirement Research Foundation, 16, 31, 89–90
Rhoades, Kitty, 53
Robert Wood Johnson Foundation (RWJF), xiv, 2–3, 26–27, 149–150, 185; "Better Jobs, Better Care" initiative of, 134; Environmental Scan of, 31; Independent Choices projects of, 14, 106; National Resource Center for Participant-Directed Services and, 90, 199; preference studies of, 86–88; VD-HCBS and, 140. *See also individual projects*
Roberts, Ed, 10, 45

Routledge, M., 11
RTI International, 16
Rutte, Mark, 167

Sannicandro, Thomas, 123
Schoeps, Dan, 31
Schoultz, Bonnie, 84–85
Sciegaj, M., 11
SEIU. *See* Service Employees International Union
self-advocacy councils, 92
Self-Determination for Persons with Developmental Disabilities projects, 14–18, 91–93, 109–111, 185
self-determination programs, 85, 95, 108; cost analyses of, 111–112, 112t; expansion of, 125–126
self-direction, 39–41, 83–98; advantages of, 4–5, 187; constraints on, 129–135; cost studies of, 40, 88, 99–118, *103*, 104t; demographic impacts on, 119–122; disadvantages of, 188–189; expansion of, 38, *39*, 119–137, 139–155, 185–189; federal promotion of, 23–33; future of, 106–108, 186–203; health outcomes with, 87; history of, 2, 9–20; international examples of, 12, 14, 157–183, 190; key components of, 63; philosophical shift to, 12; program recommendations for, 190–199; public policy support of, 123–127; state implementation of, 44–63; state participation in, 37–38; systemic recommendations for, 200–203. *See also specific programs*
Self-direction Initiative (Mich.), 109–110
serious mental illness (SMI), 31–32, 86, 146–152, 154, 186, 198–199. *See also* mental health care

service coordinators, 129, 130
Service Employees International Union (SEIU), 45, 48, 134–135, 201–202
"Settings Rule" of HCBS, 126, 185
Shulkin, David, 31
Shumway, D., 83
Simon-Rusinowitz, L., 132
skill-building objectives, 67, 69, 135–136, 181
Slade, Eric, 150
Smull, Michael, 208n1
Snethen, G., 152
Social Security Act, 10, 11, 32
Spaulding-Givens, J. C., 151–152
spinal cord injuries, 20–21, 54
State Units on Aging (SUA), 140
Stern, Andrew, 135
Stone, Robyn, 23, 28, 34
Substance Abuse and Mental Health Services Administration (SAMHSA), 26–27, 31; Access to Recovery program of, 148–149; Cash and Counseling program and, 89–90; Community Mental Health Services Programs and, 148; mental health self-direction programs of, 150
substance use disorders, 20–21, 146, 153–155, 198–199
Supplemental Security Income (1974), 10
support brokers, 2, *3*, 6, 129–130, 154; for mental health care, 145–146; training of, 191
Swaine, J. G., 96
Swan, Lou, 120–121
"system navigators," 124
System Transformation Grants (Va.), 55–56

take-up rate, 41

Temple University Collaborative on Community Inclusion of Individuals with Psychiatric Disabilities, 32
Tennessee: managed care organizations in, 56–59, 131–132, 200; nursing home care in, 56–57, 113, 187; self-direction cost studies in, 101; self-direction participants in, 44, 56–62. *See also* CHOICES waiver
Texas: mental health self-direction programs in, 149, 152; peer specialists in, 153
The Arc, 94, 130, 138
Thomas, K. S., 11, 146
Thompson, Debbi, 186–187
training, 134; of authorized representatives, 196; of case managers, 191; of in-home workers, 196; by parents, 115–117; of peer specialists, 153; of support brokers, 191
Transformed Medicaid Statistical Information System (T-MSIS), 41, 194
Trump, Donald, 18
21st Century Cures Act. *See* Cures Act

Ujvari, K., 127–128
UN Convention on Rights of Persons with Disabilities, 158
United Domestic Workers of America (UDWA), 45, 48
United Kingdom long-term care programs, 151, 158, 170–175, *171*
Utah, 148–149, 153

Veteran-Directed Home and Community Based Services (VD-HCBS), 4, 26, 38, 140–145, 192; current scope of, 140–141; evaluations of, 31, 142–145;

Veteran-Directed Home and Community Based Services *(continued)* future of, 145; growth in, 39; recommendations for, 197–198; unique aspects of, 141–142. *See also* home and community based services

Veterans Health Administration (VHA), 26, 27, 30–31; Geriatrics and Extended Care Office of, 141; long-term service and support options of, 139–141, 145, 164, 205; recommendations for, 197–198; TennCare CHOICES program and, 60

Virginia, 189; managed care organizations in, 131; self-direction participants in, 44, 53–56

Von Schwanenflugel, M., 11

Washington, 124–125, 186, 201
Webber, M., 151
"welfare state," 167
West Virginia, 73–74, 189
Wisconsin, 13, 96, 197; IRIS option in, 51–53, 72–73, 189; self-direction participants in, 44, 49–53
"woodwork effect," 100, 102
World Institute on Disability, 14–15, 24
Wyatt v. Stickney (1971), 13

zero spending, 105

www.ingramcontent.com/pod-product-compliance
Ingram Content Group UK Ltd.
Pitfield, Milton Keynes, MK11 3LW, UK
UKHW041917140426
5217IPUK00013B/200